How Your Child Learns Best

Brain-Friendly Strategies You Can Use to Ignite Your Child's Learning and Increase School Success

How Your Child Learns Best

Brain-Friendly Strategies
You Can Use to
Ignite Your Child's Learning
and Increase School Success

JUDY WILLIS, MD, MED

FOREWORD BY GOLDIE HAWN

SOURCEBOOKS, INC.
NAPERVILLE, ILLINOIS

Published by Sourcebooks, Inc.
P.O. Box 4410, Naperville, Illinois 60567–4410
(630) 961–3900
Fax: (630) 961–2168
www.sourcebooks.com

Library of Congress Cataloging-in-Publication Data

Willis, Judy.
 How your child learns best : brain-friendly strategies you can use to ignite your child's learning and increase school success / Judy Willis.
      p. cm.
   1. Learning, Psychology of. 2. Brain. 3. Education—Parent participation. I. Title.
 LB1060.W5444 2008
 370.15'23—dc22
                              2008018046

Printed and bound in the United States of America.
VP 10 9 8 7 6 5 4 3 2 1

To you, the parents, who take your love for your children and enrich it with opportunities for them to reach their highest potentials as joyful, successful learners. Thank you for passionately nurturing the bodies and minds of these future caretakers of our planet.

CONTENTS

FOREWORD

Dr. Judy Willis is a trailblazer. Speaking as a mother and grandmother, she is also my hero! I met Judy when I read her article on the neuroscience of joyful learning. I was overjoyed to know there was someone in the field of education who was addressing the importance of creating a more joyful classroom. I called her straight away. A vibrant voice resounded in my ear, and we discovered a great commonality.

I am the founder of the Hawn Foundation, which is dedicated to creating a more mindful approach to learning. Mindfulness supports more joy and self-awareness. Our mission also includes helping teachers, children, and parents learn more about how the brain functions. We have brought physical education into our schools—why not mental education? Dr. Judy Willis has taken the reins and is one of the pioneering forces who supports new and exciting ways to help parents understand and be a part of helping their children learn in a fun and exciting way.

This book, parent-friendly and without brain-speak jargon, is filled with specific enjoyable activities including games, investigation, and interest-based enrichments that will increase your child's connections to what he or she learns at school. Dr. Willis's book is what parents have been searching for and need now more than ever.

As I see it, our children are little seedlings, all different, all full of budding potential. The educational system today unfortunately does not teach the child; it teaches the child to test. The beauty of this book is that now, you as a parent can help individualize school subjects for your child, because you can make the subjects come alive through everyday experiences, whether waiting in the local grocery store line or on journeys to exotic places together on the Internet.

I recall that when my children were in primary school, I became increasingly alarmed that their early education was leaving them behind, and they were getting lost in the process. Their talents and individuality were being repressed by rote memorization and the stress related to the fear of potential failure. I took a deep breath, went to the principal, and told her that my children weren't having any fun in school, that they dreaded it, and that I was seeing stress-related symptoms. I suggested she bring more personalization and subjectivity to their learning in order for them to connect more deeply to subjects and engender deeper, more lasting understanding and retention. She heard my frustration and was receptive to my ideas, and she began to change some strategies. One great example of her new direction was an English project that involved children photographing their families and then writing about it.

I knew nothing about neurology and how the brain worked. I didn't have a Judy Willis book on my bookshelf that I could reference to understand how children's little brains worked—much less my own. I have since learned so many important facts about brain development from her. By learning the basics of brain function (and it's not difficult), we pick up a magic wand that empowers us to help our children.

With technology moving so fast—cell phones, computer games, and MP3 players, not to mention the untamed media— it is more and more challenging for our children to focus for long periods of time. How does this constant input of static affect the brain? How do our children process all this information? How can they learn when there is an overload of incoming noise? How can we best help them? In this book, Judy leads us through the amazing, fantastic, magical brain in ways that illuminate us.

Judy speaks tirelessly all over the world to teachers, school superintendents, and policymakers. She is recognized as one of the leading experts in brain-friendly learning. She shows us how to help our children truly learn and remember facts, as opposed to simple rote memorization, which is like sand that disappears from a squeezed palm.

At last, we parents have a reference book to enlighten our own brains and help guide us in assisting our children's growth and flowering.

In closing, may I say that Judy is a vibrant, curious, brilliant woman who is passionate in her pursuit of new ways to help children learn joyfully. Through this book, she is offering us the gift of insight. Dive in fearlessly. You will find a treasure trove of wonder. You will experience a lot of "a-ha" moments, and it may change the way you see your children forever.

Thank you, Judy, for continuing to inspire and teach.

—Goldie Hawn

Judy Willis is now on the board of the Hawn Foundation.

INTRODUCTION:
From Stethoscope to Seating Chart

"Teach your children well…and feed them on your dreams"
—Stephen Stills

There are disturbing changes underway in today's school systems. Funding is frequently tied to scores achieved on standardized tests, which primarily evaluate rote memory. Teaching "to" tests like these inevitably focuses resources and curriculum on the lower-scoring students. The pressure to bring up test scores for these struggling students limits time for the kinds of individualized learning that challenges all students to reach their highest potential, and teachers have less opportunity to encourage creative thinking and incorporate hands-on activities. When education is not enriched by exploration, discovery, problem solving, and creative thinking, students are not truly engaged in their own learning. Because teachers are required to emphasize uninspiring workbooks and drills, more and more students are developing negative feelings about mathematics, science, history, grammar, and writing. Opportunities to authentically learn and retain knowledge are being replaced by instruction that teaches "to the tests."

Neuroimaging and new brain-wave technology provide evidence that rote learning is the most quickly forgotten, because the information is not stored in long-term memory. As students lose interest in lecture-and-memorize classes, their attention wanders, and disruptive behaviors are a natural consequence. Even for children who are able to maintain focus on rote teaching, the disruptive responses of their classmates are encroaching more and more on teachers' instruction time as they try to maintain order.

The good news is, there is hope for education.

> Rote memory focuses on learning by repetition and recall of facts, rather than learning by understanding a subject.

This is an exciting and pivotal time in brain research. Neuroimaging and brain mapping are being used outside the confines of medical and psychological study, and the resulting work has opened windows into the functions of the thinking brain. We now can view what happens in the brain as information from the senses is categorized and organized into short- and long-term memory—scans can literally show learning taking place!

My personal revelations about education came to me not as a classroom teacher, but as a neuroscience researcher. In 1970, as a pre-med college student, I was using one of the first-generation electron microscopes to examine synapses connecting brain cells in baby chicks. My heart still races as I recall one particular night. As I sat alone in the darkroom of the science center developing my electron micrographs, I noticed a greater collection of protein in the synapses of some chicks that had been trained to follow a moving light. It was visible proof of something that had been, until that moment, only an abstract concept: the idea that learning changes the brain's structure.

Throughout twenty-one years of education, including college at Vassar and Williams and medical school at UCLA, and fifteen years of neurology practice and research, I have been vitally interested in the neurology of learning. I finally realized I could apply the growing body of research about how the brain learns best to develop sensible, scientific strategies to help improve students' attitudes and academic success— "neuro-*logical*" strategies, as it were.

To best achieve my goal, I knew I would need professional training in education. I returned to college to obtain my teaching credential and masters degree in education.

At the same time, my youngest daughter was in elementary school. I volunteered one morning a week at her school, as I had done with my older daughter. My girls are ten years apart, however, and I found there was a huge difference in their experiences. By the time my younger daughter was in school, the impact of teaching "to the test" was disheartening. Where once children were enthusiastic participants in learning, they now were passive recipients of facts and work sheets. Ten years earlier, my older daughter's excitement would bubble over in the car and at the dinner table about the new things she learned and did in school. Ten years later, in those same classrooms, with the same excellent teachers, my younger daughter had to be prodded to tell us anything she learned about or liked in school that day. She and her classmates were bored and inattentive.

So here I was, finishing school and ready to teach, but losing faith that I could make a difference. If the creative teachers I'd known for a decade were being held back by stifling curriculum mandates, we were facing a serious problem.

I decided I would start by seeing what I could do to rekindle my daughter's enthusiasm for learning. If I could apply my neurological strategies successfully to help Alani, I would stay the course, become a teacher, and apply what I learned to my students. And when I discovered that I could reignite Alani's excitement for learning by linking her school topics to her own strengths and interests and to the real world, I knew I had stumbled onto something wonderful.

Once I became a teacher, I began using these strategies with my students, and they not only became more engaged with school, they also scored higher on standardized tests. At the request of teaching colleagues, I began writing papers for educational journals and speaking at seminars and conferences. I talked about the new discoveries being made pertaining to learning and the brain, and how these findings can be used to create classroom and home strategies that ignite children's imaginations. The teachers who come to my talks are delighted to learn about empirical research upon which they can develop curricula that engages students' highest levels of thinking.

The school years are critical times in a child's development of self and her relationship to the world. This is when your child gains access to a new compendium of tools she needs to understand and participate successfully in the world. I have written this book to offer you the valuable techniques and activities I have developed, based on the latest neuroimaging research and supported by cognitive testing. By using the brain-friendly strategies outlined here to boost learning at home, you can help even the most defeated child recapture the wonder she once experienced.

You will find specific suggestions for improving your child's attention span, memory, higher-level thinking, and reasoning. You'll also find practical information about how to evaluate the type of learner your child is, and which strategies are best suited for his learning-style preferences within each subject area. You will be able to help your child build academic skills, lower test-stress while increasing test scores, increase class participation, bolster weak spots to overcome challenges, optimize gifts, enrich talents, and, most importantly, reconnect with the joy of learning.

KEEP ALIVE YOUR CHILD'S NATURAL ENTHUSIASM TO LEARN

Children are naturally curious and have magnificent senses of wonder. They want to learn and explore. Often starting at age three or four, especially if they have older siblings, children look forward with great excitement to the day they start school. Once they begin, however, many no longer see it as a wondrous place. Children often begin to begrudge the time spent in school and resent having to do homework. How sad that is.

It doesn't have to be that way. Strategies that incorporate brain-based learning research can take children's natural curiosity and enthusiasm and build upon them to enrich their minds and sustain their inherent love of learning.

When you become active in your child's education, you can supercharge classroom lessons to connect with your child's individual needs, gifts, and challenges. Learning can become active and include creative exchanges of ideas. You can bring life back into your child's learning while helping her build the critical thinking, problem solving, and reasoning skills that are being sacrificed with a rote memorization approach to teaching

HOW DO YOU KNOW WHAT SCIENTIFIC CLAIMS TO TRUST FOR YOUR CHILD?

Information obtained through brain imaging during the learning process has yielded evidence about which strategies most effectively reach and excite the brains of children. Unfortunately, as with many scientific discoveries, the increased interest in this research has prompted a cottage industry of consumer products claiming to be "brain-based." Every day there are new claims of ways to improve learning and memory, from herbs and vitamins to meditation and hypnosis.

I have compared the promises of some of these self-proclaimed educational experts with the actual neurology research, and I have found many disconnects between the objective scientific data and the conjectures made by people lacking the background to properly assess the research. I am concerned about many of the conclusions being made and strategies being proposed as "scientific," and if you're reading this book, you probably are, too.

How can you know what is valid, evidence-based research? How can you use that knowledge to support and supplement your child's schooling?

I assessed the most recent neuroimaging and brain-mapping research to determine which studies are valid based on scientific method. I then connected that information with my training and experience as a classroom teacher to provide strategies (my own and those from other successful educators) for you to use at home to further your child's learning skills. When you follow these suggestions, you can help your child receive the best possible education during the years of maximum brain potential.

Your child deserves to have a sense of wonder about learning. When you use the practices described in this book to work with your child at home, he will develop the skills he needs to follow his own natural enthusiasm to understand and investigate the world around him. You will be your child's guide and partner as he becomes smarter in school and wiser in life skills.

HOW TO USE THIS BOOK

If you are interested in the neurological background information upon which the strategies offered in this book are based, read Chapter 1. If you're not that into science and prefer to move ahead, dive right in to Chapter 2, which describes the different styles of learning that children have, allowing you to identify your child's best learning style and his particular strengths. You can then proceed to the subject-based chapters to find the strategies best suited for his learning needs and strengths.

Chapters 3–12 provide ideas for tailoring learning experiences to your child's learning strengths and offer "neuro-*logical*" strategies for each subject area and type of academic task, from vocabulary testing to essay writing. There are also suggestions for dealing with the more general problems of organization and motivation that are so critical, especially in view of the current classroom climate. Each chapter offers specific interventions and enrichments that you can match to your child's individual needs and gifts to help build brainpower to its highest potential.

It is important that your child has fun at home and doesn't feel that he is just doing more of the same work he just did for six hours in school. Observe his physical and verbal responses to see if an activity is right for him. Yawning, wandering attention, easy distractibility, looking at the clock, very short answers, or excessive

Continued

doodling may indicate this is not the best activity for him. As you tackle activities together, look for signs that he is enjoying himself, and then watch for these in future activities. Relaxed engagement looks different in different children. Some indications can include pulling his chair closer to the table, speaking louder, making longer comments, and asking questions. After the activity, ask your child what he enjoyed. This will help you with future plans and help him recognize that he really did enjoy himself, so the dopamine-reward cycle will kick in when you do the activity again.

YOUR GOALS FOR YOUR CHILD

Take a moment to consider what goals you have for your child right now. Once you establish your goals and identify your child's learning strengths, look for suggestions about achieving those goals in each subject chapter. If you want to increase your child's interest in reading, for example, turn to the section about reading motivation. If your goal for your child is to score higher on math tests, you'll find descriptions of the different challenges children have regarding math tests. For each subject area and type of academic task, you will find solutions to suit your child's learning strengths. Here are some goals you may be considering for your child:

- Becoming a joyful, successful learner
- Building greater self esteem and confidence
- Being self-motivated through intrinsic gratification and increased awareness
- Achieving higher grades on homework, reports, and tests
- Adopting a mindful approach to homework and developing personalized study habits
- Using self-initiated organizational strategies
- Becoming comfortable asking questions in school and at home
- Enjoying the challenge of creative problem solving in school and in everyday life
- Learning to see mistakes as opportunities to learn
- Planning ahead so that procrastination is a thing of the past

- Stimulating increased interest and enthusiastic participation in academic, athletic, cultural, artistic, leadership, community, inter-personal, and global activities
- Finding opportunities and experiences in the real world to motivate self-propelled learning
- Building a widened range of interest and a greater sense of wonder about and respect for the world and its people
- Establishing a lifestyle in which learning is woven into daily events

Whatever your goals, this book contains brain-friendly approaches to achieve them, enrich your child's educational experience, and help her brain develop to its full potential. Enjoy this path to a better brain.

PART I:

Building Better Brains

1

THE SCIENCE BEHIND
BETTER LEARNING

"We can't hold on to our youth, but what we can hang on to is the thing we've been told a zillion times: You have to find the light in your life you had when you were a little girl or guy that made you happy."
—**Goldie Hawn**

This chapter explains how your child's brain turns information into knowledge and transforms short-term memory into long-term memory. You'll learn what you can do to help your child build and strengthen these critical skills.

THE KEY TO BUILDING BETTER BRAINS

Everything we learn comes to the brain through our senses. But the brain has built-in obstacles to sensory information input. It is an amazing organ, but it is not able to process the billions of bits of information that bombard it every second. To deal with the barrage, it is equipped with filters to protect itself from input overload and focus on the data most critical for survival.

How your child's brain responds to environmental sensory data determines what information gets his attention. Only selected information passes through his lower brain filter (called the reticular activating system, or RAS) to enter his thinking brain. The RAS is particularly responsive to novelty, surprise, color, and unexpected/curious events when selecting which sensory input to allow into the thinking brain.

Once information makes it through the first filter, there is a second filter in a part of the brain called the amygdala. The amygdala is part of the emotion-processing limbic system network. How well your child stores the sensory input that makes it through the amygdala filter is greatly influenced by her emotional state at the time she receives the information. When stress is high, the amygdala diverts the information to the reflex automatic system, where nonthinking reactions, such as fight/flight, dominate. When the amygdala is in a safe state and emotions are positive, the information is passed on to the reflective, memory-making, and thinking networks in the brain.

There is something that helps sensory input make it through these two filters—a chemical neurotransmitter called dopamine. When learning is associated with pleasure, dopamine is released. This surge increases focus, helping the brain stay attentive.

As a parent, understanding how information enters the brain to become knowledge and long-term memory is a powerful tool for enriching you child's brainpower. Using brain-friendly strategies empowers your child to respond to the most useful sensory input from her environment and turn that data into retained knowledge.

RAD Learning

There are two essential brain *processes* and three main brain *systems* that are keys to building better brains. The processes are *patterning* and *neuroplasticity*. The three systems are what I refer to as *RAD*, which is short for:

R: *Reticular activating system* (RAS)
A: *Affective filter in the amygdala*
D: *Dopamine*

If you want to learn more about these systems, the information in this chapter goes into detail about the neuroanatomy and chemistry of learning. If you are ready to jump into the strategies, you can move on to Chapter 2, identify your child's best learning strengths, and then proceed to the subject-based chapters to find the strategies best suited to his learning needs.

The Reticular Activating System (RAS)—The Brain's Sensory Switchboard

The RAS is the attention-activation switching system located at the lower back of the brain (brain stem). It receives input from the nerves that converge into the spinal cord from nerve endings in the arms, legs, trunk, neck, face, and internal organs. The RAS sets the state of arousal and vigilance of the rest of the brain. It is the RAS that selectively alerts brains to changes in their environment that impact their survival—sounds, sights, and smells that may indicate danger or signal opportunities to find food, mates, or shelter.

In humans, the RAS has evolved to become responsive to more than just the basic needs for survival in the wild, but it is still a filter that is most attentive to changes in our environment. The RAS is key to "turning on" the brain's level of response and alertness.

The RAS's response to the sensory information it receives determines the speed, content, and type of information available to the "higher" brain. Although millions of bits of sensory data bombard the RAS every waking second, this filter limits access to about two thousand bits per second.

In successful learning, children are stimulated to pay attention to important information by getting the attention of their RAS. Listening to lectures and doing drills and worksheets are not novel or engaging experiences, so they do not contain the sensory stimulation sufficient to power information through the RAS's brain filters.

The Amygdala—Where Heart Meets Mind

The sensory information that children receive—the things they see, hear, feel, smell, or touch—stimulates the intake centers of their brains beyond the RAS.

The areas most active when new information first enters the brain are the *sensory cortex* areas in each lobe of the brain. Each of these regions is specialized to analyze data from just one sense (hearing, touch, taste, vision, and smell). This input is identified and classified by matching it with previously stored similar data. The sight of a lemon, for example, connects with the visual cortex in the occipital lobes. The feel of the lemon is recognized by the somatosensory (touch) centers in the parietal lobes.

This sensory data must then pass through the brain's emotional core, the *limbic system*, especially the *amygdala* and *hippocampus*, where emotional significance is linked to information (sour taste is yummy in lemon sherbet but yucky in unsweetened lemon juice). On receiving sensory data, these emotional filters evaluate its pleasure value. That decision determines if the information is given further access to the higher brain, and if so, where the data will go.

When the brain perceives threat or the child feels stressed, these brain filter centers go into survival mode and divert the sensory data away from the thinking brain and into the automatic centers (fight/flight). Because there are usually no tigers in our homes, children really don't need the same threat-filter response their prehistoric predecessors did. Yet those filters still exist in human brains and can be activated by the type of stresses children experience in some classrooms. Bullying, attention difficulties, confusion, or boredom may trigger these filters, blocking the absorption of sensory input related to learning. The fight/flight response is engaged because the stimuli are perceived as negative experiences, and learning becomes difficult.

If your child is frustrated, bored, or confused because she already knows how to multiply fractions but is doing yet another worksheet multiplying fractions, or if she's confused by the difficult vocabulary words in the story the class is reading, her amygdala responds to those stresses by taking up much of the brain's available nutrients and oxygen. The brain then goes into survival mode. The high activity in the amygdala blocks entry of information to the thinking brain and memory. This is why learning strategies that reduce children's anxiety are important: They lower the affective (emotional) filter in the amygdala and allow information to reach the thinking centers. When your child is stressed, the amygdala directs information to the *reactive*, nonthinking brain. When your child is relaxed, comfortable, and interested, the amygdala directs the information to the *reflective*, thinking brain.

When you understand the functions of these filters, you can also use them in positive ways. If learning experiences are associated with pleasure, connected to topics of interest, or related to satisfying goal achievement and other positive experiences, sensory data will be considered valuable and permitted entry into the higher, thinking brain. With well-planned learning activities that sustain attention and interest without producing frustration, confusion, or boredom, these filters can be recruited to help the brain focus on the sensory information of the learning activity.

Next to the amygdala in the limbic system is the hippocampus. It is in this *consolidation center* that new sensory input is linked to previous knowledge and to memories of past experiences retrieved from memory storage. Positron emission tomography (PET) scans show that when children are given new information, their brains activate their stored memory banks. Their brains are seeking relationships or connections between the new information and stored memories of past knowledge or experience. When new information is consolidated with prior knowledge, the newly coded *relational memory* is now ready for processing in the frontal lobes and long-term memory storage

Dopamine—Working to Prime Your Child's Brain

Dopamine is one of the brain's most important *neurotransmitters.* (Some of the other neurotransmitters in the brain include serotonin, tryptophan, acetylcholine, and norepinephrine.) These neurotransmitters are brain chemicals that carry information across the spaces (*synapses*) that form when one nerve ending connects with another. During the last trimester of fetal development, the brain creates thirty thousand synapses per second for every square centimeter of cortical surface.

The brain releases dopamine when an experience is pleasurable. As a pleasure-seeking organ, the brain also releases dopamine in expectation of rewarding, pleasurable experiences. This has several advantages. Dopamine release increases attentive focus and memory formation. When dopamine is released during enjoyable learning activities, it actually increases children's capacities to control attention and store long-term memories.

Learning activities that can induce the release of dopamine and create pleasurable states in the brain include physical movement, personal interest connections, social contacts, music, novelty, sense of achievement, intrinsic reward, choice, play, and humor. The dopamine released during these activities is then available to increase attention and focus.

Internal motivation is valuable in goal setting and persevering with homework, studying, and focus in class. Especially when the goals are related to personal interest, children will build on their strengths and enjoy the dopamine-pleasure response from their goal-directed achievements. Many of the strategies in this book are connected to building dopamine-pleasure brain responses.

RAD LEARNING = Reticular Activating System + Amygdala's Filter + Dopamine

Helping your child turn information into knowledge

R = Reticular activating system (RAS): Use changes in the environment, mindful focus activities, teachable moments, and multisensory lessons to turn on the brain's attention via this information intake filter. The RAS alerts the brain to change and gets it primed to interact with new information based on past experience (existing brain patterns of prior knowledge). The RAS selects for intake the sensory input (information) it "values" for survival or pleasure potential.

A = Amygdala: Games and activities that reduce stress and increase pleasurable associations with learning keep this second brain filter from blocking information from the higher, thinking brain. Stress, boredom, frustration, or confusion block the flow of information through the amygdala to the thinking brain. However, when learning is associated with pleasure, the amygdala "stamps" that information with increased memory impact. Activities that build curiosity, positive emotional associations, and reminders of pleasurable prior experiences and academic successes expedite knowledge passage through the amygdala's filter.

Continued

D = Dopamine: This neurotransmitter's release is associated with pleasurable experiences and when the brain expects a pleasurable experience. Dopamine release also increases focus, attention, and executive function in the frontal lobes. Neuro-*logical* strategies are available to accelerate learning through the dopamine-pleasure cycle.

FROM SENSORY INPUT TO HIGHER THINKING

The brain has highly developed nerve communication networks, especially in the prefrontal cortex, where higher thinking takes place. When sensory information from what is heard, felt, seen, and otherwise sensed is not blocked by the RAS and amygdala filters, the information can reach the powerful thinking and reasoning networks in the prefrontal lobes. These higher thinking networks process new information through what are called *executive functions*, including judgment, analysis, prioritizing, and decision-making.

It is in the executive function networks that new information is *mentally manipulated* to become memory. When your child's prefrontal cortex actively processes new information with mental manipulation such as problem solving, planning, or predicting, his executive functions take ownership of the new information and it is transformed from short-term into long-term memory.

HOW THE BRAIN BUILDS MEMORY

When your child's brain turns sensory input into memory, she learns. The construction of new memories allows her brain to learn by experience and predict the outcome of her behavior. Memory is a survival requirement for animals that must learn, store, and recall how they should respond to physical needs and changes in their environment. They reactivate stored memories to recall and predict. Where did they go to find food? What places were dangerous because of predators? Where was the safe cave that provided shelter?

Each time your child remembers something, he is also reactivating a neural network that his brain previously created. When he adds new memories related to information already in brain storage, the neural circuit for that pattern or category of knowledge grows larger as more connections form between nerve cells. In essence, the more information stored in the brain's networks, the more successfully we respond to our environments. The more we learn, the more information stored in our neural networks, the more likely our brains are to relate to new information—hence, learning promotes learning.

Types of Memory

Rote memory is unfortunately the type most commonly required of students in school. Rote memory involves simply memorizing, and soon forgetting, facts that are often of little personal interest, such as a list of vocabulary words. Usually these facts are not paired with interesting connections that would give them meaningful context or relationship to children's lives or past experiences. There are no neural networks (patterns) to which these isolated bits of data can connect, so permanent memories are not constructed.

The good news is that by using personalizing, connecting, and motivating learning strategies, your child will spend less time memorizing. Instead, she will be able to link new information to her previous knowledge, existing categories of stored information, and personal experiences. What remains to be memorized will be easier because you will discover which activities and strategies help her build upon her learning strengths to efficiently construct permanent memories more rapidly and enjoyably.

Working memory, or short-term memory, holds data in a child's mind for less than a minute. The challenge students face is in moving information from their working memories into their long-term memories. If this does not take place in less than one minute, that information can be lost. (Think about the last time someone gave you driving directions that seemed so clear when you heard them, but evaporated once you made the second right turn.) To keep working memory from slipping away, it needs to enter the network of the brain's neuronal circuits.

There are study activities, such as vocabulary word meanings or math formulas, you can use with your child to increase her mental manipulation of facts so the information is retained as long-term memory without tedious drill and repetition.

Long-term memory is created when short-term memory is strengthened through review and meaningful association with existing patterns and prior knowledge. This strengthening results in a physical change in the structure of neuronal circuits.

Relational memory takes place when your child links new information to something he already has stored in his memory. His brain actively seeks these connections when it encounters new information. If no links are found and no strategies are employed to recognize connections that exist, his brain won't transform the input into memory. However, by using *pattern recognition* strategies, your child will make those links and construct permanent relational memories. Studying for tests is more efficient and successful.

Building Knowledge through Patterning and Prediction

Patterning refers to the meaningful organization, coding, and categorization of information in the brain. It is through the patterns constructed and stored in neural networks that our brains recognize and make meaning out of the millions of bits of sensory input received every second. The greater your child's experience in sorting information into categories, the greater her chances of finding relevant patterns in new information. When you provide your child with a rich environment, interesting experiences, and sorting (categorizing) activities, you help her build her patterning tools.

Prediction is what the brain does with the information it patterns. Patterning allows the brain to store information and add new learning to existing categories. Prediction occurs when the brain has enough information in a patterned memory category that it can find similar patterns in new information and predict what the patterns mean. For example if you see the number sequence 3,6,9,12…, you predict the next number will be 15 because you recognize the pattern of counting by threes. Through careful observation (another skill to practice with children that will be described later), the brain learns more about our world and is able to make more accurate predictions about what will come next. Prediction is often what is measured in intelligence tests. This predicting ability is the basis for successful reading, calculating, test taking, goal setting, and appropriate social behavior. Successful prediction is one of the best problem-solving strategies the brain has.

Activities that allow your child to recognize, play with, and create patterns are powerful memory-building tools. I once observed a preschool in which children were engaged in a variety of patterning activities. In one section of the room, two four-year-olds were playing with Legos. They were not building a structure; they were simply sorting the pieces and finding patterns. One child separated the pieces by color, regardless of size or shape. Her pile's pieces were all red. The other child said, "I know what you are doing. You are keeping the same color together." Both children giggled as if a great discovery had been made.

Then the second child said he had a guessing game for the first child. He sorted the Legos by size. To my surprise, he went beyond just collating the same size cubes. He also included cylinders and spheres if they were about the same size. He was actually recognizing that patterning by size could go beyond shape and color—he was discovering volume.

I was already impressed and thought that was it, but not for these two kids. The other child said, "I'm ready to make a guess." She then moved a Lego wheel of about the same size as the other objects into the pile and asked if she was right. Her partner said, "I think so, but try again to be really, truly, really, really sure." She then placed another piece in the pile, this one a small ball about the same size as the other objects and said, "They are all the same smallness." She had not only detected the pattern and correctly predicted what would match it, but she had also verbally described it!

I don't know who taught these children the skills of patterning and predicting, but their high-level thinking in these areas was quite advanced and, more importantly, they enjoyed their activities. I *predict*, based on past experience, that if they continued to have those kinds of positive learning experiences, they went on to be successful in math, reading, and much more.

Neuroplasticity and the Continually Growing Brain

Neuroplasticity (often shortened to *plasticity*) includes the growth of new neuronal connections and the *pruning* of unused connections between neurons. Neuroplasticity is a physical reshaping of the brain in response to life experiences and mental manipulation of information. Plasticity growth adds new memories by linking new information onto existing memory networks. This includes the construction of more connections between neurons (dendrites, synapses, and more). When more of these bridges connect neurons, information traffic flow is more efficient. Neurons can share information faster. Pruning, as the name implies, is the brain's elimination of nerve pathways that are not being used so they won't drain its limited supply of nutrients. Pruning is a "use it or lose it" phenomenon.

LEARNING PROMOTES LEARNING

Neurons that fire together, wire together. When more connections form between neurons, there is greater potential for further learning. Each time your child participates in any endeavor, a certain number of neurons are activated. When the action is repeated, such as rehearsing a song or reviewing a list, the same neurons respond again. The more times one repeats an action (practice) or recalls the information (review), the more dendrites sprout to connect new memories to old ones (plasticity), the stronger the connections between neurons become, and the more efficient the brain becomes at retrieving that memory or repeating that action.

The learning activities in the following chapters build better brains by increasing your child's ability to select the sensory input on which to focus (RAS), powering the appropriate information through the brain's filters (RAS and amygdala), and connecting learning with positive experiences (dopamine release). Through games that build successful patterning, she will construct and store durable relational memories. With enjoyable, learning strength-compatible review activities, her brain's neuroplasticity will build more efficient neural networks with which to store and retrieve long-term memories. Each brain-strengthening process paves the way for the next success, as learning promotes learning.

It is a great cycle to build lifelong learning.

Let's get started!

2
YOUR CHILD'S LEARNING STRENGTHS

Discovering Intelligence and Learning Styles

They Are Poetry

Why doesn't she like to talk?
Because there is so much to look at in her mind.
Why doesn't he like to run?
Because the ants he watches move slowly.
Why doesn't he like to write?
Because his words get tangled in a tango.
Why doesn't she like to read?
Because the letters float like cookie crumbs in milk.
Why doesn't he like to draw?
Because his thoughts take a nap on the way to his pencil.
Why doesn't he like to sing?
Because he likes to listen.
Whey are they all unique?
Because they are poetry.
—Malana Page Willis

When you help your child tap into the way she learns best, you will help her find a comfortable and compatible approach to any subject, which increases her potential to enjoy high achievement. The more your child knows about the way she learns best, the more insight, strategies, and self-awareness she will have to use her learning strengths to achieve her greatest potential as a joyful learner.

There are several different ways to look at learning, including multiple intelligence designations and learning-style preferences. These two approaches overlap—the learning proficiencies that are the hallmark of specific intelligence strengths match the learning-style preferences found in children with those intelligences.

This all can sound a little confusing and academic, so in order to designate which brain-friendly strategies in this book will help your child best, I have devised two classifications of "learning strengths." The strategies that follow are suited to these learning strengths, a categorization that incorporates both multiple intelligence and learning styles.

Before we discuss the learning strengths, however, let's take a look at the more formal definitions and characteristics of multiple intelligence and learning styles. As you read through these categories, consider making notes or underlining qualities you recognize in your child. Those notes can help you decide which of the two learning strengths best describes your child.

MULTIPLE INTELLIGENCES

Multiple intelligence theory suggests that rather than intelligence being an all-or-nothing entity, it is made up of distinct learning proficiencies that can work individually or together. There are generally eight agreed-upon classifications of intelligence strengths. All of us are presumed by this theory to have all eight intelligences in varying amounts. Your child's learning may be most efficient and successful when he applies his strongest intelligence to the task. Here's a quick overview of those eight intelligences:

Linguistic intelligence includes sensitivity to sounds, rhythms, and words. Proficiencies in this intelligence include organizational abilities, logical deduction, memory sensitivity to spoken and written language, mnemonics, and structured, sequential notes or instructions.

Logical-mathematical intelligence includes proficiencies in logic, patterning, conceptualization, and abstraction.

Musical-rhythmic intelligence includes sensitivity to auditory tone, pitch, and rhythm. Proficiencies include auditory patterning and auditory memory.

Visual-spatial intelligence includes sensitivity to the relationships of objects, concepts, or images in different fields or dimensions. Proficiencies in this intelligence include mentally creating and visualizing spatial relationships, as in mapping or diagramming, and starting with a big-picture conceptual overview before filling in details.

Bodily-kinesthetic intelligence includes sensitivity to physical, spatial, or sequential movement through time and space. Proficiencies include sense of time, proportion, prediction of sequence, and visualization of movement.

Interpersonal intelligence includes perceptiveness and sensitivity to others' moods and feelings. Proficiencies include the ability to interact with and lead people with understanding by interpreting their intensions, needs, emotions, and desires.

Intrapersonal intelligence includes understanding of and confidence in one's own beliefs and goals. Proficiencies include an ability to reflect upon one's own thoughts and feelings, introspection, analysis, and reflection.

Naturalist intelligence includes perceptiveness of things existing in the natural world, such as plants and animals. Proficiencies include organizing things into categories, detailed observation, and pattern recognition.

LEARNING STYLES
Learning-style preferences refer to the way children prefer to approach learning and how their brains most successfully process information. Where intelligences are seen in *what* children relate to in the things, information, and people around them, learning-style preferences are reflective of *how* they relate and which way of presenting information is most likely to stick with their neural-network patterning.

There are dozens of different names for learning-style preferences, though three main ones dominate, and for the purposes of this book, I will consolidate these into three general categories.

Auditory-sequential or analytical learners tend to process information in a parts-to-whole manner. These children respond to logic, order, and sequence. Auditory-sequential (AS) preference is evidenced in children who respond best to spoken information. These are often children with linguistic and logical-mathematical intelligence strengths who tend to learn best by evaluating patterns and connections in information they hear. AS learners often respond well when they study information methodically—making timelines, lists, and other sequences using facts about the information they need to study. They also respond to talking or reading aloud to themselves and being quizzed verbally when they study.

AS learners prefer dealing with one task at a time in organized working spaces. Because they tend to be analytical thinkers, they prefer solving existing problems rather than creating their own. They use logic and deduction. If your child is an AS learner, he might enjoy expanding on a concept or theme by reasoning out and predicting logical implications that follow from a rule or guiding principle. AS learners usually prefer learning activities that have one correct answer and can be broken down into logical, sequential steps.

Visual-spatial learners usually are high in visual-spatial (VSK) intelligence and process information best when a topic is introduced as an overview before the details are taught, in a whole-before-detail or global introduction. They think primarily in images and prefer visual explanations, videos, diagrams, computer simulations/graphics, and demonstrations. They enjoy success when learning is less structured and more creative and interactive.

Because children with visual-spatial learning-style preferences tend to see or visualize patterns and connections, they enjoy solving novel problems with more than one solution. They choose or create their own problems and evaluate them through reasoning and intuition.

VSK learners enjoy starting with a larger concept and then adding details to that concept through inductive reasoning. To do this, they often like to see the final product and then, without instruction, use their intuition to figure out how to get the final product or solution.

These children like discovering or creating relationships between themselves and what they are about to study.

Kinesthetic preference learners generally have the proficiencies found in children with bodily-kinesthetic intelligence and many of the proficiencies found in children with visual-spatial intelligence. They like to touch what they are learning and respond well to learning activities with movement, role playing, and hands-on exploration with math manipulatives and science experiments, and may need to move during breaks rather than just change to a different sedentary activity.

THE TWO LEARNING-STRENGTH CATEGORIES

The two learning-strength categories I have devised, visual-spatial-kinesthetic (VSK) and auditory-sequential (AS), incorporate commonalities between learning styles and dominant intelligences. You will find strategies to support these designations throughout the remainder of the book.

When you identify your child's learning strengths and find the strategies that suit him best, you will open up opportunities for success in all academic areas.

Visual-Spatial-Kinesthetic (VSK)

Individuals with this learning strength demonstrate a sensitivity to the physical, spatial, and temporal relationships of objects, concepts, or images in and through space and time.

Proficiencies in this intelligence include mentally recreating and visualizing spatial relationships, seeing the big picture, prediction of sequence, visualization of movement, good time-coordination sense, physical coordination in fine and gross motor skills, and putting together puzzles or broken objects.

VSK learners respond to:

- A topic being introduced as an overview before the details are taught, in a whole-before-detail style
- Exploring the big picture or concept before focusing on details
- Discovering or creating relationships between themselves and what they are about to study
- Images and visual explanations, videos, diagrams, photographs, magazine pictures, maps, computer simulations/graphics, and demonstrations

- Visualization of patterns and connections, visual memory strategies, video learning, books with pictures and diagrams
- Learning with their own art, maps, or diagrams
- Creating analogies for strong relational-memory building
- Using movement of objects or their bodies to learn information, solve problems, and convey ideas
- Opportunities to discover things or solve problems creatively before reading or listening to detailed instructions
- Novel problems with more than one solution
- Choosing or creating their own problems and evaluating them through reasoning and intuition
- Hands-on experimentation and object manipulation to deduce patterns
- Dramatizations, pantomime, puppet shows
- Making models, crafts, floor puzzles, manipulating Legos and blocks
- Moving letters on magnetic boards, writing on chalkboards or whiteboards, and prefer typing over writing
- Step-on number lines
- Nature walks, field trips

Challenges for Some VSK Children

- Tuning out or becoming distracted during passive learning, extended explanations or directions, and prolonged sitting
- Being able to write down all the steps that took place in their brains when they solved problems
- Being challenged by memorization more than linguistic learners
- Having trouble organizing time and prioritizing activities
- Experiencing difficulty with verbally communicating their visualizations or concepts

Auditory-Sequential (AS)

Individuals with this learning strength demonstrate sensitivity to sounds, structured patterns, logic, order, sequence, and words.

Proficiencies include several (but usually not all) of the following: organizational abilities, logical deduction and concept building (parts-to-whole construction of knowledge), evaluating patterns and connections in information they hear, memory sensitivity to spoken and written language, vocabulary, and foreign-language aptitude.

AS learners respond to:

- Clear rules to follow to learn a skill or do an activity; structured, sequential notes or instructions
- Problems already existing rather than self-created (they tend to be analytical thinkers, and may then use logic and deduction to expand on a concept or theme by reasoning out and predicting logical implications that follow from a rule or guiding principle)
- Dealing with one task at a time
- Categorizing and sorting
- Processing information in a parts-to-whole manner—doing things in well-defined steps and instructions (recipes, instructions)
- Written and spoken language, including changes in tone, pitch, and rhythm
- Memorizing facts presented in a logical, methodical way
- Graphic organizers connecting parts to whole, compare/contrast, making timelines, mnemonics
- Songs or music, audiobooks, connecting music or rhythmic movement to learning, and reading aloud or repeating information to themselves when studying

Challenges for Some AS Children

- Grasping and mentally visualizing some nonverbal concepts and special relationships
- Understanding the big concept without first thoroughly understanding the steps that build it
- Recognizing the physical, spatial, and temporal relationships of objects, concepts, or images in and through space and time.
- Memorizing facts without first understanding the logic that connects them

DISCOVERING YOUR CHILD'S LEARNING STRENGTH

As a way to evaluate your child's learning strength, consider which learning experiences he finds most enjoyable and which he dislikes or finds frustrating. Does he connect more to what he manipulates, listens to, or sees? Imagine your son visiting a zoo or museum. Is he more likely to run right to the habitat of his favorite animal and tell you what he sees (VSK)? Does he want to start at the first cage or habitat and move in an orderly way throughout the entire zoo, reading the display cards or listening to the audio headsets at each destination (AS)? When he gets home, does he move toy animals around as if creating a zoo (VSK), draw sketches of animals (VSK), create stories about the animals (AS), diagram the zoo in map form (AS), or request books about his favorite animals (AS and some VSK)?

Kids Who Don't Fit

Keep in mind that children rarely fit all characteristics of one learning strength and don't necessarily respond to all activities and strategies designated for their learning strengths. All children have some characteristics of both. As you're reading through this book, you may want to try various strategy options described for both learning strengths, and over time, you may find that the best fit comes from one or the other.

In addition, practicing the suggestions for both learning strengths can help reinforce learning goals while building proficiencies in your child's nondominant learning strengths. This is part of the benefit of multi-sensory learning.

MULTISENSORY LEARNING

Even though each child has individual learning strengths, it benefits all children to exercise multiple learning systems and neural networks. If your child is doing well with a subject by working through his "learner strength," it can be a good opportunity to encourage him to incorporate something different. For example, if your son always wants to study with note cards and is doing well in vocabulary, suggest that he try to learn the new words by drawing pictures or acting them out. His success on his next vocabulary test will give him more confidence in his artistic or dramatic abilities when it comes time for the class play or school art show, and it will also give him more versatility in studying for tests or preparing reports.

When children have access to learning activities that include multiple avenues of access (sensory connections) to the information, multiple brain regions are connected to the lesson. Multisensory input results in enriched, reinforced information transit to memory storage along more than one pathway. This redundancy of pathways and storage regions results in a greater likelihood of memory retention. Creating duplicated storage areas also results in faster, more accurate recall, and stored memories can be retrieved by a variety of stimuli. That's a good thing, too!

SYN-*NAPS*: REFILL THE TANK

Young brains are simply not equipped for sustained periods of high concentration. Neuroimaging demonstrates what happens when children's brains don't get the breaks they need: the brain's messenger chemicals—neurotransmitters such as serotonin, dopamine, tryptophan, and epinephrine—are depleted by long periods of forced concentration. When your child is entering a state of depletion of neurotransmitters, she can become fidgety, distracted, and unfocused. It is best to have your child take a brain rest before neurotransmitter depletion occurs and before stress builds up in the amygdala, inhibiting new information intake. If the neurotransmitters are not being replenished as fast as they are being used, or if amygdala hyperactivity is beginning to block new information input, memory efficiency drops rapidly. In this burnout state, new memories can't be stored efficiently. These neurotransmitters rebuild with time, but only if the brain is rested.

It is neuro-*logical* to plan periodic rests during which your child's neurotransmitters are replenished, so her higher reasoning centers can return to the learning session fully alert and refreshed. We'll call them "syn-*naps*." The use of the word "syn-*naps*" is an example of the use of wordplay to help build memory. The synapse is the gap between nerve endings. Neurotransmitters like dopamine carry information across this space separating the axon extensions of one neuron from the dendrite that leads to the next neuron on the pathway.

If a learning activity involves complex material, brain rest can be necessary after as little as 15 minutes. During these rests, the newly learned material has the opportunity to go from working memory to relational memory (although it will not become permanent memory until time and practice follow).

Having plans for enjoyable syn-*naps* activities is much better than the common practice of having a snack. Associating food with a break from studying can lay the foundation for future negative behavior patterns, such as eating to feel better emotionally. Instead, your child can change pace by moving about the room, stretching, singing, playing a musical instrument, tossing a ball, or rehydrating with a glass of water. Return to academic study after the syn-*naps* with a pleasurable activity, so your child won't associate the return to learning with an end of pleasure.

You know your child's body language better than anyone. When your child is not alert and focused, no amount of repetition will drive the information into his memory storage banks, and it's time for a syn-*naps*.

SHARE THE KNOWLEDGE

After you decide which type of learner your child is, consider letting him know what you think, and why. Ask for his opinions. Helping your child discover how he learns best gives him insights into self-awareness. Children who understand their learning strengths begin to develop their own strategies suited to those strengths. The more your child knows about his unique abilities and talents and the way he learns best, the more strategies he will have to use his learning-strength strategies to achieve his greatest potential as a joyful learner.

Sharing Strengths and Strategies with Your Children's Teachers

If your child's learning strength doesn't match the type of instruction she receives in school, the result can be frustration, underachievement, lowered self-concept, and learning difficulties. Your child may be judged as having a learning disability or attention disorder, when in fact she is a creative, perhaps gifted, thinker. The rush to label children with LD or ADD implies a permanent condition and can become a self-fulfilling prophecy, when the root of the problem could simply be a disconnect between your child's way of processing information and the way she's taught in school.

When you offer your child opportunities to use her learning strengths at home, mastery becomes greater and learning more powerful. When you share this information with her teachers, learning disability labels can be reevaluated and behavior understood as the learning-strength differences it really represents, and it can be responded to appropriately.

Most classrooms are best suited for AS learners who sit still, take notes, and learn by listening carefully (although only a small portion of AS learners are actively learning during such passive experiences). VSK learners, especially boys, need more opportunities to use their learning strengths. Misbehavior at school may be attributed to a lack of motivation, and teachers are understandably upset and angry when they interpret misbehavior as purposeful or as something that the child could change "if he only would try harder." When you help your child's teachers recognize that behavior reflects individual differences in temperament, not motivation, it helps them think about the fit between the child and the situation, and allows them to make the necessary adjustments.

Many educators lack the knowledge and expertise in neuroscience and cognitive science to support students with different learning strengths within the constraints of the typical, increasingly rigid curriculum. When you help your child's teachers understand your child's learning strengths, they are better able to create more opportunities to connect with those strengths.

So what should you do?

Consider sending a note or scheduling a brief conference with your child's teachers early in the year to present information about your child's best learning strengths and the types of homework or reports that are most engaging and productive for him.

You may have suggestions for homework alternatives that you find are best suited to your child's learning strengths. Perhaps, for example, you're concerned that the time your son spends looking up definitions in the dictionary and copying them word-for-word is not productive and fails to help him retain them when tested. Instead of complaining that the assignment is worthless, you might send a note suggesting that he use the vocabulary words in sentences or as part of a story, so he demonstrates his understanding of their meaning.

When you find strategies that are particularly successful for your child, save evidence of his successful work, or let his teacher know which activities are particularly helpful with different subjects and types of assignments. To reinforce development of a mutually beneficial relationship with the teachers, let them know you are looking forward to learning about anything they observe in class that you can add to the strategies and study techniques your child uses with you at home. When you send these teachers follow-up notes about how your child responded to their suggestions at home, they will appreciate your acknowledgment of their input. You will establish a teamwork approach that will increase your child's enjoyment and his success with that teacher.

Another way to show your appreciation for the effort your child's teachers are making is to offer to help in the classroom or with jobs they need done, such as photocopying, filing, or planning class parties. Not only will you be helping, you also will have the opportunity to observe your child learn in a different setting and gain more insight into what works, and doesn't work, for her.

If problems in communication come up, there are strategies you can use to achieve the best outcome for your child. I have been involved in conflicts of various magnitudes between teachers, parents, administrators, counselors, and students, in each of my roles as parent, teacher, neurologist (prescribing or refusing to prescribe medication for behavioral "issues"), and mediator.

Begin by considering what you feel would be the ideal outcome. You can then adopt a positive approach, seeking solutions instead of following the fruitless path of placing blame. Talk to your child to be sure that any complaints she expresses are true and not simply attempts at getting your attention.

If you feel sure your child is having a problem the teacher might help solve, your approach can be cooperative rather than accusatory. "I am concerned that Bev is not able to stay focused during class discussions," instead of, "You don't seem to keep the class under control, and when they all call out without raising their hands, Bev is frustrated and confused."

If your child is in upper elementary school, it can be useful to include her in the discussion you schedule with the teacher. When she participates in discussion and conflict resolution, she is building important life skills.

Increased communication with your child's teachers brings about alignment of school learning and the things you do together at home, and achieves a coordinated approach that will increase enjoyment, engagement, and active learning.

The Result: Increased Interest, Motivation, and Success in the Classroom

When you enrich schoolwork with learning strategies best suited to your child's learning skills and strengths, more efficient neural connections are made. Memory retention and classroom success is likely to reduce or eliminate much of what may have been labeled as "acting out" or hyperactivity by teachers. Connection of school topics to your child's interests and learning strengths increases his engagement and participation in the classroom.

Your child will respond with joy and optimism, and she will be excited about learning.

PART II:

Reading

3
LAYING THE FOUNDATION FOR READING SUCCESS (AGES 3–8)

"SITTING ISN'T LEAVING!"

On a hot afternoon, after a climb up a few hundred steps in a historic lighthouse on the Oregon coast, I was weary but ready for the next adventure. I had been motivated to make it to the top because I knew it would be worth climbing those stairs, both for the view and for the lighthouse's historical significance. Back in the parking lot, I heard a boy of about five complaining to his parents in the overtired and frustrated whine any parent recognizes. He didn't want to go to any more lighthouses. They were "stupid and boring," so why should he have to go? His parents tried to reason with him, promising that the lighthouse room at the top would be "so interesting." They were using the same fruitless logic we parents use when trying to coax children to eat vegetables because they are healthy. He remained completely unmoved.

As the child became more angry and resistant, his parents suggested he sit in the car and calm down, and then they would continue the discussion. This boy knew what that meant. There would be no discussion, and he would have no say in the outcome. So he just put it out there and proclaimed in a loud, nasal reproach, "Sitting isn't leaving!"

The emotions he was feeling are much like those of children who struggle with learning to read. The frustration, impatience, and anxiety about making mistakes build and build as teachers and parents try to convince children to climb the lighthouse steps that are the bizarre phonics of the English language.

Reading comes easily to some children, but most struggle with some part of the complex process, such as recognizing words, sounding out words with letters that have several pronunciations, memorizing high-frequency words, reading orally with fluency and expressiveness, understanding vocabulary, or comprehending stories. When your child is asked to face stressful reading challenges, he feels much like that little boy facing the daunting staircase. For some children, learning to read is so frustrating that they stop caring about books completely. The child who loved hearing you read bedtime stories over and over suddenly just gives up. If learning to read is this hard, why not just play a video game or watch television?

Learning to read should not be a discouraging, joyless struggle. You can observe your child as he tries to read, and see which skills are weak, where he struggles, and where he succeeds. Because you know your child's learning-style strengths and what interests him, you can make reading a goal he can achieve with a positive attitude. You can select the strategies offered here that match your child's specific challenges and learning styles, and by doing so, keep up his motivation.

Unlike learning to speak, learning to read is not a natural process for your child's brain. Neuronal networks must be gradually built up, exercised, stimulated, and extended through activities that help your child develop reading skills neuro-*logically*. Using games, rhymes, and songs along with the words in these pleasurable verbal and auditory experiences, your child will pattern neural pathways that connect letters to sounds and recognize the patterns of words and then sentences. When you add the support of helping him learn the high-frequency words, prefixes, suffixes, and roots, the payoff is wonderful—words on a page are translated in his brain into meaningful, exciting sentences that become a springboard to the world of reading.

Why Reading Is a Challenge: It's Unnatural

Reading is not a natural part of human development. Unlike spoken language, it does not follow from observation and imitation of other people. There are specific regions of the brain devoted to speech and processing oral communication, yet there is no specific center of the brain dedicated to reading. Instead, the complex task of reading requires that multiple areas of the brain work together through networks of neurons. This means there are many potential dysfunctions in structure and information transfer that can interfere with successful reading. For children to become joyful, successful readers, they need to develop the neural pathways that connect the parts of the brain that turn print into words, and words into thoughts and memories. Considering how inter-dependent and intricate these reading networks are, it is astonishing that anyone is able to read at all!

SECTION I:
DEVELOPING PHONEMIC AWARENESS IN YOUNG CHILDREN (AGES 3–6)

There are two key things that are highly correlated with good readers: early phonemic awareness, and parents who read for personal pleasure. When your child sees you reading for pleasure and you share interesting facts or part of a story with her, she sees that reading is fun. When you show her how you use reading to follow a recipe or assemble a toy, she learns that reading is valuable.

Phonemic awareness is a little trickier. It's about your child coming to understand that letters have associated sounds. *Phonics* involves connecting sounds with specific letters or groups of letters (that is, that the sound /k/ can be represented by c, k, or ck spellings). Phonemic awareness starts when you read to your child and sometimes point to the words as you read them. This lets your child see that the letters symbolize sounds.

The best activities to increase the development of phonemic awareness and, later, phonics and word recognition in young children are patterning games. If your child has strong patterning skills, he will be able to recognize and remember the patterns found in letters, words, and sentence structures, and he'll be ready to become a proficient reader.

Learning to observe carefully is the first step toward building strong patterning skills in your young child.

OBSERVATION ACTIVITIES

Your child needs to be a good observer in order to recognize patterns. Try using the following games to build your young child's observation skills:

- Play "color detective": As you drive together in the car, have your child say "red" each time he sees a red car. Then ask him to be on the lookout for another color.
- Play "shape hunt": Ask your child to lead you around the house and point to all things that are shaped like a circle (or square, etc).
- Place a few household objects on a tray and allow your child to examine them. Then ask him to close his eyes as you remove an object. When he opens his eyes, have him try to recall which object is missing. Gradually increase the number of objects on the tray as his skill improves.
- For a syn-*naps* change of scene, spend some time with your child observing the details of a leaf. Encourage her to tell you all the things she notices about the leaf. Try this with other objects indoors as well as in nature. Natural-history museums with collections of rocks, butterflies, and bird eggs are great sources of objects that are similar but reveal differences upon closer observation.
- Read a very familiar story or poem aloud, and leave out a word or sentence. Make a game of asking your child to say "I noticed" when you leave something out. After a few tries, give him the opportunity to recall the missing words. You'll be building his memory skills along with his auditory observation.

PATTERN IDENTIFICATION ACTIVITIES

The brain recognizes and stores information by seeking out familiar patterns. Learning takes place when your child's brain recognizes something new as fitting into one of its stored patterns, and links the new sensory input with that memory circuit. Try the following activities to practice pattern identification with your child.

Button-Matching Games

Take a large bag of assorted buttons (you can purchase these at most sewing stores for a few dollars) and make small groups of buttons that share simple characteristics, such as color, shape, or number of holes. Have your child select a button from the bag that he thinks fits with your cluster. If he is correct, ask him why his button matches. As your child progresses, add more complex patterns, such as flat versus indented, multicolored versus single color, and metal versus plastic. **Always be present when toddlers have access to buttons or other small objects, because they are a choking hazard.**

AS learners will enjoy telling you about the patterns. Your child might want to find patterns in a sequence, such as objects with three, four, or five sides, or may make up a song or rhyme that has sound patterns. AS learners might especially like to make up rhymes about their button patterns if you start them off with a model rhyme such as:

> *Some buttons are red,*
> *Some buttons are blue.*
> *Buttons with two holes*
> (or however many holes yours has)
> *Are in the pattern made by YOU!*

VSK learners may find matching buttons elsewhere, such as on the shirts in his closet, which adds movement to the activity. Ask your child to look for a piece of clothing in his closet he believes has buttons that match the ones you gathered. For example, if you group together various two-hole buttons and he thinks he knows the pattern, he can look for shirts with two-hole buttons to show you. The movement will refresh his synapses.

In addition to buttons, you can also sort clothes (pants, shirts, socks, shoes; outdoor/indoor; summer/winter), utensils (forks, knives, spoons), shapes (triangles, squares, circles), or pictures cut from magazines (people, animals, objects, toys, machines, transportation vehicles).

Guess My Category

In this activity, your child decides the categories, sorts the figures, and has you guess the pattern of things taken from his collection of small toys, plastic animals, or toy vehicles. Toy categories might include zoo, farm, or pet animals; objects that are hard or soft; or things that move people, such as toy cars, trucks, bicycles, and buses. When you guess, explain your reasoning to your child. This will prepare him for the next activity.

What Belongs? What Doesn't Belong?

To increase the challenge and build more connections to the way words and letters form patterns, group together three items with a shared characteristic and have your child describe what they have in common.

Next, group together three items that are in the same category and include one that does not belong. Have your child select the one that does not belong and explain why. When your child becomes proficient with these more obvious categories, create increasingly complex groupings. For example, if you first sort coins into groups of pennies, nickels, and dimes, and your child recognizes that a dime does not belong with the pennies, you can progress to pattern sequences. Line up a sequence penny-penny-dime, penny-penny-dime, penny-penny-dime. Ask your child to choose the next three coins that would fit with the pattern you set up. This builds patterning skills for reading and sequencing skills for number sense, or *numerancy*, the basis for learning arithmetic.

AS learners with musical interests may observe a pattern you play on a piano. Then they can demonstrate that they recognize the pattern by copying the movements of your fingers and touching the same piano keys in the same order you did. As your child advances, he can try to sing or play the next note in the sequence. Start easy, just playing the white keys left to right, singing notes in a scale, or singing the first few notes of a familiar song. Gradually build up to more complex patterns, such as playing every third key or singing a pattern of the same note soft-soft-loud-soft-soft-loud or short-short-long-short-short-long. Then switch roles, and let your child create the pattern for you to predict or continue.

VSK learners will enjoy going around the room pointing to objects they believe fit into a pattern. Your child may think of a pattern and point to things that fit it, such as things that are blue or things that are toys. You then guess his pattern by making predictions. For example, if you recognize the pattern as toys, walk to another toy and ask, "Is this in your pattern?" Take turns as pattern selector and pattern predictor. The complexity of the pattern can be increased to include more specific categories such as long pants, things that roll, shoes that have laces, etc. Children will also enjoy doing this activity in the park or on a walk.

Similarities and Differences

When your child has mastered large similarities and differences in patterns, such as red cars and black cars, try engaging in the following activity. While driving in the car, ask your child to point to cars that are four-door or those that are two-door, houses that have flat roofs or pointy roofs, or signs that are all capital letters or signs with both lower-case and capital letters.

This game becomes more complex and expands compare-and-contrast aspects of pattern recognition when you encourage your child to tell you other similarities and differences he notices: between two cars, houses, leaves, dogs, family photos, or photos of himself at different ages.

For the photo activity, find two photographs of your child taken about a year apart. Have him tell you all the details he finds in each of them. Ask him which picture was taken when he was older and how he can tell. Venn diagrams, which are explained on page 49, are helpful for this type of compare/contrast activity. You can write the words you child dictates, or she can draw sketches below your words on a large Venn diagram.

VISUALIZING PATTERNS AND ACTIVE LISTENING

Visualization is an essential skill for prereading, and it can be developed in young children through active listening. Before your child can visualize the images represented by words on a page, she needs practice visualizing words she hears spoken. Visualization of words that are heard builds the brain's pattern recognition and pattern development skills.

AS learners

AS learners can describe what they "see" mentally when they hear you read. After you read a book to your child several times, encourage him to describe the visual images in the sequence in which they occurred in the story. This builds his auditory and sequencing learning strengths to their optimal potentials for reading.

VSK learners

VSK learners can draw the visual images that come to mind as you read or reread a familiar book. When your child draws her visualizations, her brain connects images with word sounds. This develops the neural networks needed to later connect written words with word sounds and images when she starts to read.

SECTION II:
KEY SKILLS FOR BEGINNING READERS
(AGES 4–8)

Research shows that the crucial window of opportunity to deliver help for reading problems is during the first two or three of years of school. The National Institutes of Health confirms that 95 percent of poor readers can be brought up to grade level if they receive effective help early. While it is still possible to help an older child with reading problems, those beyond third grade require much more intensive help. If help is given in fourth grade rather than in late kindergarten, it takes four times as long to improve the same skills by the same amount. Here are activities to enjoy with your child that will help you work on key reading skills during these critical early years.

HIGH-FREQUENCY WORDS

Simple words such as "I," "and," and "the" make up ten percent of all words in print. The twenty-five most commonly used words comprise about one-third of written text, and the hundred most commonly used words make up about 50 percent of the material we read! These words are called *high-frequency words.* Once your child knows the most frequently used words in print, he will have access to a vast world of literature and be able to enjoy reading most books he chooses.

The challenge for beginning readers is that many high-frequency words in the English language are not phonetic, which makes them more difficult to learn. Some examples of high-frequency nonphonetic words are those with the letter combination "ough." Just consider the many ways that the letter combination "ough" is pronounced in the words "though," "trough," "through," "bough," "rough," and "ought." Learning these high-frequency nonphonetic words by sight as whole words will have a high payoff for your child, especially if her school uses a phonics-heavy reading program, such as Open-Court.

A little bit of knowledge can go a long way when that knowledge is particularly useful. It may not seem like a great achievement to learn fifty words of a foreign language, but if you've traveled to a foreign country and had to ask for the restaurant, hotel, museum, beach, rest-room, hospital, and perhaps the names of a few foods, you'll remember how that small vocabulary can be as essential as your passport. Your sense of comfort and well-being is increased because you can communicate your basic needs and priority interests.

Similarly, when children master high-frequency words, the payoff is also great because high-frequency words open the potential for creating or reading innumerable sentences, and boost a child's confidence to persevere with reading. Your child will also be more willing to study vocabulary words later when she discovers that the more words she recognizes, the more easily she can read.

As you try the following activities with your child, remember that by the time children are ready to learn high-frequency words, they benefit from knowing the reasons for doing things. Share with your child your reasons for doing the activities you're using to help him become better reader, such as memorizing high-frequency words. When I give short explanations to my students about how a learning activity will change and grow their brains, they enjoy the information about their own bodies and are more interested in doing the activity.

One second-grade student said, "I like it better when I know why you want us to do something, especially if it is something that is not too much fun." His classmate added, "When teachers tell us why we have to know something and why it is good for us, it doesn't make it easier, but it makes me want to do it more."

FIFTY HIGH-FREQUENCY WORDS

a	had	of	they
all	have	on	this
and	he	one	to
are	her	out	up
as	him	said	was
at	his	saw	we
be	I	she	went
but	if	so	were
came	in	that	with
for	is	the	you
from	it	their	your
go	me	then	
got	my	there	

AS learners

AS learners may prefer creating their own way of sequencing the list of high-frequency words, rather than the alphabetical order given here. AS learners may also enjoy sorting cards with the words on them into different patterns (by their number of letters, ending letters, all short/tall letters) as a way of becoming more familiar with the words.

Experiment and let your child choose which pattern is best for him. One powerful way for anyone to memorize word lists is to put them in order of how pleasing one finds them to be. As simple as that sounds, adding an emotional punch to memory by personally relating to the words in terms of like or dislike increases the passage of the memory through the amygdala and increases dopamine release. Students using this ranking strategy remember word lists with much higher success. My students love it! Note: When working with the fifty high-frequency words, it is best to start with five words a day or every few days, and review previously learned words before starting on the new ones.

VSK learners

VSK learners are especially likely to enjoy reading success with high-frequency words because they can relate to the words using their visual, spatial, and kinesthetic strengths rather than having to accommodate the auditory emphasis of phonics. The following practice activities can help your VSK learner memorize high-frequency words.

- Encourage your child to copy the words onto paper (especially in different colors).
- Create large wall posters that list the words. VSK learners feel pleasure that supports their perseverance when they can use sticky notes to cover up words they master. They also are able to see visual evidence of their increasing success in the decreasing number of words left to learn.
- Allow your child to sort the words in many different ways. VSK learners may be thrown off by the visual similarity of the words listed alphabetically and may prefer other ways of sorting them.
- Use flash cards and labels around the home. When your child sees a word, the whole word is viewed and remembered like a photograph.
- If your child likes typing, he can look at the high-frequency words on the computer screen, using a free downloadable activity at www. usoe.k12.ut.us/ATE/keyboarding/resources/presentations/1hfw50. ppt. This activity has one high-frequency word per page for your child to see, say, and even type if he enjoys that interactive activity. If he doesn't like typing, he can just repeat the words as you listen. You can also use the "jump in" method described later in this chapter (page 53) so he doesn't become discouraged by multiple errors.

FREQUENT LETTER PATTERNS

Just as there are high-frequency words, there are also high-frequency letter pairs found in many words, such as "th," "ch," "sh," "st," and "sl."

The most frequent letter pairs are:

al	es	it	se
an	et	nd	st
ar	he	of	th
as	ha	on	to
at	hi	or	
en	in	ou	
er	is	re	

The second set of most frequent letter pairs are:

ac	ge	mo	so
ad	gh	ne	ta
ai	ho	nh	te
ay	ic	no	ti
be	id	nt	ts
ca	il	ol	ul
ce	im	om	un
ch	ir	oo	ur
co	la	os	us
de	ld	ow	ut
ea	le	pe	ve
ed	li	qu	wa
ee	ll	ra	we
el	lo	ri	wh
fe	ly	ro	wi
fi	ma	rs	wo
fo	me	sh	
fr	mi	si	

To help your child become familiar with the high-frequency letter pairs, motivate her to practice through her interests and learning strengths. If she likes sports, she can list words that include the letter pairs and are related to sports, such as thro*w*, ser*v*e, and t*os*s. Or she can draw or paste sports pictures on top of her lists. If she likes animals or cartoon characters, she can use the letter pairs to make lists of words that relate to these things and put the words under pictures of the animals or characters.

Begin practicing high-frequency letter pairs with words that have the letter pair at the beginning, such as *th*ing, *th*row, *th*at, and *th*en. Later, you can practice learning high-frequency letter pairs or even triplets that commonly appear at the end of words, such as "ly," "ed," "ing," "ate," and "ion." After learning high-frequency letter pairs, your child will recognize the familiar letter patterns and have a head start on reading new words.

AS learners

- Take the starting pattern of the letters "st" and list the "st" words in alphabetical order, by meaning, or by ending patterns.
- List the high-frequency letter pairs and sample words based on similar sounds. Emphasize the sound when practicing the list aloud together.
- Learn a number of words together that contain the same letter pair and also rhyme.
- Make sentences that use several words with the same letter pairs, and repeat the sentences to develop patterned auditory memory. For example, "I *swat* the fly from my *sw*eet cookie after my *sw*im." For words with similar endings such as "ing," the sentence can be "The buzz*ing* th*ing* in the sw*ing* that can st*ing* is a bee."
- Visit http://www.fonetiks.org/ for oral pronunciations of word combinations in a variety of words.

VSK learners

- Clap or give a high-five to emphasize the "st" or other high-frequency sound of a word. Say three words, and have your child clap when he hears one with the "st" or another starting or ending sound.
- Use magnetic letters that your child can move and sort. For example, your child can place "st" on the magnetic board and change the ending letters as she says the new words she makes.

- Encourage your child to have fun making written or typed letter pairs and sample words. Use different colors for the letter pair than for the rest of the word.
- When you use the errorless learning activity (described on page 53) for high-frequency letter pairs, ask your VSK learner to make the note cards or computer lists. Use letters that are larger than or in different fonts from the rest of the word.

WORD PATTERN RECOGNITION

When your child begins to read words at home or in school, she will need to recognize increasingly subtle distinctions, such as the similarities and differences between letters "p" and "q." You can boost her progress by practicing word pattern recognition, making the complexity of the patterns you help her discover gradually more and more challenging.

All children have letter confusion and number confusion in their first year or two of reading in school. But if your child's teacher tells you she is making more errors than normal in confusing letters, associating the wrong sound with a letter, or distinguishing a rhyme, you should request a formal reading analysis from the school specialist so if intervention is necessary, it can begin as soon as possible.

AS learners

- Use changes in your vocal pitch, speed, tone, or volume to emphasize auditory patterns or parts of words that sound alike. Say a series of words, emphasizing the similar endings or beginning sounds, and have your child repeat them with the same emphasis on that part of each word.
- Discover rhythm patterns in books by Dr. Seuss or titles like *Goodnight Moon*, which appeal to AS learners with musical-rhythmic and sequencing strengths.
- Play word-category sequencing matching games, such as matching root words correctly with their "ion" ending (*cau* with *tion* for "caution" or *sta* with *tion* for "station"). Try these categories for sequence matching:
  - Word endings: words ending in "ook," such as book, look, cook, brook, and hook

- Words with similar meanings: pal, friend, buddy
- Words with similar roots: "fract," meaning break, as in fracture or fraction.
- Words with similar prefixes: "ex," meaning from or out, as in export, exhale, exchange.

• Show your child how to match objects with cards that have words written on them. Say the word on the card and ask your child to repeat it. Then match words with the objects, such as the names of friends or family members with their photos; cards with the names of foods with pictures of the actual food; names of objects with pictures of the objects cut from magazines.

• Help your child recognize the repeating patterns in written words, such as hibernate, decorate, and collaborate, by changing your voice as you say them to make the common sounds more distinctive. Your child can then repeat the word with his own way of making the ending sound different, say, by stretching the sound out, or saying it louder or in a higher pitch.

• Encourage creativity and humor when studying word roots, prefixes, or suffixes. Create nonsense words with your child, using the part of the word he is learning to create funny words. For example, when your child is studying words with the "ogy" sound ending, such as *biology*, in which the ending means "the study of," he can review other real words such as *mythology* and *psychology*, and then create his own, such as "soccerology" and "candyology." If he creates an imaginary word that has a real-life equivalent, such as "codeology," tell him the correct term (cryptology), and add it to his list of words. This kind of learning becomes a game with positive emotional connections that make for stronger relational and long-term memories.

VSK learners

• Use paper or plastic cutout letters of frequent combinations such "ion" or "ate," and add other letters to make words.

- Explore letters and words using tactile materials such as magnetic letters, felt letters, tracing letters in sand, and modeling letters with clay.
- Practice word construction with wooden puzzles with movable letters.
- Use a variety of visual activities to emphasize patterns in word families, spelling patterns, prefixes, suffixes, and word roots (see the list of common English roots and prefixes/suffixes on page 47). Patterns in new words can be emphasized with different colored highlighters on paper, dry-erase pens on a small whiteboard, or colored chalk on a blackboard.
- Encourage your child to draw sketches representing several action verbs ending with "ion," such as flotation, celebration, or decoration.
- Play a version of Pictionary using only words with specific letter patterns (prefix, suffix, and root). Draw pictures or observe a partner's drawings to identify the word.
- Play a game where you keep a root, such as "smith," and move different letters in front or behind the root to build new words: blacksmith, silversmith, and even informal words that may have originally been derived from the root, such as smithereens. "Smith" is defined as "one who puts things together" and "smithereens" refers to small, broken pieces. That type of wordplay and creative exploration of word relationships can appeal to children who enjoy moving letters.
- Make parent-modeled and child-copied physical movements that correspond to the sound pattern to be learned. Have your child stand like a robot and rotate a quarter-turn each time you say the part of a word with the chosen beginning or ending sound. For the word "rotate," have your child stand facing forward when you say "ro" and turn a quarter-turn when you emphasize the syllable "**tate.**" For "hibernate," have your child face forward when you say "hiber" and rotate as you say "**nate.**" To add verbal skill to the kinesthetic skill, have your child say the common ending as he rotates.
- The preceding robot-rotating activity also is a fun way to include whole-body movement, which you can do when you practice separating words into syllables. Have your child rotate for each syllable

in the word "hibernate": "hi"… rotate… "bern"… rotate… "ate" rotate. For reinforcement, he can also clap. To help with recalling the information aurally, he can say the syllables as he rotates. These activities can be especially useful after a period of sitting still.

COMMON ENGLISH ROOTS

act: to do or start (*active, activate*)

am, ami: to love or like (*amorous, amicable, amigo*)

annu: yearly or over a year (*annual, annualize*)

aud: to hear (*audible, auditory, audition*)

bene: good (*beneficial;* also the Latin root for *benign*)

bio: life (*biography, biology*)

biblio: book (*bibliography;* also the Spanish word for "library," *biblioteca*)

cap: to seize (*capture, captivate*)

chron: time (*chronometer, chronicle, chronological*)

cogn: to know (*cognition, recognize*)

corp: body (*corpse, incorporate, corporation*)

cred: to believe (*credible, credence*)

duct: to lead (*conduct, air duct, aqueduct*)

fid: trust (*fidelity, fiduciary, confide*)

fract: to break (*fracture, fraction*)

geo: earth (*geography, geology, geode*)

graph: to write (*autograph, graphic*)

loc: place (*location, local*)

log: speech or reason (*logic, logistics*)

man: to make or do (*manage, manipulate*)

mem: recall (*remember, memory, memorial*)

nom: name (*nominate, nomenclature, nom de plume*)

nov: new (*novice, novel*)

path: feel (*sympathy, empathy, pathos*)

ped: foot (*pedal, pedometer*)

pod: foot (*arthropod, podium, podiatry*)

continued

phon: sound (*phonograph, phonics, phone*)
scrip: write (*inscription, script*)
soci: to join (*society, sociable*)
struct: to build (*construct, structure, instruct*)
terr: earth (*territory, terrain*)
uni: one (*united, unicycle, unicorn*)

WORD-CATEGORY BUILDING

Your child can learn to identify words more rapidly and with greater accuracy if her brain develops categories for storing data about similar objects or words. But because beginning readers do not automatically understand category cues such as prefixes, suffixes, or roots, it takes some practice to build the categories that will help them quickly identify new words. The goal is to help your child recognize the patterns and connections between the more than forty speech sounds and the more than one hundred spellings that represent them. As she becomes more familiar with the patterns, she will build brain familiarity and circuitry to identify letter patterns and words automatically and use those patterns to decode previously unknown words. Two highly effective category-building activities you can try with your child are multisensory learning and the construction of graphic organizers.

Multisensory Learning

If your child learns the word "drum" by seeing the word (visual input), hearing the word (auditory input), and tapping her hands on a table as if playing drums (tactile-kinesthetic input), it will give her three brain storage categories for the word "drum." These multiple storage locations will help her recognize the word more quickly when she sees it again because her memories of "drum" are located in more than one sense-memory center. If your child uses strategies from multiple learning strengths, she will learn and store the memory through several sensory systems and remember the information more easily and more successfully, thanks to the brain's duplication of that memory storage.

Graphic Organizers

Graphic organizers are visual representations (such as charts, maps, webs, diagrams, timelines, and outlines) that encourage children to construct personal meaning from information. Graphic organizers provide different ways to relate, compare, contrast, and associate information, and help children recognize relationships and pattern new information for memory storage. This means a child needs to do less rote memorization because he sees relationships (visually) and codes information (kinesthetically) into brain-compatible patterns. The patterned information then connects with previously stored related memories and enters long-term memory.

All graphic organizers have the advantage of being flexible, so your child can add new information when she chooses. They are introduced here for practicing patterning in the context of early reading skills, but they are also suggested for many other uses throughout this book. You can familiarize yourself with them now, or come back when you want to use a graphic organizer for another learning activity.

Venn Diagrams

In their simplest form, Venn diagrams consist of drawing two circles that partially overlap each other, like links in a chain. They are used to compare and contrast similarities and differences. In the non-overlapping parts of each circle, information is placed that is true only of that circle's topic (differences). In the region where the circles overlap, information is placed that is true for both topics (similarities). Older children can write their own words in the diagram; younger children may dictate words to you or draw pictures in the diagram.

For example, if you're comparing boats and cars, begin with the similarities. You could include "provide transportation," "can have motors," and "can carry people and things." These similarities would be placed in the overlapping section. Then, list some of the differences. In the separate section for boats, you could include "float on water" and "can have sails." In the separate section for cars, you could include "move on land," "have tires," and "passengers must wear seatbelts."

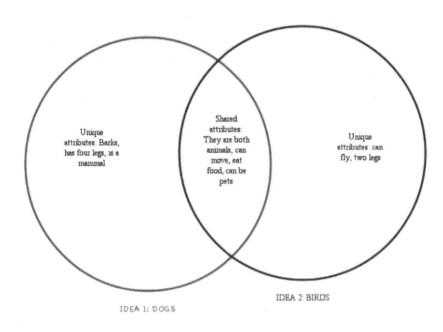

Unique attributes: Barks, has four legs, is a mammal

Shared attributes: They are both animals, can move, eat food, can be pets

Unique attributes: can fly, two legs

IDEA 2: BIRDS

IDEA 1: DOGS

Figure 1: Venn diagrams are useful for comparing two things, particularly with younger children. Shared characteristics are listed in the overlapping section of the two circles, allowing for easy identification of characteristics that are shared and those that are not. String or colored yarn can be used to make the circles on the floor, and using objects and pictures is strongly encouraged. Interactive Venn Diagram activities can be found under "Venn Diagrams" at http://nlvm.usu.edu/en/nav/category_g_3_t_1.html

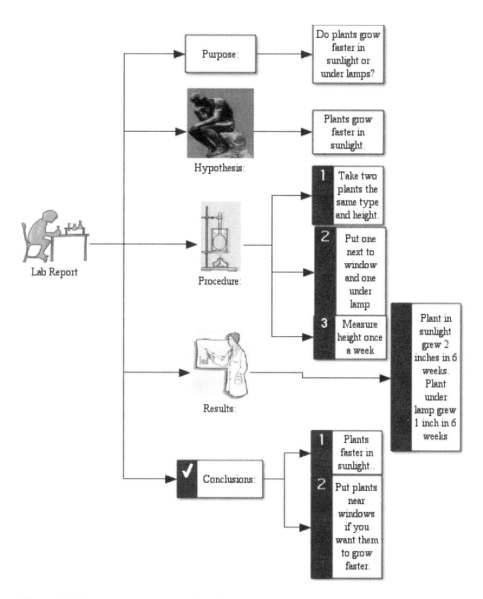

Figure 2: Event reports or timelines link words by time (events, instructions, stages, phases) and demonstrate sequential, memory-friendly linear relationships.

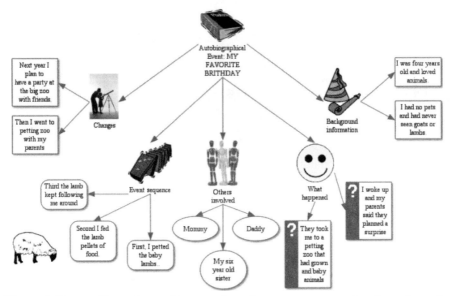

Figure 3: Tree and branch graphic organizers have a tree representing the main topic (the autobiographical event, such as a birthday), branches representing subtopics (what happened, who was there, future plans), and leaves from those branches (event sequence of petting and feeding the lamb).

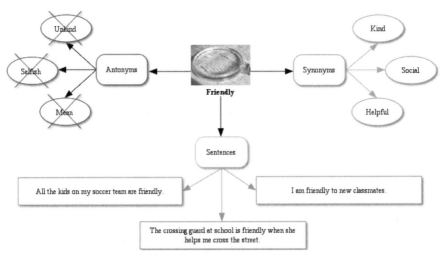

Figure 4: Information webs allow children to connect with prior knowledge by writing down ideas that come to mind while learning a new vocabulary word, planning a report, or reviewing information before a test. For example, to practice vocabulary, a child might put a word in the center of the web and have offshoots that include a sketch or picture representing the word, the word used in a sentence, its part of speech, and its synonyms and antonyms.

Graphic organizers effectively complement the brain's style of patterning, which relies upon encoding and consolidation. Encoding takes place when information enters the brain from the senses and is the essential first step for memory capture. The information must then be consolidated and stored so that it can be patterned into a more lasting form and reach the final stage of enduring retention in long-term memory. Graphic organizers promote this enduring process of patterning because they rely upon the visual presentation of information, which stimulates the brain to build relevant connections to new information and related stored memories. They match the brain's natural tendency to construct meaning, forming and enlarging patterned memory circuits.

The best graphic organizers engage your child's imagination and ignite positive emotions through a creative process that allows her to recognize, sort, and discover patterns for herself. The use of graphic organizers to connect information in meaningful relationships also allows your child time to reflect on the information. The result is that she goes beyond regurgitating rote memorization to the higher cognitive process of using the information in significant ways.

STAY MOTIVATED WITH "JUMP IN" WORD PRACTICE

Children require high levels of success in order to be motivated to continue practicing something difficult. After a day of making mistakes during reading at school, no child is excited by the idea of more frustrating practice at home. You can boost your child's reading success with errorless "jump in" word identification, which ratchets confidence.

Here's how it works: Show your child a word that is on one side of a card. He can either choose to wait and have you say the word, or "jump in" and say the word correctly himself. He doesn't need to pronounce it if he doesn't feel he knows how. The following are step-by-step instructions.

1. Choose a list of words. These can be high-frequency words, vocabulary words, or words that are important to a unit of study. To improve general vocabulary, you can encourage your child to tell you words related to high-interest topics, such as sports or animals,

that he likes to read about in magazines or books. These can become vocabulary words that, once learned, increase the readability of books or magazines about his high-interest topics.

2. Prepare a list of the words on your cards, and include three columns next to each word, labeled "correct repeat," "correct wait," and "correct response."

3. Start by building reading confidence. Show the word on the card and without any delay, read the word aloud.

4. Then, ask your child to repeat the word with you. Place a check in the "correct repeat" column for repeating the word properly.

5. If your child doesn't repeat the word with you correctly, just read it again and have her repeat it correctly with you. Don't write anything on the list until she does the correct repeat and then check that column.

6. As she becomes more familiar with the words, add a delay of a few seconds between the time you show the word card and when you say the word. If during this delay she "jumps in" and says the word correctly, make a check in the "correct response" column of your list.

7. If she waits through the delay for you to read the word and then repeats it correctly along with you, check that as a positive response in the "correct wait" column. Check this column because she knew to wait and then say the word correctly with you. The practice continues to be errorless and nonthreatening because there is acknowledgment for both correct waits and correct responses.

8. With continued errorless practice, the word becomes automatic and is learned successfully.

9. Show your child the progress she has made on the checklist you keep for "correct wait" and "correct response" to increase her intrinsic reward and motivation.

You can also use the errorless practice method to help your child master facts in other areas, such as states and capitals or vocabulary words and definitions. For example, in biology, one side of the card could name an organ of the body and the other could name the system that the organ belongs to—"femur" on one side and "skeletal system" on the back, or "heart" on one side and "circulatory system" on the back.

4
STRATEGIES FOR ORAL READING SUCCESS (AGES 4–8)

Fluency is the key to oral reading success. It's the ability to recognize words quickly enough not only to read aloud, but also to put the right expression or inflection in your voice, such as exclamation, questioning, or surprise. Some children can read silently but don't have the experience, confidence, skills, or word memory to read aloud with fluency. Even children who are fluent readers with you at home may have low confidence and may read hesitantly in class during oral reading.

The goal of this chapter is to provide you with activities and strategies to get your child eager for oral reading by building his fluency. Powerful motivators are needed to encourage your child to struggle with so many new words, as it is a challenge even for the brightest children. Motivation comes from choice, the pleasure of shared reading, and games that emphasize how punctuation and verbal expressiveness increase the emotional power of words. Enjoy bringing the excitement of fluent, expressive reading into your child's reading toolkit!

BOOK CHOICE
Choice is a powerful brain motivator. Let your child select books she likes from the library, and help her select books of different levels of difficulty. If your child chooses books instead of them being forced on her, she is more likely to read them independently, as well as with you. If your child is not comfortable reading aloud, choice is especially important for books used for oral reading.

Some of the books your child selects will be too advanced for her independent reading level and should be read to her by you. She can follow your finger as you point to the words you read, but if she doesn't enjoy it, don't force it. Reading development needs to link books and reading to positive, pleasurable memories and experiences.

SHARED READING

After you read an age-level-appropriate book aloud to your child several times, he will begin to recognize frequently-used words and words of high interest. For example, if you read him a book about robots several times, he'll be interested in words that relate to robots, such as electricity, battery, motor, transformer, mechanical, remote control, etc. He might automatically add his voice to yours and point to them when you read the words "remote" or "transformer" aloud. If he doesn't, you can have a brief conversation in which he is the "expert," and you ask him about the word in relation to his toys or the cartoons he watches. After he tells you about "transformers," reread the sentence in the book with that word and ask him to repeat this unfamiliar but high-interest word with you after you say it aloud. Then reread the sentence a third time, point to the word, and see if he jumps in and says it. If not, start to say the beginning of the word, and he'll eventually complete it. In subsequent readings, he will jump in with the word before you say it if you point to the word and wait a few seconds before you say it.

VS learners especially enjoy seeing words during shared reading, while AS learners enjoy hearing and predicting the word from the pattern they recognize in the words before it.

In addition to your child's favorite books, you can try shared reading with ABC books, nursery rhymes, and Dr. Seuss books, where the rhymes help your child predict the words. Talk with your child about the mechanics of reading books during this shared experience, such as explaining as how print goes from left to right, and let her turn the pages.

PRACTICE AND PREVIEW

Emotional comfort is essential for fluent oral reading. These brain-friendly de-stressing strategies can support your young reader and enable her to grow in comfort and confidence as well as skill.

- Pick books for oral reading practice that are at or just below, but not above, your child's successful independent level of reading. This is not the time to build new vocabulary, but rather an opportunity to work on fluency, pacing, and expression while building confidence.
- Before the actual reading session, have a general discussion with your child about the book she's about to read. Let her tell you why she selected it, what she likes about the cover, which are her favorite illustrations, and what she predicts will happen based on the illustrations and book title. If she already knows the story, ask her about her favorite characters and when in the book they are happy, sad, frightened, and excited. This discussion increases your child's comfort level with speaking about books, which carries over to her oral reading skills.
- Preview new vocabulary that your child will encounter in the book. Prepare a list of unfamiliar words in the book and use word-recognition strategies while reading so your child will not be stopped by these words. There shouldn't be too many new words if the book is at your child's independent, comfortable reading level.
- Review punctuation. Preview the reading together, looking for punctuation such as commas and question marks. Talk about the "codes" of punctuation. Remind your child that comma "codes" tell him when to pause, and question-mark "codes" tell him when to raise the pitch of his voice at the end of the sentence. (See page 58 for more on this.)
- For a syn-*naps* activity with a change of pace, read a few paragraphs with a monotone voice and without responses to punctuation codes. Then reread the same paragraphs again with expressiveness, changing your voice to show the emotional power of words and the increased meaning that punctuation adds. Ask your child to tell you which reading he enjoyed listening to more, and why.

EMPHASIZING PUNCTUATION

As your child reads aloud, he should be looking ahead for punctuation codes to see if his voice should pause, sound questioning, or express surprise and excitement. Learning to emphasize punctuation is a key goal of oral reading. If your child is having trouble recognizing and anticipating punctuation while reading aloud, try the following strategies.

- Highlight punctuation codes in different colors, such as periods in blue, question marks in red, and exclamation points in green (in library books, you can use small sticky notes of different colors).
- After you read a book to your child for the first time, go back and reread the sentences with special punctuation codes aloud to yourself before your child begins shared reading with you.
- Have fun exaggerating punctuation cues, and alternate how you emphasize them, such as putting long delays between commas, using very loud volume with exclamation points, or speaking in funny accents for dialogue in quotation marks. Your child will be more comfortable using the appropriate voice expressiveness for the punctuation after having a laugh about the exaggerations you two make together.
- As you read aloud, use exaggerated facial expressions that match the type of sentence you are reading to your child (also called "visual modeling"). Furrow your eyebrows for a question, and widen your eyes for an exclamation point. When you make these movements and expressions more pronounced, *visual learners* will respond to the visual cues and *auditory learners* will respond to your verbal expressiveness. You can add variation to visual modeling by having your child watch your faces in a mirror as you take turns reading aloud with expressiveness.
- After you have read a book together several times using exaggerated expressions, gradually drop your volume on future readings, and let your child's voice and expressiveness dominate. Continue allowing her to point to words and punctuation until she no longer needs that support. Let her read as slowly as she needs to as she builds her comfort with punctuation and expressiveness.

- As your child reads, offer compliments that specifically acknowledge the ways in which she improved, such as using more inflection or increasing speed. For example, "I liked the way you spoke louder when the sentence had an exclamation point."
- Encourage your child to sometimes practice oral reading with books that come with a CD or tape. Ask him to listen to the reader and follow along in his book. The reader is likely to read very expressively and is a good model for your child. (See the following section on tape-assisted reading.)
- To increase your child's confidence in reading aloud in school, review the school read-aloud books in advance at home (contact the teacher to get a list of books). Preview the pages the class will read aloud the next day, and practice reading those together aloud.

Tape-Assisted Reading

Tape-assisted reading allows your child to read and reread books along with a recording. There are various tapes, CDs, and computer programs to choose from in which the narrators read books with high expressiveness. Engage your child's interest by picking books he is interested in or chooses himself. After the first listening, have your child listen to the tape and follow along with a finger, pointing to the words and punctuation he hears and sees (with your help if needed). In subsequent listenings, as your child gains experience with the words and punctuation, he should stop pointing to the words. Now you can encourage him to read with expression in his voice, the way the narrator does.

You can also make your own tapes or CDs for tape-assisted reading. Create tapes for books your child enjoys hearing you read, or favorite selections from the library. Also look for books that emphasize different aspects of fluency. When making your own tapes, you can use the format of commercially available tapes as a guide. They often use a bell or other sound to alert the child to turn the page.

You can emphasize phrasing during tape-assisted reading by using two variations of the read-along book strategy (simply make a photocopy of the book so you have two copies). The first variation can include added cues about punctuation, such as slash marks placed between phrases that should be read together, such as, "When I went shopping for clothes with my mom, // which was never fun, // she always promised to let me buy at least one thing I really liked even if she didn't like it.// But do you think that it ever worked out that way?" // (using the photocopy is best in this case). The second read-along variation uses the original book without these marks, so your child can move from supported oral reading to more independent oral reading.

As your child listens to you read aloud, engages in shared reading, and reads along with tapes, he will grow in the visual and auditory components of reading, and his desire to read successfully will be continually motivated. That motivation will serve him well when he needs the perseverance to continue climbing the steepest lighthouse stairs that remain as he moves to mastery in reading comprehension.

AS learners

AS learners respond to the rhythm and order of words. Your AS child will enjoy oral reading practice in books that include rhymes. You can encourage her to create her own rhyming sentences to match first lines of rhymes in the book. Rhymes often have more cues for pauses, such as separate lines after commas. Sequential learners enjoy practicing oral reading with books about their interests that also have logical sequences, such as the changing seasons, building of boats, or the lifecycle of butterflies.

Listening and singing along while reading the lyrics to expressively sung songs can increase your AS child's comfort reading expressively. Invite your child to enjoy a syn-*naps* and sing or play a song she naturally performs with musical expressiveness, or listen to a song and follow along on sheet music. Notice together how variation of whole notes and half notes make the song more interesting. Suggest she now play or sing the song with all whole notes. Do the same with volume, where she plays or sings the song without, and then with, appropriate changes in volume, so she learns to appreciate the value of differences.

AS learners often excel at logical deduction, word games, and vocabulary. Your child can become more a confident oral reader by telling stories and playing verbal word games, such as Twenty Questions. Encourage your AS child to describe an exciting event, field trip, school assembly, or movie he watched. You might tape record him if he is expressive in these descriptions, and as you listen together, he will recognize the value of his verbal expressiveness.

If you child enjoys doing systematic processes, such as cooking with recipes or building models from instructions, he may enjoy making his own recordings of stories. He can record over errors or sentences he wants to read more expressively. If he is comfortable with the sequences of using the recording system (or computer recording software, such as iWEB or GarageBand, which allow him to create personal podcasts), recording activities can positively reinforce his oral reading success.

VSK learners

VSK children seem "wired" for code and pattern recognition. They particularly enjoy using highlighters to underline new vocabulary words or punctuation clues, and they respond well to using these visual cues to read more expressively. With library books, they can draw sketches on paper to remind them of the meanings of new vocabulary words. If your VSK learner likes larger visual input, you can find large-print books and he can put sticky notes that enlarge the symbol above punctuation codes or create his own sketched symbols, such as a megaphone, to remind him to speak more loudly just before an exclamation mark.

Your VSK learner might enjoy a kinesthetic syn-*naps* of acting out or tapping out a rhythm to match your oral reading before he reads aloud himself, perhaps using the tapping beat as support for his fluent reading the first few times. He can also retell stories with puppets. Your VSK child can cut pictures from magazines and paste them onto colored paper stapled together in book form to create and tell a story about the pictures.

5

BUILDING AND ENRICHING VOCABULARY (AGES 7–11)

"The difference between the right word and the almost-right word is the difference between the lightning and the lightning-bug."
—Mark Twain

In the two previous chapters, we focused on how you could help your young child recognize words through word and letter patterns, high-frequency vocabulary practice, and building oral reading fluency. The next step in reading goes beyond word recognition and addresses how to read sentences correctly—*understanding* what you read, also known as reading comprehension. Increased vocabulary builds upon your child's recognition of words and enhances his understanding of the reading process. As your child extends his understanding of words and sentences, he transforms from a mechanical reader into a scholar who employs reading to enrich his knowledge, pleasure, and communication effectiveness. One of the keys to this transformation is building a larger, richer vocabulary.

When you share engaging games and activities with your child that are fun and build vocabulary, you'll give him a whole key ring. Start discovering new words together in everyday life, collecting words of personal value on cards or charts, visualizing words with patterns, pictures, sharing word stories, and playing word detective. Help your child experience words through all his senses, and he will fill his brain's word basket with gusto.

THE IMPORTANCE OF VOCABULARY

Vocabulary knowledge in young children directly impacts their later success in learning to read, and vocabulary size in early elementary school is a strong predictor of reading comprehension in the years to come. The number of words young children are able to learn varies greatly from two to eight words per day (or seven hundred fifty to three thousand words per year). If there is low brain processing and little manipulation of words in a child's early years, there is less stimulation and development of the reading neural networks he will need later.

Here's a brain-stimulating approach to enrich your child's vocabulary. Your child can learn many new words and gain ownership of a new vocabulary through active word processing—"doing things" with words, such as acting them out or creating word maps and diagrams.

In neurological terms, this "ownership" involves the development of new connections in the brain's neural network that link new words to known words through patterning and categorization.

New Words Are Everywhere

One of the simplest ways to build your child's interest in new vocabulary words is to help her notice the words in her everyday life as well as in her areas of special interest. You can incorporate interesting vocabulary words into your conversations with your child, and play games in which you use higher-level words instead of more familiar words. When you embed a new word in a sentence that gives hints (contextual clues) about the word's meaning, your child will enjoy guessing its meaning. Instead of saying, "You look exhausted from your soccer game," ask, "Are you *fatigued* from playing soccer?" You child then can respond, "If 'fatigued' means 'tired,' I sure am."

Add positive emotion to new words by incorporating them in funny sentences, puns, and jokes, and you'll hear your child do the same. Gently encourage your child to elaborate on the words she uses. When she uses unspecific slang words such as "stuff" or "that thingy," suggest that she can be a creative speaker, just as she is a creative artist, guitar player, or soccer player, if she finds more informative words to substitute for slang. Promote the habit of asking you or others for creative word suggestions if she needs help. Driving in the car can be an ideal opportunity to review words. Use the words "vacant" and "occupied" as you pass by homes or shops, and you'll see her flexing her mental muscle when she suggests richer words for you to use. After a few weeks of this "rich vocabulary" game, when you say, "Hey, look at that cool car," she is likely to respond, "It is an *extremely* bright shade of *amber*."

A family word challenge can even be a daily ritual, in which family members keep track of how many times during the day they say a "word of the day." Even if the selected day's word is familiar to older family members, they still can participate so your child feels the family bond and gets the message that the whole family values using rich words. At dinner, family members can take turns revealing the number of sentences they used with the day's word and how they fit those sentences into their conversations with others.

You can incorporate words from a "Word of the Day" calendar for children or from "Word of the Day" websites, such as the English Language Learner (http://www.learnersdictionary.com). You can also have your child select a word describing an intriguing illustration from an illustrated children's dictionary. Try asking your child to do a "Point and Shoot" by closing her eyes and pointing to a word in a favorite book you read to her that she can't read independently. If the word she points to is one she already knows, have her keep going until an unknown word comes up. That can become a word of the day.

Discovering New Words in Books

Encourage your child to select books from the library or bookstore based on his own personal curiosity and interests, and he'll be highly motivated to understand the words they contain. Help guide your child's selection so his vocabulary gradually grows without using books whose level of difficulty cause frustration. Aim for a selection with about ten percent new vocabulary words. When you read new books together in the shared reading activities described later in this chapter, you'll know after a few readings which words are giving your child trouble. Jot these down or put sticky notes on the page as you are reading, so the flow of reading is not interrupted.

You can also use index cards to track the new words your child learns while reading. After each chapter or story, work together to figure out the meanings of new words by rereading the sentences and looking for clues based on the surrounding content (contextual cues). See if there is a familiar root, prefix, or suffix that suggests the word's meaning, or use the word in other sentences that give her more direct clues about its meaning. After she works out the definition and perhaps uses the word in her own sentence, ask her to write or dictate the meaning in her own words for you to write on an index card.

Punch holes in the upper corners of these new-word index cards, and link them together with a key chain or binder hook. After a word has been practiced and stored into long-term memory (such as through the activities on pages 72–77), your child can take the index card of the word he now "owns" and tape it into his personal vocabulary notebook. He can organize his personal word-ownership notebook in any way he chooses: alphabetically, grammatically (action verbs, nouns, descriptive words), or by the letter patterns he sees in the words (roots, affixes, tall letters). Provide him with special pens or crayons with which to write each newly "owned" word in the notebook, perhaps with a picture. Then celebrate his growing vocabulary by encouraging him to share his book with family members.

Storytelling and Discussion

The following activity makes word learning a naturally flowing and enjoyable activity, whether done at home or while out and about with your child. Here is an example from the classroom.

After I read *Goldilocks and the Three Bears* to a second-grade class, I asked for volunteers to summarize the story and describe a similar story from a book or movie. As a way to inspire student-centered discussion, I also invited students to share their opinions about what type of person Goldilocks seemed to be. I wanted them all to feel like experts and be engaged enough to participate in the discussion and make the personal connections that build strong memories.

I allowed the students to control the discussion and did not interrupt for about five minutes. After several student comments and classmate responses were completed without my interrupting, I begin summarizing what students said and embedding new vocabulary words in my reflection of their ideas back to the class.

Student (S): Goldilocks was like a robber because she took things that weren't hers.

Teacher (T): So you think Goldilocks did something that was against the law, something that was *illegal?*

S: Yes, she broke the law. Could she go to jail for that?

T: What do you think? Do people go to jail when they do *illegal* things? For what *illegal* things do people go to *prison?* (Here I used the word "illegal" twice and also substituted "prison" for "jail." At this point, the idea was not to explain the difference between jail and prison, but to add another word that could be used when referring to incarceration.)

After a discussion about illegal things in which I responded with a sentence that continued to substitute "illegal" when students said "against the law," I asked what they thought the word might mean. I asked if there was a part of the word that is another smaller word. When one student suggested that the word "eagle" was in the word "illegal," I didn't detail the spelling differences but instead acknowledged that the sound of "eagle" was indeed heard in the word "illegal." When a student gave the response of "legal," we made a game of opposites where students volunteered a pair of actions, one legal and the other illegal (borrowing with permission and stealing, taking medicine your doctor gives you to get better and using illegal drugs).

This process continued for about ten minutes—about the length of time the students' attention spans could hold before they lost interest and shut down. Other words were discussed and illustrated as we continued with overall story comprehension and character analysis. For example, "rescue" was substituted for "save," "enormous" for "very big," and "terrified" for "scared." There was no test or formal summary of the words, but I did write them on the board and encouraged the students to write them down, too.

VISUALIZING WORDS THROUGH PATTERNS AND PICTURES

Visualization is an excellent strategy for all children to use to help remember the meanings of vocabulary words. The more mental energy and creativity your child puts into her visualization, the stronger the neural network being built will be. This section includes two different visualization activities you can try with your child. For AS learners, the visualization may be more effective if they hear the information from someone else, by whispering quietly while they read independently, or after verbally summarizing what they read. VSK learners usually can go directly from what they see or hear to visualization, but the details of their visualization are improved when they add another step, such as movement, color, or manipulation of objects.

Visualization Activity: Finding patterns in letters

First, visualize a simple word in your mind, and describe what you see to your child. For example, "I'm picturing the letters that spell out the word 'but,' starting with one tall letter, *b*, then a short letter, *u*, and ending with one tall letter, *t*. In my mind, I am making the tall letters very tall and the short letter between them very short." Then, ask your child to visualize the same thing, and describe the visualization: "Now you visualize the word 'but,' and in your mind's eye, picture the tall, short, tall letters *b-u-t* and tell me what you see." After your child describes her visualization, suggest that you look together at the high-frequency word list and see if there is another tall-short-tall word. Your child might locate the word "had" and describe her visualization of that word.

Visualization Activity: Word pictures

You can help your child recognize words by finding creative ways to mentally picture and draw the word using its letters. The following example is based on a conversation I had with a student who wanted to recognize the nonphonetic word "bicycle." She loved to ride her bicycle and was reading a beautifully illustrated book showing the development of bicycles over time. You can modify this example based on your child's interests and vocabulary words.

Teacher (T): "I see the word 'bicycle' many times in this book you chose, and I know you love to ride your bicycle. I'll give you something to start your brain picture. Imagine two letter *c*'s as wheels and a y between them as a kickstand. I'll start by writing my visualization of the *c*'s and the *y* on this paper. What do you think we can do with the letters *b*, *i*, *1*, *e* that we have left?

Student (S): "I put the *b* and *i* in front as handlebars and the *1* and *e* as the back fender and reflector. Then, I imagine the word 'bicycle' in the shape of a bicycle, using the letters to make a bicycle." The student then drew her visualization on the board and added the word-picture to her journal.

T: "Can anyone find another word from the book that could be drawn as a picture made from the letters?"

S: "I found the work 'hill,' and I can see in my mind's eye the tall and short letters, so I'll draw them on a card making the *h* and two *1* letters very tall."

T: "Can you draw the word 'hill' in the shape of a hill? Good. Now let's write the word 'hill' on the back of your picture to use for a practice card."

AS learners

AS learners visualize best when they have the framework of a sequence for the word, such as a graphic organizer that helps them connect images with the word through an orderly parts-to-whole structure. The *Information web* organizer described in Chapter 3 connects a new word with prior knowledge. The word is located in the center, with various offshoots, such as a sketch or picture, representing the word, the word used in a sentence, its part of speech, and its synonyms and antonyms.

Your child then can describe her graphic organizer verbally to hear her own words and process the information auditorily. The actual drawing and writing of the graphic organizer adds tactile-kinesthetic memory, which means the information has now entered the brain through three different pathways. When your child reviews the information web, the memories will be reactivated, and after a few reviews with visualizations, she will "own" the word.

VSK learners

Children who connect well with movement enjoy creating mental images, especially if the visualization is followed by a related physical activity. In this way, both visual and kinesthetic memory circuits are activated. Here's one to try: Have your child spell a word (for example, "fill") while looking at the word, saying the letters, and acting them out. He can stand for the tall letters and squat for the short ones. Stand and say *f*, squat and say *i*, stand and say *l*, and remain standing and say *l*.

WORD STORIES

Write down the words your child has the most trouble with during oral reading. Discuss the words and draw sketches or find pictures in the book related to the words. Working together, create a fun story using these words. The following word-story activities allow the brain to add words to more than one mental category. For example, if your child is having trouble learning the difference between the words "stray" and "stay," there can be a connection to a category called "things dogs do" (sit, bark, stay, stray) as well as a connection to the category "*st* words." The neural pathways created to these two stored mental categories will allow your child to recognize the word "stray" by association with either of the two memory storage categories. There will be two ways of accessing the pronunciation and meaning of the word "stray" when it appears again in written text.

AS learners

AS learners benefit from conversations that include troublesome words. If a word difficulty is the difference between "stay" and "stray," for example, ask, "When you have a dog that will **st**ray from home, would you like him to learn how to **st**ay? (Emphasize the "st" sound in both "stray" and "stay.") When your child answers, have her write the two words in the sequence in which you say them, "stray" before "stay," then repeat them back in the same sequence, as in "I want my stray dog to stay." She can use both the auditory sentence and the sequence that goes from a five- to a four-letter word (stray to stay) to remember the two word spellings. Another option is to put the two words into a short rhyme that your child reads to you and practices aloud to herself. "There were five letters in 'stray'; then one ran away, and only four letters now 'stay.'"

VSK learners

VSK learners can incorporate movement into learning words with a subtle one-letter difference, such as "stay" and "stray." Ask your child to picture a dog that doesn't know how to *st*ay, and then to picture that dog wandering away from home. Continue the story that the dog is then picked up with other *st*ray dogs and brought to the animal shelter that keeps dogs safe after they *st*ray from home.

Your child can reinforce the difference between the two words by writing the shorter or more familiar word (in this case, "stay") on paper, or building it using magnetic letters. After the word "stay" is built or written (with help if needed), have him place or write the letter *r* inside the word "stay" so the dog won't stray. Again, there have been three sensory systems stimulated in the mental manipulation of these two words (visual, auditory, and kinesthetic-writing), resulting in pathways to multiple storage centers and easier memory retrieval.

MY OWN WORDS: INTEREST-GENERATED VOCABULARY ACTIVITIES

Word-learning activities chosen by interest and sustained by learning strength give your child word ownership. Ownership happens not by looking up words in a dictionary but by your child explaining a word's meaning in her own words and using the new word in ways that are meaningful to her. As syn-*naps* activities, your child can create her own word list from high-interest books or magazines, or a perhaps create a list of words she has heard and wants to know more about. Use the following learning-strength games and activities to help her own those words.

AS learners

- Use free websites, such as Puzzlemaker.com, to create computer-generated word puzzles and word searches that appeal to your child's sequencing and part-to-whole learning strengths.
- Give your child opportunities to hear and speak words and their meanings by rhyming, singing, listening, and discussing them.
- Break down the word-learning process and follow a sequence when learning new words. Your AS child may prefer listening to you use a word in sentences before he is ready to try using it in a sentence himself.
- Encourage your child to make audio recordings of words and their definitions. AS learners enjoy the auditory feedback of hearing their own recordings and listening to their words with definitions they say (or in rhyming poems they create independently and with help from rhyming websites, such as www.poetry4kids.com).
- Play "Word Detective" for an on-the-go vocabulary review, such as while in the car or waiting in lines. This activity appeals to an AS learner who has strengths in deductive reasoning, sequential learning, and/or auditory memory.

    Here's how it works. Select a vocabulary word and gradually give your child clues about the word's meaning in sentences, so she can deduce the definition. Add increasing information about the word's meaning in your clues until your child has the satisfaction of being correct. She will almost always get the correct answer as you continue to give stronger clues, and the number of clues she hears will add auditory reinforcement to the word in memory.

    For example, if the word is "opaque," the sentence clues may start off with, "The room had opaque windows." Continue to give more specific sentence clues until she suggests the definition or uses it in another sentence. You could say, "The room with opaque windows seemed darker than the other rooms in the building," or "The opaque windows didn't let in much light, but they did let in some." Then, if she figures out the definition, you can continue the game with another sentence of your own followed by one she creates. You could say, "We couldn't see clearly enough through the opaque windows to know what was outside," and she could say, "The window was opaque, so I didn't know if it was foggy outside."

- Use a "story-making" strategy to help your child build auditory memory and add positive emotional connections to the memory. This can be another on-the-go or waiting-in-line activity. Start the story with a fun sentence that uses a new word, perhaps related to one of your child's interests. For example, for the word "swift," you could start the story with, "My speed was swift, but I couldn't seem to outrun the creature I heard on the trail behind me." Encourage your child to figure out the meaning of "swift" from contextual cues, and then add his own sentences to build an ongoing story. His sentences can link in any way he likes to your preceding sentence. Consider tape recording the stories, so they can be replayed for future review. As a series of ongoing syn-*naps* activities, your child can listen to and draw illustrations for the story, and write down the vocabulary word for each image. There will now be a picture book to go with the audiotape for future vocabulary review or to share with younger siblings.

- Talk about situations in your child's life that relate to new words. This will help her connect a word with prior knowledge, and builds it into the patterns of relational memory. For example, to review the word "enthusiastic," you might ask your child, "When you find out you are going to do something you really love, like going to the zoo or playing soccer, you might say you are *excited*, but you could also say you are *enthusiastic*. About what other things could you say you are enthusiastic?" You child might answer, "Before my birthday party." Encourage her to use the word in her sentence: "I'm enthusiastic before my birthday party."

VSK learners

- Play "Domino Words" for a fun syn-*naps*. Here's how it works. Make cards that include a vocabulary word on one side and a picture of the word on the other. Have your child select interesting pictures of objects, people, or places from magazines or the Internet that represent words she wants to include in a word journal. If she is interested in transportation, for example, she can cut out or download pictures related to transportation, and you can help her write the word on one side after she tapes a picture on the other side of the card.

Once you have several categories of cards prepared, you're ready to play Domino Words. You'll need at least ten cards each from at least three different categories, such as transportation, foods, zoo animals, farm animals, or items of clothing. Also include three blank cards.

Mix the cards and blanks. Deal four or five to each player (older children can handle more cards). Place the remaining deck in the middle. Take turns using one of the word-picture cards in your deck to match the category of a starter card pulled from the deck (animal-to-animal, machine-to-machine, etc.). Model your thoughts aloud, and encourage your child to do the same: "A lawn mower is a machine, so it matches the card with the dishwasher." If either of you don't have a matching category card, pick from the pile. If you pull a blank, you get to choose a category for the blank card.

"Aha" moments arise in my students when they play this game. For example, when two chosen categories of cards are machines and transportation, one child may match his sit-upon lawn mower to another child's truck and say, "I know we call the lawn-mower card a machine card, but since you can sit on it, it also can be transportation." Celebrate your child's category-relationship breakthrough!

• Play "Match Card Solitaire" using the word-picture cards from the preceding activity. Your child can flip through the deck independently and use the pictures and words (and later, just the words) as you watch her sort the cards directly into category baskets designated for the categories of the cards (transportation, foods, etc.) When she is ready to just use the word sides of the cards, she can play alone and check her accuracy by looking at the picture side of the card before placing it in the proper category basket.

• Help your child connect descriptive vocabulary words to objects with a fun "label my things" activity. If the word is "dilapidated," for example, she can put a note card or Post-it on her well-loved, frayed stuffed animal. For the word "precious," she could put a card with the word on her most prized toy or photograph. If the word is "sanitary," she can put a card with the word on a sealed Band-Aid. It is fun for your child later to go around the house and see labels. After the word descriptors have been up for a few days, encourage her to remove the cards and place them on other objects that suit the definitions. If she describes her thinking as she applies the definition labels, she is further reinforcing the memory of the word's definition.

• Play "Be the Word/Feel the Word." Here's how it works. After learning the definition of a word, such as "electron," for example, suggest that your child visualize an electron orbiting the nucleus of an atom, and ask him to imagine or make the sound of the buzz of electricity as it whizzes by. Have him sense the tingling associated with the electron's negative charge by rubbing a balloon against the wall and then near his arm so he feels the hairs move. He then can draw a sketch of his experience, describe the experience verbally, or describe it in writing using his own words. Multiple brain pathways will be stimulated to carry the new information into long-term memory.

Here's another example, using the word "inspect." You and your child can move about the room carefully examining details of the electric outlets and light switches, pretending to be electrical inspectors or fire-prevention agents.

• Remember that actions speak louder (and build stronger memories) than words. For the first introduction of a new vocabulary word, act it out and have your child pick the word he thinks matches your pantomime from a list of three you write down. Later, have him act out a recently learned word or make a physical response, gesture, or facial expression that reminds him of the word. Then, you try to guess his word.

• Take a picture. Thanks to digital cameras, your child can be the star of her own vocabulary show. Photograph your child acting out vocabulary words to create reminders of physical movements for words. I have a great class photo taken when I asked my students all to show me a "haughty" expression after I first prompted them that it might be the expression a rude king or queen would make after being served tea in a dirty cup by an unwashed servant.

Create bulletin-board or computer slide-show displays of the photos. You can use these for subsequent review, and they can be saved for younger children as tools to help them build their independent vocabulary beyond classroom lists. You can also make magnetic strips for each set of vocabulary words, and your child can put the words on a magnetic whiteboard and use dry-erase markers to create different sentences that include the word along with pictures.

- Show your child how to tap out the rhythm of a word's syllables on a tambourine or with maracas.

- Draw words in interesting ways that show their meanings. For example, the vocabulary word "shadow" can be drawn with shadows of each letter. "Dollar" can be written with a dollar sign ($) in place of the two "11" letters. (You can inform your child that the origin of the dollar sign came from superimposing the letter *s* over the letter *u*, from the initials of the United States.)

- Perform a learning activity. Boil water in a teapot and watch the steam *evaporate*. Hold a mirror over the steam and talk about the *condensation* of the steam (water vapor) on the mirror. Then watch as the condensation on the mirror increases, becomes denser, and forms drops of water that then *precipitate* back down to the pot. If your son follows this activity by drawing a diagram of the experience, he will be adding another sensory modality to his memory of the three vocabulary words. Utilizing these multiple storage centers for the same words will result in a greater likelihood of memory cues activating one of the brain regions where the meanings of these words are stored, making the words easier to remember.

- Visit fun word websites during a syn-*naps*. Go to puzzlemaker.com or use its software to create word puzzles, such as crossword puzzles, hidden word searches, cryptograms, or one of the other twelve puzzle types available for word practice. These puzzles can be saved and used for review in the ensuing weeks, and new puzzles can be made out of the same list of words for variety in review. Another fun website, Flexicon, offers vocabulary-building activities that allow your child to use a crossword format to create word challenges appropriate for his abilities through a variety of learning-style options. (http://games.msn.com/en/flexicon/default.htm?icid=flexicon_hmemailta-glineapri107)

• Vocabularyworkshop.com is another example of a website offering a variety of opportunities to interact with words to build mastery. Activities including hangman, word search, hidden word, word matching, word scramble, concentration, reproducible word cards, graphic organizers (word webs, concept circles, word squares), and crosswords.

KEEP GOING!

A basketball by itself is fun to bounce for a while, but simply having one is unlikely to build motivation to learn all the things that can be done with it. Practicing passing and throwing drills goes one step further, but even drills on their own become repetitious and don't inspire skill building. But when your child sees all the things experienced basketball players can do with a ball, such as dribbling, passing, and throwing it into a basket in an exciting, interactive game, his motivation for acquiring basketball skills increases.

If you offer your child strategies and practice opportunities to build his successful manipulation of that basketball, it becomes much more than a big ball to bounce. He experiences the satisfaction that comes from seeing practice pay off in increased skill and success. He becomes motivated to continue to practice because he has connected with the pleasure of becoming a basketball *player*.

Similarly, vocabulary instruction that focuses on repetitive, unin-spiring activities like looking up definitions in a dictionary is not going to motivate your child to learn new words. But when you help your child develop interest in and awareness of words beyond the formal vocabulary lists he is given at school, he is on the path to becoming a real reader. Like the basketball player who builds skills by putting the ball through the basket, having your child actually put new words to use increases his successful aim at reading comprehension.

To take the analogy one step further, once your child understands the big picture of basketball, he becomes more interested in reading the sports page or biographies of favorite players. When you inspire him through motivating literature and learning activities, he enjoys knowing that you are showing him the big picture of why reading is a worthy basket at which to aim. He will pay more attention to the words he sees, hears, and uses. He will be motivated to build his reading skills by using enjoyable, learner-strength-compatible strategies to understand challenging words and recognize relationships between words. Interest and curiosity will stimulate him to build his neuronal circuits and gain ownership of new words, and from there increase his comprehension of what he reads.

6

READING COMPREHENSION (AGES 7–11)

"Tell me and I'll forget. Show me and I may remember.
Involve me and I will understand."
—Chinese Proverb

Reading comprehension is necessary not only for your child's ability to enjoy literature, but also for him to be successful in the classroom. The enjoyable activities in this chapter will help your child build strong relational memories (one of the big keys to reading comprehension), read with purpose, discover relationships, and visualize, summarize, synthesize, and remember what he reads. When your child has background knowledge about what he reads—existing brain patterns on which to hook new information—he is more likely to remember what he has read. In this chapter, you'll also learn how to activate your child's prior knowledge and connect his personal interests to the plots, settings, characters, and messages of stories. Prior knowledge, connections to personal interest, and reading with a purpose all increase your child's emotional connections to reading, yielding stronger memory storage of the information and greater reading comprehension success.

THE POWER OF RELATIONAL MEMORY

Memories are formed when the brain matches new information to existing related memory. Prior knowledge already stored in memory patterns provides a place to which new input can link. This linkage of new sensory input with existing memory is what turns short-term memory into long-term memory.

Activate Prior Knowledge

Before your child reads a story or chapter, help him activate any existing memory circuits that relate to what he is about to read. Remind him of prior knowledge, past experiences, and interests that will make the reading more meaningful and memorable. Discuss things he is already interested in that will be included in the book, and encourage him to tell you what he remembers about things he has experienced that are similar to events that come up as he reads. For example, if the book is about a child taking a trip, first look at photos about a trip your family took. If the story is about a new baby, ask your child to recall how he felt when his baby brother or cousin was born. When those memories are stimulated, your child's neural networks and stored patterns are primed to seek and connect with related new information in the reading.

Add to your child's background knowledge by using videos related to the book's topic. If a book is about mountain climbing, watch a video about Mount Everest to stoke interest and provide a background of knowledge onto which your child can hook the new information he will encounter in the book. If the story takes place in Colonial times, watch a video or look at a few Internet sites relating to that theme. Perhaps you could do a Google Earth search together about the country in which the story takes place and see what it looks like today.

Once you start reading, periodically stop and reactivate prior knowledge (every few pages for first-year readers, every few chapters for upper-elementary readers). If a character in a book is flying on an airplane but your child has never done this, think of another situation involving similar emotions. Perhaps your child has spent a night away from home and can relate to the feelings of worry the character has about traveling away from his parents, mixed with his excitement about visiting his best friend who moved to another part of the country last year.

Connect to Your Child's Interests

Ask questions that prompt your child to discover similarities between herself and characters in the book she's reading. What personal goals, interests, hobbies, fears, personality traits, values, or hobbies can she find in common? For example, point out the connection between your child's generous act of sharing her lunch with a friend and the character in the book who gives a classmate a pencil to replace the one his mean brother took out of his backpack before school. Your child also can make comparisons and turn the differences into memory-sticking analogies, such as "Sam likes green eggs and ham like I like yellow eggs and bacon."

Emotions are important as well. If a school book is about a leader of a colony during the Colonial period, ask your child what qualities she would want to see in the leader of a club she was thinking about joining. Encourage other emotional connections about times when she had feelings of curiosity, joy, disappointment, anger, or sympathy similar to those of a character in the book.

Sometimes there are questions at the ends of chapters or the end of a book that can help your child connect personally to the story he is reading. The themes in children's books are often similar and involve problems between two characters, a personal decision that is difficult to make, or danger from some thing, person, or event in a character's life that requires action. There are usually points at which these common themes can connect with experiences in your own child's life to engage him in the story so he is focused and his brain is alert to the coming events.

If the reading has connections to current events in the areas of news, politics, sports, entertainment, or science, any of these can be an activating topic to prompt your child to engage further with the book. Watch the news together or find articles in the newspaper that relate to the book, and have discussions that link book topics with things happening in your city or town.

READING WITH A PURPOSE

Goal-directed reading, or reading with a purpose, starts with your child knowing why a book is important enough to be worth his effort. In addition to calling upon real-world interests and connections with prior knowledge, consider other ways your child can develop personally meaningful goals to keep him engaged and focused during reading.

Help your child see the big picture, predict outcomes, and formulate questions throughout his reading to sustain his focus, interest, and connection to the book.

Preview and Predict

Prediction-based strategies create opportunities for your child to personally and emotionally connect with a book, yielding greater comprehension and memory storage. Preview the "big picture" for your child before she begins reading a book that could be a challenge (especially if she is a VSK learner). Your child's brain will then be ready to look for these themes as she reads the book. Discuss the general topic of the book, such as making a new friend or building a tree house. Look together at the features of the book, such as title, chapter names, subheadings, and pictures to predict what the book might be about, and ask why she makes her predictions. In addition to priming her brain for reading, this also will help her develop analysis and judgment skills. Ask questions about the book topic that piques your child's interest. Offer tantalizing but brief descriptions of the theme or story organization. Read aloud an interesting passage from the book so your child can look forward to the things she'll read in the coming pages.

KWL Activity

One of the most popular and brain-compatible prediction strategies is called the KWL activity, in which a child makes lists for each of the following: *what I **K**now, what I **W**ant to know*, and later, to be filled in as a concluding activity, *what I **L**earned*. The KWL strategy gives your child opportunities to activate his prior knowledge as she considers a given subject. The "what I **K**now" list increases her personal investment and focus because she wants to see if her predictions are correct. The "what I **W**ant to know" list adds the focus of goal direction. After she writes or dictates what she wants to know, you can ask if she'd like to find out other things, such as: "What does the title have to do with the book (or story)?" "Where does the story take place?" "Who are the main characters, and what will they do?" "How does the illustration on the book's cover relate to the story?"

As you read the story together, your child can add to the "what I Learned" column to help her summarize new information and reactivate new neural networks to build long-term memories. When she finds answers to her questions or predictions, she can also add these to the list. The list can help refresh her memory before she reads the next chapter, and the final "what I Learned" list makes a great study guide for a test.

BUILDING LONG-TERM MEMORY

As we've learned, information enters the brain as sensory input. Each time the brain receives new information, it stays in short-term (working) memory for only seconds, unless it is related to a pattern or category of information that exists in the brain's long-term memory storage. If the brain recognizes a familiar pattern and connects the new information with the existing neural storage network, a relational memory is started. With further mental manipulation (that is, practice, use of the new information, and relating it to other memories), the relational memory becomes permanently stored in long-term memory.

Graphic Organizers

We've also discussed the fact that graphic organizers take the information found in books and make it brain-ready for the patterning of relational memories that become long-term memories. As your child relates to things, emotions, places, and characters in books, graphic organizers can help him chart and see relationships more clearly, increasing the patterning of memories. The graphic organizers illustrated in Chapter 3 can be used to help your child remember sequences of events, relationships between characters, and different settings of a book. The following structures are especially effective for increasing relational memory and reading comprehension:

- Tree and branch diagrams can link details to a main topic. The name of a book can be the trunk, character names can be branches, and facts about the characters can be leaves off the branches.
- Timelines can be used to plot sequences of events or changes in a character over time. If your child has never made a timeline, he can practice by making timelines for familiar activities of his choice

that are done in sequence, such as making a sandwich, dressing for team sports, or logging onto the computer. He also can practice the strategy by making a timeline of his life from birth to his current age, with branches for important events.

- Venn diagrams can be used to compare or contrast information from two (or more) topics, such as two books by the same author or different books about similar topics. Venn diagrams also can compare/contrast two or more aspects of a subject, character, or topic in a given book. Your child can demonstrate her personal connection to characters in the book by diagramming the similarities and differences between her life, personality, or hometown with the character or town in the book.

Journaling

If your child enjoys writing more than she likes discussing her responses to what she reads, journaling can build reading comprehension while allowing her to respond to parts of a book she finds personally significant or interesting. She also can write letters to book characters in her journal to build personal connections with the book that increase her relational memories.

Encourage your child to include quotes, paraphrase conversations, and briefly summarize parts of the plot in her journal that cause her to pause and think, or ask her questions such as these: Which character reminds you of someone you have met or something about yourself? Can you recall and write about a time when you faced a problem similar to one confronted by a character in this book and how you reacted? Did reading this book give you any ideas about what you might have done differently in your own experience? Can you describe a situation when you have been surprised, frustrated, frightened, angry, sad, or confused like the character in the book?

Note Taking

Older children who need to remember more facts from their readings, especially in textbooks, can benefit from practicing note taking at home if they have not been taught successful note-taking skills in school. As with most new strategies you want to teach your child, first consider modeling what textual information is important enough to warrant note taking. Read part of the text aloud as your child follows along in the book. When you come to a phrase or section that you think is important for your child to include in her notes because it is critical to the theme, plot, or characters of the story, say a few words about why you think it is important enough to include in your notes as you write it down. Next, take *reciprocal notes*. Read a few paragraphs together, and take turns writing notes and saying why you think the information was important to include. The non-note-taker can then offer suggestions about other items in the paragraph she considers valuable to include.

Asking Questions

Keep a list of questions handy to help your child continue to read with a purpose, relate to the book on a personal level, and make predictions about what happens next, such as:

- What evidence is there that this book is fiction?
- What does the title have to do with the book (or story)?
- Who are the main characters?
- Why do you think the picture on the cover was chosen for this book?
- Why do you think this illustration is here? What does it say?
- What do you think the character should do about his problem?
- What would you have done differently, or why do you think the character made a good decision?
- What do you think will happen next?
- What do you hope to find out in the next chapter?

Summarizing

After each section of reading, have your child summarize what happened and describe personal connections to the story. You can demonstrate by reading a section of one of your child's favorite fairy tales, and then summarizing and describing your personal relationship to it. For example: "In this chapter of *Goldilocks and the Three Bears*, Goldilocks tasted the three bowls of porridge and discovered the first two were either too hot or too cold, but the third was just right. When I read that for the first time when I was your age, I didn't know what porridge was. I thought it might be some kind of soup because it was in bowls. Then I remembered that it was breakfast time because the bears had just woken up, so I changed my mind and decided porridge might be a hot cereal, like oatmeal. I didn't know why that was important to the story until I found there was a pattern to the way Goldilocks would try things that belonged to each of the bears.

"I thought I might be like Goldilocks because I liked cereal and I fit into beds and chairs that were right for a child. When I read the rest of the story, I wondered if what Goldilocks was doing was stealing, or if she was doing what she had to do to survive? I'm still not sure. Do you have an opinion about that?"

You can also have your child summarize another favorite story, movie, television show, or sporting event so he has the experience of condensing material into a summary before he tries it with books. Encourage those same personal connections with his book-chapter summaries to increase the emotional sticking power of the facts.

READING COMPREHENSION CHALLENGES

Unless your child understands what he reads, he won't appreciate the plot, the richness of the characters, or how the story might relate to his own life. Without comprehension, reading is just connecting strings of words without forming lasting memories and deriving pleasure from these words.

To comprehend what he reads, your child's brain takes in new information and has to process it through a variety of neural networks using patterns, categories, and relational connections to build the new data into understanding. Constructing meaning from text is not a separate reading skill, but rather is a combination of vocabulary recognition, remembering main ideas, keeping track of important details of plot, locations, and characters' names, and connecting personally to a story to build relational memories.

Reading comprehension is a thinking skill that can be sharpened with several very effective brain-based strategies. You can use these to help your child build reading comprehension, and through that, he can discover the true joy of reading for pleasure and increased knowledge.

Vocabulary Confusion

AS learners benefit from verbal preinstruction of new vocabulary words that will come up in the reading. If the book is a textbook, the vocabulary words may already be in boldface print in the chapter and may be defined in the glossary. Your child can read these words before reading the chapter (and refer back during reading if you put Post-its on the glossary pages for each word). This will help her stay comfortable and connected to the text.

VSK learners may benefit from other types of preinstruction. You can prevent your child from becoming frustrated by doing activities to increase his familiarity with new vocabulary words in advance. You can use any of the VSK vocabulary-learning activities from Chapter 2, such as pantomime, diagramming, making index cards for match games, making puzzles of the words on puzzlemaker.com, or using graphic organizers, visualizations, and writing analogies using the words and definitions.

Connecting Personally to a Book

To increase personal connections to the text and connections to relational memories, encourage your child to do more predicting or adding of personal impressions.

AS learners can respond personally to the comprehension notes they take and discuss these responses with you. It involves one level of understanding when your child writes down important facts as notes, but when he adds personal impressions and connections to his notes and discusses them with you, his relational memories of the text increases. You might want to try an activity called "Note-taking–Note-making," which starts with drawing a line down the length of a page that divides it in half. On one side, your child writes factual notes, and on the other, he adds his questions, comments, and personal similarities and connections.

VSK learners can use more visual and physical activities to connect to a book, such as visualizing themselves in the action as if they are watching a filmed version of the book with themselves in a major character's role. Your child might enjoy diagramming the story as a summary activity, acting out parts of a chapter, or reading lines of text as if it is a play script. Even if there are not dialogue quotes, you can show him places in the narrative where the "voice" of a character is heard, and encourage him to read those paragraphs with a dramatic flair to sound the way the character might.

Deciding What's Important

AS learners who are overwhelmed by selecting which items to include in notes or summaries about their reading can build their note-taking skills by simply listing three or four key points they feel might unlock the meaning of what they just read. If your child is a part-to-whole learner (as are many AS learners) who feels most comfortable when she knows the sequence from beginning to end, she may benefit by knowing how the story ends, looking at review questions before reading the chapters, or even reading a summary of the book on the jacket or on an Internet bookseller's site. Other ways to learn key points is to look at the tables of contents in literature books or the bold subheadings in textbooks for cues as to what is important.

In addition to the activities suggested for connecting to text, you can strengthen your child's relationship to a book by isolating what is important using highlighting strategies (described on pages 91–92). You can then have a discussion to flesh out key words and, when your child is ready, she can then add the parts of the discussion she found helpful to her notes or dictate a summary of the chapter into a tape recorder to play back before starting the next day's reading.

Summarizing Texts

Reciprocal reading activities can be useful for both VSK and AS learners who have trouble summarizing text. Read a small section of text aloud while your child follows along, and then ask him to summarize what you just read to consolidate the information in his memory. Then, you can switch roles, so he reads and you summarize the same section. Here you can add things he missed in his summary that are important for understanding the story. Because you incorporate the information he missed in your summary, he will not feel criticized for what he didn't include, but he will learn more about what should have been included. Reciprocal reading gives your child more confidence to join in class discussions.

If your child still has trouble summarizing or recognizing the main idea in a paragraph or story, he can practice summarizing familiar stories from other books he has read or stories he has heard multiple times. Summarizing movies or television shows also can help improve text summarizing.

AS learners are likely to prefer giving their summaries verbally and possibly recording them instead of writing them down. After you listen to your child's verbal summaries, or after she listens to her recording once or twice, she can strengthen visual and sequential memory by writing the information down in list form. Her strength for sequential thinking can be called upon to increase memory if she arranges her list or graphic organizer in a sequence she thinks is appropriate, such as time of events or importance of facts from a textbook.

VSK learners benefit from hearing your summary and repeating back what they think you are saying in their own words. If your child leaves information out of his summary, he might not have realized he didn't say it, because he has a big-picture concept of the section. His global-thinking brain may not slow down enough to realize there are facts he didn't report. You can help him recognize that he knows more than he said by repeating his verbal summary back to him. When you say what you think you heard him say, he may realize he didn't explain the summary clearly or left things out. Similarly, when he paraphrases your summary back to you in his own words, he is making brain connections to the information by rephrasing and therefore is building greater comprehension while also building listening skills.

Remembering Main Ideas

Your child can practice finding and remembering the main ideas of paragraphs or pages by answering a prepared list of guiding questions, such as: "Who is the subject of the paragraph (chapter)?" "What is the most important information or most important thing described in the page or paragraph?" "What previous plot information relates to things the main character did in this section?" "Does this section include or add information about any conflicts and solutions?" "Has the action moved to another setting?" "Have new characters been introduced?" When your child practices finding the answers to these questions in the texts she summarizes, she will internalize them and will continue to ask herself these questions when she reads independently.

AS learners feel more confident if they continue their summaries in a consistent pattern and reflect back on written lists of summaries of the preceding paragraphs or chapters before responding to the guiding questions. They can then extend their sequential thinking to make connections between the new and prior events and discuss some of the guiding questions. Your AS learner may again benefit from tape-recording his responses to the questions and playing these back before his next summary or guided-question response or before a test.

VSK learners may find it helpful to write in the margins or take notes in a reading log at intervals to summarize key points after completing verbal responses to guided questions. Your child might first want to visualize the information in his mind, draw sketches, or add the new information to his previous diagrams, timelines, or graphic organizers before and after discussing the questions or summary with you. He can refer to these before answering the questions about the next section. These also become valuable review and test study aids. When my students have memory problems, I encourage them to take good notes and permit them to use certain parts of their notes, diagrams, or sketches when they take tests.

Sitting still, formulating ideas into well-organized thoughts, and relying on the fine-motor-skill activity of writing can overwhelm VSK learners. To help bridge the gap between what your child is thinking and what he can say or write in response to your guiding questions, he can engage both large- and fine-motor skills through activities such as drawing. Encourage your child to draw a series of pictures (with or without words) depicting the plot of a story on butcher-block paper spread across a wall, table, or floor. He might next write the information on smaller cards that he can then mix up and rearrange in proper order across the floor. During early practice sessions of arranging his cards, he can refer to his large drawings. Later, this rearranging of the mixed cards can be an independent activity if he numbers the cards on the backs. Then when he arranges them in sequence, he can check his accuracy by flipping them over and checking the numerical sequence. This physical movement and orientation in space accesses the VSK learner's neurological learning strengths and keeps him energized and attentive.

Understanding Complex Writing

Highlighters can be used to help your child comprehend more difficult literature or texts. She can use colored highlighters to emphasize different parts of the text in colors she codes for importance. (You might get an old copy of the textbook from her teacher or photocopy pages from her schoolbook.)

Another highlighting strategy can improve understanding through a form of rereading. Most children don't have the patience to reread what they don't understand, or if they do reread, they are already mentally frustrated and their filters are not in the ideal state to let in the information. The following activity uses highlighters to make rereading simpler and more effective. Give your child three different colored markers and ask her to highlight in yellow anything she doesn't understand. Then, without trying to reason out the information, ask her to simply reread the paragraph, this time highlighting anything she still doesn't understand in light blue. Have her repeat the same process with the green highlighter on a third reading. (You can also do this without markers by underlining first in dotted lines, second in dashes, and last in uninterrupted lines.)

During this process, your child will come to understand more of the text each time she reads it, and this will be evidenced by the decreasing amount of text she underlines with each reading. The process of underlining focuses attention on the phrases she underlines. When children are obliged to return to these lines, they focus on them and build comprehension through concentration and persistence. Your child will find the activity enjoyable (colored markers are fun) and the success is immediately evident (less underlining each time, because with rereading, more is understood). After using highlighting, some children discover that they can achieve the same degree of understanding with focused rereading without highlighters.

After highlighting important chapter or text information, it is valuable for your child to read the underlined sentences again at the end one reading session and before the next. AS learners may want to tape-record their reading of the underlined sentences, and VSK learners may want to put them into diagrams or charts.

Memory Retention

An important strategy for improving your child's memory retention is to remind him to refer back to information earlier in the book or consult his notes on earlier chapters when he is confused about his reading. Explain that it is just like referring back to examples in his math when he is stuck on a problem, or rereading his lines just before a rehearsal of a class play.

Mnemonics is a strategy that uses the pattern-seeking brain to look for associations between the information it is receiving and what is already stored. Mnemonic devices are associations we use to help us remember facts. Because the brain looks for relationships, when your child can attach facts to personal, meaningful, or even humorous sequences, the facts will be more easily remembered.

Especially at the beginning of a book, where a number of facts, locations, characters, and subplots are introduced without inherent meaning, your child can practice creating mnemonics to create organizational frameworks on which to hook new information. For example, if your child has difficulty remembering the names of the characters, he can write them on a chart and add personality traits that are revealed during the reading. To help remember the character's name and traits, he can think of words to describe the traits that start with the same letter as the character's name, such as "clever Clarissa," "funny Frank," and "gross George." Creating mnemonics can be a restorative syn-*naps* activity. The more fun your child has with these associations and the more bizarre they are, the more memorable they will be. If your child has difficulty remembering the sequence of actions or locations, he can use a timeline to make a mnemonic with the first letter of each word that describes the important event or place. If the order of locations where the plot takes place is store, treehouse, attic, movie theater, and park, the mnemonic can be "STAMP."

MEMORY-STRENGTHENING EXERCISES

The amount of information that can be kept in mind at one time is limited and different for each child. Children who have difficulty listening and taking notes in class may have low working-memory capacity, so they can't remember what they hear long enough to both listen and simultaneously take good notes—a child may miss information being said while he takes notes. To strengthen working memory, you can play memory-building games to help your child practice holding more and more data in memory. Just as physical exercise strengthens the body's muscles, a few minutes each day of memory muscle-building will pay off in strengthened memory.

AS learners

- See how long a word you can say that she can spell forward, then backward.
- Practice memorizing poems that she enjoys, and recite them together when taking a walk or as a bedtime ritual. Try committing a new line to memory each night so she builds memory capacity enough to be able to recite a poem with eight, twelve, or even sixteen lines.
- Remind your child of songs she remembers accurately, and suggest she try setting poems she wants to learn to tunes she knows or creates.

VSK learners

- Play memory-building games that incorporate movement memory by creating a series of body movements or hand gestures for your child to imitate. Gradually add more movements as he succeeds with the less complex sequences.
- Write lists of things your child likes, such as sports teams, favorite toys, places to visit, or desserts. He can make a long list, and you can start with a small number from that list for him to try to remember and gradually add more as his memory improves.

After he looks at the list, have him write or say as many as he can remember, in any order. Gradually increase the number to build his working-memory power.

7
READING MOTIVATION STRATEGIES (AGES 7–11)

There is a wonderful cycle that you can put into play to motivate your child to become a lifelong reader. When your child's interests, strengths, and talents are used to connect him to literature, he builds reading skills by reading the books he enjoys. Increased reading skills result in more satisfying reading experiences and greater engagement with, connection to, and memory of what is read.

Enjoy the discoveries you will make about your child and his world as you share experiences and activities that motivate his enjoyment of, and success in, reading. Once you are aware of the power of choice, interest, and your own modeling of reading on your child, you'll find opportunities all around you to draw him into wanting to read. Family reading nights, the daily newspaper, series books, recorded books, and reading celebrations can become lifelong influences on your child's positive connections to reading.

FOLLOW YOUR CHILD'S INTERESTS
When your child reads passionately and for personal interest, he experiences the dopamine-pleasure response in the brain and receives increased neuronal stimulation in the frontal-lobe networks of reading fluency, comprehension, and higher-order thinking. You know your child's interests better than anyone else, and these can be the motivating forces that inspire him to read. Children are attracted to books that connect to their enjoyable past experiences, such as travel, the ocean, space exploration,

insects, or people they consider heroes. As your child reads more books in areas of high interest, the increased depth of the specialized knowledge he acquires helps him stand out as a high learner to his teachers and classmates. Expertise in most any area is respected and can increase his self-concept and confidence in other academic areas. Reading about topics of interest and gaining more depth of knowledge in these areas stimulates his higher-order thinking, which extends into other learning successes.

Learn about your child's interests, and provide opportunities for her to read about them. Keep various books and magazines available around the house and see which ones she picks up. Visit libraries, used and new bookstores, or bookseller websites with your child to help reveal her interests and promote new ones. What captures her attention as she browses the library or bookstore shelves? If she enjoyed books about certain topics or by specific authors in the past, ask the librarian for additional suggestions. If she has a favorite book or author, go to an online bookseller that makes suggestions based on your past purchases, and look for suggested books that are similar to her favorites. Help your child find passions and interests that fall outside her school curriculum. When she participates in these experiences, she feels the power of igniting an area of high interest. That feeling will be recaptured when she finds ways to translate her outside interest or knowledge into a topic of study at school.

INSPIRE WITHOUT PRESSURE

Do not force your child to finish every book he starts or quiz him on the contents of all recreational reading, and do not make a big deal of it if he does sit and read a book for pleasure. You want to avoid making him feel pressured and reluctant to pick up a book again. Allow him to bring up the topic of a book, and then you can join in a conversation with him about it and show your encouragement. Offer to read a chapter aloud, or ask him if he'd like to read his favorite paragraph or chapter to you because you are interested in the topic.

You are a role model for your child. When he sees you reading books, not just for specific reasons but also for enjoyment, his regard for books increases. Just as important, if he sees you being challenged by more technical books, he will feel more comfortable about difficulties he has reading more complex texts and novels. Talk about your own reading challenges with your child. If the computer software book you are reading is dense with facts and you need to take frequent breaks or take notes, let your child know how you are feeling and what you are doing. Say, "This is hard reading. That's why I keep getting up and moving to another chair or adjusting the lights. I need to give my brain a break, or syn-*naps*, so I can get through it and learn what I need to know." Or, "There is so much to know about real estate law, and it is not all interesting. Sometimes I read the same sentence two or three times, and I even have to write things down so I can understand and remember what I read. But I really want to pass the test and get my real estate broker's license, so I'll stick with it and keep thinking about the day when I reach my goal."

If you had trouble developing an interest in reading or had a harder time than your classmates when you were learning to read, that is also good information to share with your child. He may see you reading books with tiny print and with many pages (and no pictures) and think you were just "born that way" or are much smarter than he is. If there was a special interest that connected you with certain books that you didn't like at first but grew to enjoy as you became more familiar with the subject and vocabulary, be sure to share those memories with your child. He wants to be like you. Knowing about your frustrations or embarrassments helps him when he is struggling in the same ways.

Activities to Inspire Reading

Along with physical activity, play, and self-motivation, **Parent Read-Aloud** is an activity that shows up on brain scans as being associated with the dopamine-pleasure cycle. To tap into the brain-friendly benefits of reading to your child, choose books that he finds highly interesting or that coincide with special seasonal events (holidays, popular movies, special events, the start of soccer or Little League season, etc). If books that you read aloud have some challenging vocabulary above your child's independent reading level, it's okay, because you'll be doing the reading and can explain the words' meanings as they come up.

Family reading time shows your child that reading is valued by all family members. Schedule special times when family members read books of their choice, emphasizing the pleasure of reading. Each family member can plan for the evening by selecting favorite passages from a book to share or describing its plot or characters. Because all family members are reading, there will be no television or video-game playing that might distract any reluctant readers. If everyone reads the same book, you can even have book club-style discussions. Take the lead by suggesting discussion topics, and eventually older siblings, and even your youngest child, can enjoy taking turns as discussion leader.

When your child reads aloud in these comfortable surroundings, he builds the fluency skill of reading with expressiveness. You can extend family reading time or Parent Read-Aloud to build additional fluency skills and reading interest by allowing your child to perform a scene from his book or story, either spontaneously or after writing a short script. Adding costumes or a variety of hats or props can make the activity even more fun. You could even videotape the performance, which increases engagement for many children and gives gentle feedback about their fluency and expressiveness.

The **daily newspaper** can also stimulate reading in several enjoyable ways. Younger children may prefer the comics, while older children may enjoy the sports pages. Once your child has the newspaper open, it is likely that other articles may catch his attention, especially if there are photographs. Your child can "read" the paper with you by looking at photographs that interest him, predicting what the article might be about, and listening attentively to you as you read the article aloud because he wants to know if his predictions were correct. When an article is about a local or national news event, invite your child to discuss his impressions or reactions to the article. He might even be motivated to write (with your help) a letter to the editor or to the governmental group, committee, or person with whom he wants to share his opinions or suggestions.

Once reading becomes an enjoyable experience, it can become a sustained interest through **series books**. Entire generations have connected to reading thanks to books by authors like Judy Blume, Shel Silverstein, and Dr. Seuss, just as many of today's young readers have picked up the reading habit through books by Beverly Cleary or the *Harry Potter* series. Helping your child get hooked on reading is easier when you guide her to books that are part of a series.

AS learners

AS learners in elementary school enjoy books on tape, making their own tape recordings of the books they read, and discussing the books with you informally as a break from the more formal discussions that take place in class. These discussions with you help your child feel more comfortable participating in class discussions and prepare her for essay questions later on. Those who appreciate order, logic, and sequences may also enjoy the "choose your own adventure" books, where there are places in the story where the reader makes a choice for the character and is instructed to turn to a particular page based on her choice. An AS learner can be inspired to read a book if you prime her interest by reading a passage you select aloud that is surprising, intriguing, or related to one of her personal interests or past experiences.

VSK learners

Look for books that were the inspiration for movies and videos your child enjoys. Movies appeal to a VSK learner's preference for knowing the big picture first. He can also be drawn into reading by starting with picture books that have him look for things, like *Where's Waldo* or *Art Fraud Detective*. VSK learners may be drawn to books with photographs and illustrations, even when the text is challenging. Provide upper-elementary children with magazines such as *National Geographic* that feature images, illustrations, and photos about their high-interest areas that will encourage them to read the text.

Some VSK learners may not have the focus to dig right into a full-length book for personal enjoyment or for required school learning. Abridged books can instead be read first or along with the book assignments so your child will be able to keep up and move more comfortably through the full-length books. Abridged books will help her understand the movement of the plot and may offer a list of characters. If she finds the smaller print of school-assigned books intimidating, see if you can find a large-print version that has fewer words per line and more frequent page turns.

Many VSK learners enjoy puzzle and maze books. If your child enjoys comics and humor, a progression to books that incorporate humor can be a painless entrée into reading, especially when the characters are similar in age to your child. Some examples are books by Lee Wardlaw, such as *101 Ways to Bug Your Parents* and *101 Ways to Bug Your Teacher*. More suggestions for books for specific learning styles, interests, and age groups can be found in *Some of My Best Friends Are Books* by Judith Wynn.

CELEBRATE PROGRESS

Help your child see the visible results of his efforts by recording his progress. This may mean making lists showing the decreasing numbers of errors made during the reading of the same paragraph over a week, or the increasing number of correct responses in a stack of twenty "errorless-reading" flashcards. If your child likes making graphs, as some VSK learners do, she can use graph paper and use the horizontal axis to mark the date and the vertical axis to mark the number of correct responses on her flashcard practice sessions.

Progress does not always have to be documented with numbers. If you go back to a book your daughter had difficulty reading a few months earlier and she now can read it aloud with expression, you can both share the pleasure of her accomplishment. Some children are comfortable with their parents tape recording their first reading so they can hear it again after they have mastered the oral reading of the book.

Let your child collaborate with you on appropriate celebrations for achieving significant reading goals, such as choosing a restaurant for a celebratory dinner or allowing him to choose the next family game on game night or the next video the family will watch together. Successful mastery of the oral reading of a book can be celebrated with a tea party where you provide refreshments for the stuffed animals your daughter assembles as her audience. Your son may choose to celebrate by reading a part of a book to the family before his favorite dessert is served in his honor at dinner.

As your child's learning partner, your goal is to hold his hand and guide—but not carry—him up that lighthouse staircase of learning to read accurately, fluently, and with comprehension. With your help, those stairs won't seem so steep, and your child will see the top of the lighthouse as a goal he can achieve. Thanks to you, your child will experience the pride of reaching the top. When you hold his hand and patiently guide him up the staircase that leads to literacy, you truly will light up his life.

8
TEST PREPARATION STRATEGIES: VOCABULARY AND READING COMPREHENSION (AGES 7–12)

Test-taking should be an opportunity for children to demonstrate what they have learned and for them to receive feedback from teachers that fills in any gaps and corrects misunderstandings that became evident on the test (although ideally, these are discovered before the test through class discussions, small group work, and homework). Unfortunately, the No Child Left Behind system of evaluating the success of a school is by the students' results on end-of-the-year cumulative tests. These are usually multiple-choice tests that are more an assessment of rote memory than an evaluation of what a child actually learned and will retain as knowledge.

Because these standardized tests are likely to be the basis of federal funding of schools for the foreseeable future, and because teachers are under enormous pressure to raise test scores, the pressure of test performance can be stressful, even to a child in second grade.

Sometime in early elementary school, your child begins to take spelling and vocabulary tests. If these first test experiences are positive, she is at an advantage because she's more likely to approach future tests with confidence and open brain filters. If these first experiences are negative and your child stresses out in formal test situations, or if your child has difficulty memorizing facts, consider the "MOVES" strategy detailed in the following section. (Also keep in mind the importance of having planned review sessions over time, not just the evening before the test, and remember the value of reassurance—and of a good night's sleep!)

As you practice the MOVES strategy, you'll enjoy experiences that build your child's confidence and discover which strategies are best suited for her test-taking success. Your child will develop the study skills most suited for the way her brain learns and remembers best. The results will be evident on her test scores, and more importantly in her power as a lifelong learner.

MOVES STRATEGY

Two of the primary goals of reading comprehension for children are to *retain* and *retrieve* information from their long-term memories. In order to do this, it is helpful for your child to store the memories in several different memory banks, so they can more easily be accessed using more than one cue. **MOVES** is a mnemonic acronym students can use when they review reading material or notes for comprehension assessments. Each letter reminds them of another way to review the information through alternative sensory processing systems.

M: *Move/manipulate.* Have your child **Move** around and use a physical action to remind her of a fact, a character's traits, or a setting. Alternatively, move models, dolls, or stuffed animals to act out important plot information.

O: *Organize.* Create graphic organizers, such as timelines and character charts, to review and **Organize** important details. Practice reorganizing mixed chapter summary index cards into proper order. Plan how your child will best remember the information by using the organizing cues *what, who, when, where,* and *how.* Talk about what materials your child will study, who can help him study, when he will schedule review times in advance of the test, where he studies best, and how best to use the strategies you've discovered together to be most helpful. These organizing tips are particularly useful for VSK learners.

V: *Visualize.* Have your child **Visualize** characters, settings, and plot progressions in her mind. This will help her make mental connections to prior knowledge so the new information will link to memory categories she already has stored in her brain. Finding personal links to the information bolsters the emotional components that strengthen long-term memory.

E: *Enter.* Your child can **Enter** the information she wants to remember by typing it into a computer, writing it by hand, telling it to someone in her own words, or diagramming it. The more ways she mentally manipulates the information and transforms it into another sensory memory, the more places the information is stored in her brain, and the more ways her brain has to retrieve the memory. If her notes are written in words or diagrams, try starting with a graphic organizer with empty boxes, and fill in the information she remembers. Then go back and see what she left out. If she is listening to a tape recording she made, she can write notes or draw diagrams as she listens.

S: *Say.* **Say** it aloud. Saying/reading notes or important passages aloud adds auditory memory.

GOOD SLEEP HABITS AND SCHEDULED REVIEW

Dendrites, the fibers that link neurons together and store learned information into long-term memory circuits, grow in the brain during deep sleep. When your child goes to bed, dendrites related to the day's learning begin to grow after about six hours of sleep and continue to grow through the eighth hour of sleep—so make sure your child gets that full eight hours to cement the day's learning. It is also best to review for tests over several days instead of leaving the studying until the evening before the test. This ensures that the new neural networks and connecting dendrites have repeated stimulation and become stronger, more permanent long-term memories. In addition, planning several review sessions at increasing intervals (daily for two days, weekly for two weeks, then monthly for two months if there is a year-end comprehensive test) is a good rule of thumb for reviewing. Practice makes not only perfect, but also permanent. With good sleep habits and well-planned review sessions, the vocabulary words and text comprehension information your child works so hard to memorize for test is retained far beyond her test day.

REASSURE YOUR CHILD

Because your practice sessions with your child have included activities tailored to her learning strengths, she has studied to her best advantage. Remind her of her successes and of the different types of reviews she has done for her test so she realizes how well prepared she is. Be specific about the reviews she has participated in and the activities or projects she did that demonstrated her knowledge. The final review should be one that your child enjoys, based on her learning strength, and that allows her to feel successful, so she will approach the test with confidence.

Build further confidence and help take your child's brain out of the fight/flight mode by reminding her that this is just one assessment of her knowledge. Put the test in perspective so she will do her best and not be frozen by anxiety. If your child is taking a standardized test, remind her that many standardized tests include questions about things that have not been taught and that she is not necessarily expected to know. (These questions are sometimes included as trial questions, to see if they are valid for use on future tests.) You also can help your child practice body relaxation and breathing techniques that calm the brain, and she can use these techniques to be mindfully alert and focused before and during the test.

CONFIDENCE IS KEY

Self-esteem and hope are nurtured when we convey our appreciation to our children and acknowledge their progress, not just their products (grades). If your child is frustrated about reading comprehension tests, remind him that although he might not be a great test-taker, he shows his comprehension to you in your discussions and in his graphic organizers (or diagrams, voice recordings, test review sessions, etc.).

When your child has prepared with good effort but doesn't succeed in achieving high test scores, rather than asking what grade she received on the test, you can ask, "Did you feel good about what you *did* remember for the test?"

In school, when I was frequently eliminated from spelling bees and scored poorly on standardized state spelling tests, it was some comfort to me that when I studied predictable words assigned in advance for regular class spelling tests, then I would succeed because I knew which strategies had helped me remember their correct spellings. It was nevertheless disappointing to be so unsuccessful at the unpredictable words during spelling bees and on those state tests. One day, when I was in seventh grade, a teacher reached out to me after she gave me a copy of my state test scores that contained an abysmal score in spelling. After class, my teacher said, "I know you might be disappointed by your spelling score, but look at how high all your others are. Some of the smartest people I know are terrible spellers. I think it is because their brains, like yours, process information so fast that the details of spelling don't have time to settle in. I think that is a fair price to pay for such a smart and fast brain."

Decades later, that experience has resonated for me with my current understanding of the brain and learning. I recognized that there are indeed neuronal circuits and brain processing regions that are more developed and efficient in some people than in others. Being smart is not an all-or-nothing condition. If classrooms are not always pleasurable places for your child, you can create positive learning experiences outside them. Promoting an emotionally positive learning environment at home will help your child grow in resilience, confidence, and academic success.

AFTER THE TEST: EVALUATE YOUR STRATEGIES

As you practice more reading-comprehension activities over time and your child becomes more experienced at reading for understanding, she will be ready to think about and evaluate the strategies you have been practicing. To increase her understanding about which strategies work best for her, periodically check in and discuss the activities you have been doing, and ask how she feels they have helped her. Ask your child how she has been applying things you do together to her independent reading or reading at school, or ask if she ever stops to consider if she understands what she is reading and tries to mentally summarize the information. Does she take time to compare what she reads to what she already knows about the topic from her own experiences or previous reading? Is she making predictions about what might come next, and paying attention to see if her predictions were correct?

Help your child remember to use the reading comprehension strategies you've practiced together, and acknowledge her when she does. Ask her how the strategies helped her understand and remember what she read when she took the test. Remind her to try some of the ones she hasn't been using, for even more success next time. Create a list of the strategies you've practiced, using names your child suggests for each, and have her include examples of when she used them and how they helped her. Include suggestions you both come up with for how to use these strategies in future reading and test review.

These discussions also can identify comprehension problems that may have resulted in errors on the test. Is your child having trouble with confusing vocabulary words, difficulty recalling past information about a character in the story, or problems recalling what happened previously that connects with something later in the plot? If these kinds of problems are revealed as you review completed tests, discuss the strategies from the list that she could use to prepare more successfully next time. If the problem is with understanding vocabulary, review how she can get clues from the context of the sentence to understand what the word means. Is she remembering to look through the test to see if the information in later test questions can clarify her confusion about a question? If her problem is remembering a sequence within the story, review the use of summarizing and graphic organizers, such as timelines and diagrams of how the story progresses, to increase her memory of the plot.

PART III:

Math

9

YOUR CHILD CAN THRIVE DESPITE A FAILING MATH SYSTEM (ALL AGES)

"A #2 pencil and a dream can take you anywhere."
—Joyce Myers

AMERICAN MATH FAILURE

Once upon a time, before starting kindergarten, your child proudly recited to all who would listen that she could count to ten, then twenty, and could even add two plus two. Does she still have that excitement and joy over math? Probably not, if she is beyond first grade.

There are plenty of reasons why math is often joyless and problematic for American children. Many public schools are pressured by No Child Left Behind to teach "to the test," and as a result, math instruction is focused on the memorized facts, procedures, and formulas that appear on standardized tests. These tests also tend to evaluate math skills that are *below* the average student's ability level, so the attention is focused on underachieving students and the tests offer little to stimulate students with higher math ability.

Math is rarely taught in public schools in a way that offers students personally meaningful, real-life connections or opportunities to discover concepts through their own explorations, inquiry, trials and errors, and active learning. As a result, your child is likely missing out on creating the kinds of joyful connections that make mathematics relevant to her life and the sense of accomplishment that comes from solving engaging, appropriately challenging mathematical problems. Why would children within the now-standard math teaching environment be motivated to learn anything beyond simple grocery-store calculations?

Unfortunately, there is also a gap between the needs of elementary school children and the mathematics knowledge of elementary teachers. In a 2007 study of teachers from six countries, U.S. teachers scored at the bottom on an algebra test. Teachers in Korea and Taiwan, where students earned highest marks on international tests, had the best teacher scores. The U.S. teacher curriculum requires fewer advanced undergraduate math courses than these other countries do, and teachers here only receive math teaching instruction for a few months (or even less) during their K–8 teaching credential programs. Without a depth of mathematics knowledge, teachers cannot help children creatively understand relationships between numbers and solve problems in different ways. Instead, they often rely on memorization, and aren't well-equipped to help struggling students. Teachers can't teach what they don't know, and many elementary-school teachers are not confident in their mastered skills beyond elementary-school math.

The foundation for your child's lifetime of mathematical knowledge begins building in the elementary grades. The skills your child needs to master algebra, for example, start in the third grade. Arithmetic, algebra, and geometry are intertwined, and elementary teachers need to know far more than the standard curriculum to effectively build this foundation. If during elementary school your child doesn't master arithmetic and with it the early concepts needed for algebra and geometry, she may be doing remedial work all the way up to college.

RUDE AWAKENINGS

Consider the way children learn long division. In second or third grade, your nine-year-old is taught to solve a long-division problem with remainders: 67 divided by 8 equals 8 remainder 3. That is acceptable until the fifth or sixth grade, when he is suddenly expected to calculate quotients using decimals or fractions, not remainders. He isn't told why. The only cues he has for reporting his answers are the instructions on the textbook homework page and the tests he takes: round to the nearest tenth this time, now to the nearest hundredth; put the answer in fraction form using mixed numbers, now in fraction form with improper fractions.

There is no explanation given for which of these division answers is best, or when he should choose one quotient-reporting option over another. In most schools, children don't have opportunities to participate in classroom discussions about what these remainders or decimals mean in the real world, when actually they can mean great deal. When it comes to rate of interest on large sums of money, the difference between 8.3 and 8.375 percent can be significant. Other times, decimal or remainder answers are less consequential, such as when division is used to plan how many restaurant tables of eight will be needed to seat sixty-seven children at a pizza party (and all the tables only seat eight). Whether the remainder is 3, .3, or .375 does not make any real difference because any remainder or decimal after the number eight means that a whole additional table is needed.

Your child truly "gets" math when he sees it applied in real life and has opportunities to discover how to solve realistic problems. If you gave your child sixty-seven toothpicks and some index cards and asked him to see how he could model the problem at the pizza restaurant described earlier, he could have fun building the experiential knowledge of a real situation and better understand the concept of division.

But this type of teaching doesn't often always occur in classrooms. Because most elementary arithmetic skills are taught by rote memorization and assessed on tests of rote memory, children who are not great at memorizing isolated facts are less successful, inadequate, and lose math confidence. This results in a cascade of increased math anxiety, lowered self-confidence, alienation, and failure. It's a great loss, because it is not an ability to memorize basic arithmetic and multiplication tables that determines who has the potential to become a great mathematician or scientist. Rather, it is the child who can see patterns and develop concepts who will be the next Einstein.

Even for children who succeed with math taught "to the tests," the problem is not that they won't rise to standardized test expectations, but that they will… and they'll stop there.

If your child's math curriculum doesn't include real-life problem solving, inquiry, and discussions that connect her learning to things that are relevant to her interests, your intervention at home can prevent the confusion and alienation that often arises in math education.

> *"It is what we don't know that frightens us,*
> *and nothing stifles joy like fear."*
> **—Goldie Hawn**

WHAT YOU CAN DO

This chapter offers ways you can help improve your child's (and perhaps your own) attitude about mathematics and recognize it as a useful, relevant subject that can be learned through creative ways of understanding (instead of only memorizing facts and confusing formulas). We'll start by looking at the common causes of math negativity, and then we'll walk through some strategies and neuro-*logical* activities that can open up your child's brain to discover his math potential, develop positive attitudes about math, see the opportunities of learning from mistakes, and use logic to try to solve problems even when he is not certain of the answer. He will build confidence in taking risks and asking questions to build his math understanding. You'll learn how using manipulatives, discovery activities, real-world math, interest-driven projects that show the value of math, and math games that make necessary memorization go faster and sustain the memories longer as math appreciation also grows.

If your child is gifted or highly interested in math, turn to the pages describing activities and projects that can extend his math connections, achievements, and advancement. If your child is challenged by math, you can turn to the pages describing the activities and approaches suited to his developmental level and begin using his learning strengths and interests to foster improvement.

With your help, your child will build or rebuild a positive, can-do relationship with mathematics. When that happens, she will reconnect with the joy she once had when she proudly counted from one to ten!

MATH NEGATIVITY

The first step to mathematical success is a positive math attitude. Four in ten American adults surveyed in a 2005 AP poll said they hated math in school, and twice as many said they hated math more than any other subject. What's your attitude about math? Whatever it is, you're probably passing it along to your child. Some parents say they were never good at math so they don't expect their children to do very well. Others are concerned that they cannot help their children because they don't remember what they learned. This causes problems because children who are not successful and comfortable with mathematics in elementary school fall progressively behind throughout middle and high school.

Even parents who were successful math learners can have difficulty instilling this love in their children. They often believe that the way they learned math (usually by lecture, memorization, and worksheets) is the best way. They don't see the need for math instruction that includes investigations, cooperative group work, and objects to manipulate, such as fraction bars. Memorization and drilling practice can be just fine for students with good memories and AS learning strengths, but with the visual and tactile influences of the media, computers, and video games, AS learners make up less than fifteen percent of the school population, compared with fifty percent twenty years ago. Today, math taught with lectures and practice sheets won't connect with eighty-five percent of school children.

Regardless of your experience, if you demonstrate a positive attitude toward mathematics, your child will want become engaged and motivated to excel in it. Once you reopen the doors that have been closed by classroom instruction that didn't resonate with your child, math can be revealed as a way for her to understand and describe the world in which she lives. This happens when you offer your child experiences that inspire her to want to measure, question, and analyze things around her. When she's given these opportunities, she will want to acquire more knowledge and better tools as she comes to realize these help her achieve mathematical fluency.

The key to building your child's interest in math is to capture her imagination at a young age. When you find opportunities throughout the day to show her the ways she will benefit from mathematics and how it is useful in her areas of interest, you show her the value of math. The following brain-friendly strategies will increase your child's positive feelings toward with mathematics, and she will feel connected to what she learns. You can start with activities that unlock your child's math-blocking filters, promote long-term memory, and foster her greater understanding. You will guide her to comprehension beyond rote memorization while helping her construct a positive attitude toward mathematics.

STRATEGIES TO REDUCE MATH STRESS

If your child is anxious during math class, information entering his brain is less likely to reach the thinking and long-term memory parts of the cortex, and learning will not take place. Earlier chapters have emphasized the influence of stress that blocks the brain's intake filters. The perception of a real or imagined threat creates anxiety, and sensory input (information from the environment) is channeled away from the thinking brain and into the automatic, reflexive parts of the brain. Children who are anxious, frustrated, or bored by math don't participate in math class with their voices or their active thinking. When they are interested and feel they are capable of success, however, they participate in discussions, ask questions, and risk making mistakes.

Before children can become interested in math, they have to be comfortable with it. Let's look at some strategies to reduce math stress.

Preview the Material

If your child frequently feels confused when a new topic is introduced in class, but after a few minutes of explanation from you at home is able to understand the concept she couldn't follow, she will respond to previewing. Spend a few minutes each evening reading two or three pages of text and look at the examples that will be taught in class the next day. Your child probably won't understand everything you and she read, but when the teacher begins to explain the lesson the next day, she will be familiar with the new words, symbols, or procedures. Previewing the next day's lesson in the book will allow her to listen with enough background familiarity to reduce the reflex anxiety pattern of learned helplessness.

Consider the Stressors

Reversing negativity may take months if your child has been repeatedly stressed to the point of feeling helpless and hopeless regarding mathematics. To help your child reduce that negative baggage, work to understand the sources of her stress and determine which of these interventions might help.

Provide Opportunities for Success

Use individualized approaches that offer challenge but also give enough support that failure is rare. If your child is stressed by multiplication tables, a positive reinforcing strategy could start with him first reviewing the multiplication table for the number five, followed by filling in blanks on a worksheet, and immediately checking each written answer with a calculator. He gets instant positive reinforcement if the answer is correct. Even if it is incorrect, there is pleasure in seeing the calculator produce the right answer, instead of hearing it called out by the usual classmates who respond to flashcards before your child can even begin to think of the answer. Through the confidence built by guided practice at home, your child will sustain motivation and persevere with learning the multiplication tables with the boost of dopamine that comes with a positive experience. (More of these activities, differentiated by learning strengths, will be described in chapter 10.)

Ignite Your Child's Interest

Look for opportunities to motivate your child by demonstrating connections between math and her favorite sport, hobby, or career interest. Personalize lessons and math problems by substituting your child's name or her pet's names in scenarios and examples you use to illustrate concepts.

When a lesson or block of lessons is full of facts to be memorized, your child will often feel less stress when she sees an intrinsic reward for her efforts. Think of ways you can help your child use the facts she is trying to learn as tools for participating in appealing activities. For example, she could practice metric-to-standard measurement conversions by translating a recipe for cookie dough from a cookbook that uses metric measures into the U.S. equivalents, and then you can bake the cookies together.

Create Positive Associations

Neuroscience shows us that children can develop positive associations with arithmetic memorization by practicing positive-reinforcement games and activities. In a similar way, your child can build more durable memories if she has opportunities to recognize and savor her successes. Making a chart of "Personal Goal Achievement" can help acknowledge your child's successes. She can set personal goals, such as learning a specific multiplication table, and record her improvement as she works toward her goal. This is more motivating than a single test score that measures math knowledge at only that one point in time.

Build Confidence

Whatever you do to build your child's self-confidence will reduce learned helplessness. Show her how she can use the sample problems in texts to guide her in homework problems, and encourage her to use that strategy before asking you for help on a problem. Even if reviewing the sample doesn't give her all the information she needs to solve the new problem, she'll build the skill of reviewing sample problems to reach a higher level of independent understanding before asking for help.

To encourage this independence in class, I ask my students to do two things before asking me for help. First, they are asked to find an example in their text or class notes of an answered question very similar to the problem they are working on. Next, they are asked to carefully read the example so they can explain it to me in their own words. Usually, by then they are able to connect the process with the new problem with very little help from me. Ultimately, most children become self-sufficient at this process, and math skill and confidence grows.

If your child has become very insecure about his math skills as a result of negative past experiences, it may be more difficult to wean him from asking for help before trying to work independently to solve a confusing problem. When that occurs, you can be reassuring and uncritical as you remind him that you are pretty sure he knows what you are going to suggest he try first. Often, the confidence he gets from having you by his side as he looks for similar examples in his text, class notes, or previous homework will be enough for him to persevere independently. He then gains the reward of solving the problem on his own. It is truly one of the most rewarding teaching experiences to watch as a child has an "aha!" moment that transforms the predictable "I don't get it" into "I did it—I found an example and figured it out myself!"

Use Humor and Visuals

To insert humor into mathematics in my classes, I use narratives and draw pictures that are corny but memorable. For example, when explaining the concept of a hypotenuse, I tell my students to imagine a high hangman's gallows built with a right angle, and I then draw two perpendicular lines for the gallows. I then draw a *pot* hanging from the rope *noose* (pot in a noose). This helps them remember the word "hypotenuse" and the position of the hy-pot-en-use in a right triangle.

My equally corny story about polygons is meant to prime the students' limbic systems by adding some positive emotional power to the memory they are building. For an explanation of open versus closed polygons, I draw a closed multisided polygon and sketch a bird inside. I then "open" the polygon by erasing a portion of one of the sides. I next erase the bird and say, "When the polygon is open, Polly is gone."

Have fun with your child and enjoy a syn-*naps* creating your own bizarre or silly stories, narratives, or drawings to help her remember and mentally manipulate mathematical vocabulary words or formulas she needs to memorize. Keep track of the ones you or your child create, and share them with younger siblings when they study the same topic. The stories or drawings will be all the more enjoyable because their big brother or sister created or learned from them.

STRATEGIES FOR TAKING RISKS AND CORRECTING MISTAKES

"Without mistakes, how would we know what we have to work on?"
—William James

Mistakes are opportunities for learning. With the exceptions of errors that result from carelessness or forgotten rote-memory facts, most children make the same types of mistakes. The most common reason they do is that they tend to apply an incorrect procedure because it seems somewhat logical. These kinds of errors are the result of children memorizing procedures without understanding what they mean—many procedures in math are so similar, children easily confuse them. They memorize the rules, but don't truly learn to understand them by manipulating objects or following logical, sequential steps. For example, if your child is in upper elementary school and can add fractions with different denominators correctly, it is unlikely she can tell you *why* her system works, even if she can describe the procedure and uses terms such as "common denominator" or "least common multiple."

You can help your child go beyond memorizing rules to truly understanding why the procedures and rules make sense and when each should be applied. Using RAD strategies such as manipulating objects to "discover" the concept behind a rule and examining his errors using logical, sequential steps, your child will develop mathematical thinking power.

RAD LEARNING = **R**eticular Activating System + **A**mygdala's Filter + **D**opamine

RAD strategies for learning from mistakes described here include thinking and planning before writing, discovering the reason(s) for the error, building tolerance to examine and learn from mistakes, reducing anxiety-related errors, and striving for achievable challenge.

Think and Plan Before Writing

The goal of this strategy is to have your child carefully consider his mental toolkit of possible methods for approaching math calculations and problems. If he is not at first successful, he can correct his mistakes with this logical yet creative approach. Help him relate to math as a creative process where there are multiple routes to a correct answer. Help him see that it is reasonable to consider several options and then to use logical reasoning to select the best approach for each problem.

Practice this approach by having your child discuss his *thinking* with you before writing or saying any answer. Suggest, "This time, I don't want you to tell me what the actual answer is. Just tell me what you could do to solve the problem." After he describes one approach, encourage him to think of others, and then discuss the advantages of one over another. For example, if he's trying to find the solution to the problem "8 x 6," he might suggest three options: memorizing the multiplication table for sixes, knowing that 8 x 5 = 40 and adding another 8 to find 8 x 6, or adding a column of six number 8s. In this way, you will be helping your child build math logic, intuition, and reasoning that will extend into other academic subjects as well as into real-life problem solving.

Discover the Reason for the Error

When your child offer answers that have been thought through but still are incorrect, you can guide her to deduce and reason the correct answer so she learns from her mistake. Go through the reasoning process described in the previous step, and if she makes the error of selecting a procedure that is inappropriate, talk that decision through. For example, if the problem asks her to find the quotient of 8 and 2, and she says one way to find the quotient is to multiply 8 by 2, ask her what "quotient" means. If she says it means "to multiply," you can look it up together in the glossary and find out that it means "to divide." Other options include looking back in the math chapter for sample questions that use the word "quotient" and show sample problems worked out using division.

If she can understand and explain why she made the error, she will own the knowledge she needs to get the answer correct in the future. This deduction through mental manipulation and reasoning embeds a long-term memory of the correct processing in her neural network which can be activated to solve similar problems in the future.

She can then add the word "quotient" to her math journal (a notebook she can keep to record math ideas, questions, vocabulary, and project notes). She can also include a problem she creates using the word "quotient," an analogy ("Quotient is to divide as minus is to subtract"), or a rhyme that helps her remember its meaning ("Quotient means divide; sometimes the answer's not as wide.").

Build Tolerance for Analyzing Mistakes

Positive connections to mathematics increase your child's tolerance for mistakes. You can change a problem on which your child made an error into one that has personal positive connections. If a question involved subtraction, for example, you could relate subtraction to an upcoming family vacation. "If we have $150 per day to spend, let's subtract the expenses for an average travel day and see if we'll have enough money left to go to the water park." Because he is in a positive state of mind, thinking about something he wants to do, subtraction becomes a meaningful tool and he values it. He will want to correct test errors and understand subtraction if he understands how it is personally useful to him.

Reduce Anxiety-Related Errors

If your child worries about making mistakes on tests, that worry can overstress her amygdala and prevent her brain from accessing the information she needs to solve the problems. Help her achieve a positive state of mind to keep her neural networks open for *reflecting* instead of *reacting*.

A Positive Mood

Suggest she begin tests or error corrections by first taking a few deep breaths, thinking about a favorite place to picnic or play, or looking at a comforting object in the room. In a study of the influence of mindset on test success, children asked to think about the happiest day of their lives solved more problems accurately in five minutes than the control group. This suggested to researchers that children's positive moods raise belief in their own success, which in turn raises their brains' information processing capacities.

Errorless Math

Errorless math, like errorless jump-in reading described in Chapter 3, uses time delay so that almost every answer can be correct. Once again, you use flash cards to build accuracy and speed.

The traditional way speed is practiced in class is having students see how many multiplication problems they can do on a worksheet in a set amount of time. This is a high-stress, low-reward activity, because there is no motivation for the students to review the facts they got wrong or attempt ones they didn't finish. Also, since in a typical classroom perhaps thirty children have made different mistakes on different problems, the teacher can't review each multiplication fact so the children can't learn from their errors.

For this activity, prepare cards and a response recording list as described on pages 53-54, with places to check "correct response," "correct wait," or "correct answer." When showing your child a flashcard that lists a multiplication fact not yet mastered, you read the problem to him and then immediately say the answer. Your child then repeats the question and you answer, just as you did while he looks at the card (achieving both visual and auditory memory stimulation). He then turns the card over to confirm that the answer was correct.

After enough practice, when your child seems familiar with a particular math fact, you can show him the card and read the problem together simultaneously, but then wait about three seconds to see if he jumps in with the answer before you say it. If he is successful, turn over the card to confirm his response. If he doesn't jump in during the brief delay, proceed as before and say the answer. He then repeats the practice of saying the question and answering just as before, turning over the card to confirm his accuracy.

In either case, you or your child can place a check in the "correct response" or "correct answer" column next to the list of math facts that are on the flashcards because either he made the correct response by waiting or said the correct answer. This process can be viewed as almost errorless because if he says the correct answer, that is a "correct answer" response, and if he waits for you to say it and then repeats it, he has also made a "correct response" because he waited appropriately and then repeated correctly.

If he gives an incorrect answer, there is no box to check that says "incorrect response." Just leaving a space blank for that problem on the list gives you a record that the problem was missed, but offers no visible negative feedback to your child. There is, however, immediate correction feedback, because you ask him to try again. On the second try, say the problem and the answer without any delay, so he can't jump in with an incorrect answer and will have the opportunity to repeat the correct answer.

Allowing your child to see his progress records will help keep him motivated to increase his mastery while building math knowledge and an all-important positive math attitude.

Verbal or Gesture Cues

In this activity, you provide verbal or gesture cues to increase the probability of a correct response. For example, if your child is multiplying numbers with decimals and forgets to count the number of digits following the decimal points in each multiplier, you say the word "decimal" if he appears finished and has not placed the decimal in his product. In this way, he does not actually make an error in the final answer he writes down. Even though he needed a cue from you, he ended up writing down a correct answer and benefits from the practice and the pleasure response from his achievement.

Challenge Your Child

Very young children are usually comfortable making mistakes. You are the caretaker of that precious creative potential your young child possesses. Challenge builds skill, so you want your child to stay comfortable even if he makes some mistakes so he will be willing to challenge himself. Without challenges and opportunities to correct mistakes, his math brain won't stretch.

Does your snowboarding daughter still enjoy the beginner runs now that she is advanced, or do they seem boring? Does your guitar-playing son prefer playing songs with two chords now that he has mastered over twenty? Remind your child that when he previously built up his skills in sports, music, or video games, it became boring to stay at a previous level, and that he made mistakes as he took on challenges to progress to higher skill levels. Gradually, with effort and practice, he made fewer mistakes and enjoyed the pleasure of greater skill. If he can understand this, he'll be motivated to try other challenges and understand that mistakes are a natural part of new skill development, whether in athletics, musical instrument playing, video games, or mathematics. Encourage him to make the effort to build his brain's math muscles by trying new approaches to problems beyond the first idea that comes to mind and by attempting to solve challenging problems in his math book even if they are not assigned for homework.

If you find your child is finishing his math homework quickly, easily, and correctly, that is good information to pass along to his teacher. I have my students write down the amount of time they spend on each homework assignment, and I use that information as well as their accuracy to individualize homework into several levels of challenge. I suggest more conceptual problems for students who are already successful at doing basic procedures.

If your child's teacher doesn't offer different homework options, you might ask him if your child can substitute advanced problems in place of some of the assigned problems. If that doesn't work for his teacher and you need a way of helping your child see if his answers to the advanced problems are correct, look in the back of the book. Most math textbooks have the answers to problems in the back of the book or a corresponding website (or on a site such as hotmath.com that shows answers for homework problems for almost all math textbooks). You can look to see which problems have answers available and let your child know those are the ones to try.

Help your child understand that if he almost always gets all answers correct, he is probably not working at a high enough challenge level and that his skill won't grow without attempting more difficult problems. Again, remind him of his experiences building proficiency in a sport, video game, or playing a musical instrument and how he had to repeatedly push himself to greater challenge levels to achieve his current higher level of skill.

In addition to the strategies in this chapter, try these fun activities to revitalize your child's math brain:

• Sing a math song or share a math joke. Visit the math section of www.jokesbykids.com for math riddles by children for children. There's humor, plus a bit of math practice, in each one.
• Ask your child how many ways there are to add numbers to equal today's date.
• Play code-breaking games, such as S M T W T F S (first letter of days of the week). You can find them in math activity books or on websites like www.puzzlepixies.com.
• Change the location of your child's study area to refresh her visual background. Move to a different part of the room, use the floor, or go outdoors and use chalk to draw giant shapes, practice multiplication facts, or make chalk graphs.
• Take your child on a walk and give his brain a syn-*naps* to discover math in the neighborhood. Look for shapes and quantities in buildings or nature.

10
TARGETING YOUR CHILD'S MATH READINESS LEVEL (ALL AGES)

Just as street names, traffic lights, and road lanes increase the efficient flow of traffic in a busy city, your child's brain uses patterns to organize neural circuits into different categories. Pattern practice activities increase the brain's efficiency at recognizing and identifying new information, adding the new data onto the appropriate networks and creating more detailed patterns. Thus, patterning begins the brain's progress through the increasingly complex stages of mathematical development.

Once you are able to assess your child's level of mathematical brain readiness, you can use targeted strategies and activities to enhance his enjoyment and understanding of mathematics. This is especially important if classroom instruction is one-size-fits-all. This chapter begins with a description of characteristics at each developmental stage to guide you in identifying your child's brain readiness, and then suggests appropriate games and activities for each stage. These games and activities will strengthen your child's neural circuits and prepare her for the next developmental level.

You can always use more or less advanced activities than those suggested for the developmental level of your child. If they are too simple, he'll get bored, and if they are too advanced, he'll get frustrated. Either way, you'll know which activities are the best fit simply by seeing how engaged your child is with the activity. He needs to learn at his own pace, and you will need to be responsive to that. If you keep in mind that your math activity time together should be enjoyable for both of you, it will remain a bonding time you both look forward to and enjoy.

If it becomes unpleasant, or you find yourself focusing on your child's progress and wanting to push him along, that is your cue to stop that activity and perhaps not return to it for a few days.

Many activities suggested for each developmental stage suit all learning styles and intelligences, but some are identified as particularly enjoyable for children with VSK or AS learning strengths.

DEVELOPING NUMBER SENSE (AGES 3–6)

Characteristics of This Stage

- If your child can count to ten, does she understand that the number word "ten" represents a quantity? Stack nine blocks and ask her to count them. Next, point to the stack and ask how many blocks are in the stack. If she has to count again, she doesn't yet grasp the concept that the last number counted in a sequence signifies the total quantity and is still developing number sense.
- Children at this stage can "count up" on their hands from the finger designated as "one" to the finger designated as "three," but they do not comprehend the actual meaning of the number—they cannot visualize the difference between a group of six objects and a group of nine objects.
- During this stage, your child realizes that numbers may be used to represent objects in a grouping.

Activities (All Learning Strengths)

- Ask which cereal bowl has more and which has less. Find other quantities of things that your child can compare using words like "more than/less than," "bigger/smaller," or "greater/fewer."
- When your child can count to one hundred, start using objects to show him what ten buttons look like next to one hundred buttons. Gradually introduce the concept of numbers representing quantities by including a third cluster of about twenty buttons and asking if it is more like the cluster of ten or the cluster of one hundred. Continue the same activity with increasingly subtle differences, such as clusters of thirty and sixty, and ask if a cluster of twenty is more similar to the thirty or sixty cluster.

- Play "Mind Reader" as a syn-*naps*. Think of a number for your child to guess. After each guess, respond with the words "higher" or "lower." At different times, use the words "more" or "less" so she learns different arithmetic vocabulary. This game helps her correlate the number words and counting sequence with actual amounts or sizes. A free Internet number guessing game is available at www. prongo.com/guess/index.html.

Activities for AS Learners

- Try "counting up" by one as a pre-addition activity. What is one more than three? Show your child how to first count to three and then "count up" to the next number.
- Practice early sequencing and have your child's body and brain become refreshed with an active syn-*naps*. Count up from one and skip occasional numbers, asking your child to jump in and say the number you skipped.

Activities for VSK Learners

- Pair numbers with objects, such as two legs on a person, four on a dog; two wheels on a bicycle, three on a tricycle, four on a car. Encourage your child to find or describe other things that usually have a specific number of parts: Three colors on a traffic light, four legs on a table or chair, two eyes on a face, etc.
- Incorporate movement as a syn-*naps*. Tell your child, "Let's see how many giant steps you need to take to get from this wall to that wall." After practicing counting steps for several days, ask her to estimate how many steps she predicts it will take to go from here to there. When she compares her predictions with the actual number of steps, she'll build her patterning/prediction skills.

NUMBER SENSE (AGES 4–7)

Characteristics of This Stage

A child at this stage will not only be able to tell you there are nine blocks in a stack, she'll also be able to express "nine" in several different ways, such as holding up nine fingers and knowing that nine is more than eight. Although she may not yet be able to tell you what nine minus three equals, she'll know or be ready to understand that it will be less than nine. She will use these ideas about number symbols to make some estimations and predictions, and give reasons using words like "compared to" or "increased." She will begin to recognize that object *size* is different from the *number* of objects.

Activities (All Learning Strengths)

- Practice estimation with games that include visualization, judgment, and prediction. "How many buttons do you think are in this group?" Start by giving a choice of ranges such as, "Do you think there are between ten and thirty or between fifty and eighty in this group?" If your child chooses the correct estimate several times in a row, you can progress to asking him if the number is closer to fifty or eighty.
- Gradually introduce the concept of adding or subtracting. "With this pile of twenty buttons, tell me or show me what you can do with these extra buttons to make the pile grow to twenty-five buttons."
- Demonstrate quantity differences in measurement. Ask your child to take four steps and mark the spot with a button or coin. Then ask him to return to the start line, take eight steps, and mark that spot with a larger coin. After several more practices, ask him to estimate where he might end up after taking three steps, ten steps, etc., and mark that spot with a coin. Have him check his predictions by taking the designated number of steps and marking the actual spot with a different colored or shaped object. As he makes more estimations, followed by the actual step measurements, show him his improved skill at estimating by pointing out how the prediction markers are getting closer to the actual measurement markers.
- Build the concept that even though objects are larger or smaller, the *number* of objects is the same. When your child can predict or approximate the numbers of buttons in a pile, change from buttons to different-sized objects. It is not the size, but the quantity that relates to number of objects.

Activities for AS Learners

- Encourage your child to sequence objects based on number quantity. Using words such as "small," "bigger," and "biggest," ask her to tell you which word best describes each of three groups of objects.
- Ask her what other words can be used when she compares amounts of things. Ask your child to tell you words that compare the different amounts of the same liquid in three clear glasses. After successful practice, use measuring cups with numbers and ask her what she notices about the number each liquid reaches in the measuring cup when they are lined up in sequence from least to most and then from most to least.
- If your AS child especially enjoys word sounds, have her compare shortest, middle, and longest words or sentences that you say aloud. Encourage her to say three words or sentences starting with the shortest and going to the longest.

Activities for VSK Learners

- Ask your child to look at plates containing different amounts of dry cereal or beans. Then, ask your child to arrange the plates so the least is on the left and the most on the right. After he is successful with three different sizes, add more plates with different quantities.
- After your child can successfully move plates with different quantities from least to most, have him add five beans to each one and tell you if the order is still the same and why or why not. At this stage, he may be able to tell you that the order is the same but is unlikely to explain the concept that adding equal quantities to all plates doesn't change their relationship to each other. Eventually, he will develop that concept, which is a cornerstone of balancing equations in algebra (adding the same quantity to both sides of the equation does not change the balance of the equation).
- Give your child three plates of five, ten, and fifteen beans, ordered from least to most. Add one bean to the first plate and ask if the order is still least to most. Gradually work up to adding five beans (and then as many as necessary) to the first plate and see when your child decides to move that plate to the middle position because it

now has more beans than the plate that had been second. Extend this game by adding more plates and later by taking away beans and having him reorder the plates again.

- After trying the activities above, ask your child to draw pictures of the plates with different numbers of beans and tell you what he sees in his mind when he draws the pictures from most to least and then least to most.

EARLY CONCEPTUAL THINKING (AGES 5–9)

Characteristics of This Stage

As your child develops early conceptual thinking, she begins to understand more about the meanings of mathematical symbols and procedures. She begins to use judgment and comparison to make predictions and evaluate when and why predictions need to be modified and how to guide her modifications through deduction and strategies instead of random guesses. She might be able to understand the idea that numbers or quantities can be less than one, such as fractional parts (and, later, negative numbers).

Spatial visualization begins during early conceptual development. Your child may be able to imagine the movements of objects and spatial forms, such as recognizing that a square can be rotated to look like a diamond. Similarly, she might be able to match a correctly scaled-down picture to the original picture as being similar to each other, and explain why. Matching tasks and ordering also become conceptual when your child can order two different sets of things and then match which items from one group match best with items from the second group.

A child not yet in the conceptual stage might need to set the dinner table for each person at a time using an *appearance* of how each complete setting should look. He would get a single fork, knife, spoon, and plate and complete one person's setting before moving on to the same process for each of the other settings. A child with concept development could reason that for four people, he would need four plates, forks, knives, and spoons and set the table by first distributing the four plates, then the four forks, and so on.

Math concept development varies greatly from child to child, and your child's age is not the best predictor of his brain's mathematical conceptual development level. This neural development cannot be pushed. If you try these activities and your child is not ready, go to other activities and come back to these at a later time. It may be useful to start with the game that is well suited for your child's learning strength before trying others.

Activities for AS Learners

"Draw my picture" is a syn-*naps* that is an especially enjoyable activity for AS learners. Pair up with your child. Place various shapes drawn or cut from paper into a box. One of you gives verbal instructions for drawing a shape pulled from the box. For example, if you pull an ice cream cone shape from the box, you might instruct your child to draw a "long" (or isosceles) triangle with the pointy side down and then draw a semicircle, flat side down, over the "base" of the triangle, which is the top part of the drawing. For older children, the verbal instructions could include descriptive vocabulary words they are using in class, such as *left*, *right*, *curved*, *straight*, *diagonal*, *specified length*, or *proportional length*.

The success of the verbal communication of the speaker and the careful following of instructions by the drawer becomes immediate feedback when you both see the final drawing. The "describer" takes satisfaction in accurate communication, and the "drawer" is proud of her attention to the details of the description. You can then discuss what was most helpful and what was confusing in the verbal instructions and further build your child's math communication skills.

Activities for VSK Learners

- Use a number line on the floor with marks at 0 to 10 feet. Have your child walk from 0 to 5, counting the steps as she walks and looking down at the numbers. Have her take one more step and tell you what number she is on. If she says "six," ask her where she would be if she took one more step, two more steps, three more steps, etc. Each time, have her take the steps and see if she is correct by looking down at the number.
- After several practices at the above activity on the number line, try the process with subtracting. As your child starts on number five,

ask her to step back a step and say what number she is on without looking down. Progress to increasing the number of steps she takes back. When she is ready, ask her to predict where she will be if she starts on the number six (have her actually stand there) and takes two steps back (but this time, she doesn't take the two steps, she *visualizes* or *conceptualizes* the process of taking away or moving back two steps). If she predicts she would be on number four, have her try it. If her prediction is off, go back to the earlier practice a few more times and repeat the practice activity for short periods over the next several days before trying the prediction again.

• Build on this number line activity over the coming months by changing the intervals to 2s, 5s, 10s, and 3s so she begins to count by those numbers in preparation for multiplication.

• After success at the above number lines, your child *may* be ready to try negative number practice (although this may not occur until a later stage of conceptual development). Add a negative strip to the number line so it now extends from negative ten to positive ten. Repeat the actual practice, followed by the prediction when she is ready.

HIGHER CONCEPTUAL THINKING (AGES 6–10)

Characteristics of This Stage

Only when your child understands that moving herself on a number line or moving objects can represent addition or subtraction should she progress to procedures using written numerals. When the physical activity makes sense, she is ready to grasp the higher conceptual and abstract representations of mathematics with numbers, symbols, operational signs, formulas, and equations. She might get correct answers without this conceptual understanding, but these will be rote memorized answers without the conceptual comprehension on which to build further math knowledge, not just facts. Your child is at a higher level of conceptual development when he can manipulate objects to successfully demonstrate that three plus four add up to seven, and later that seven "take away" three is four, and describe what he is doing in his own words.

Activities (All Learning Strengths)

- Show your child that you are putting seven buttons under a cup. Take away one and ask how many he thinks are left. If he is not successful, go back to more practice with objects he can see. Try again some weeks later, and when he is able to use visualization to predict or calculate the correct number, show him that he is correct by revealing the number of buttons left when you pick up the cup. Advance as long as he is comfortable and successful, but don't reinforce error making by showing him over and over that he predicted or calculated the incorrect answer.

- The next level of abstraction uses numbers instead of objects. Start by putting number cards next to the buttons so he sees the number "7" written down next to the cluster of seven buttons you then hide under the cup. Show him the number "2" on another card and ask him to turn around as you remove two buttons from the cup. Ask him to predict how many buttons remain if you took away the number on the "2" card (don't say the number "two"). Instead of him saying the number he predicts, ask him to select the card that has the number with his predicted answer on it. If correct, he will select a card with "5" on it.

- The higher level of this activity involves your child writing the equation on paper as $7 - 2 = 5$. Request that he do the same for the next button subtraction setup by writing the equation and his predicted answer for when you remove a specified number of buttons from under the cup. When he has successfully matched correct equations to the object manipulation, he can progress to just writing and saying the equations without manipulating objects. Return to working with objects if he is stuck on an equation.

11
BRAIN-BASED SOLUTIONS FOR MATH CHALLENGES (ALL AGES)

There are many different reasons why children struggle with mathematics. This chapter will address several of the most common problems regarding brain development, math language, short-term memory, and long-term memory, and provide a variety of learning strengths directed solutions and strategies.

BRAIN DEVELOPMENT DELAY
If your child has not yet developed the neural circuitry needed to form long-term memories of arithmetic facts, such as the multiplication tables, it does not mean he cannot understand the concepts of long division carried out to several decimal points. However, to be successful at this division procedure, he does require access to the multiplication facts needed as the long division is carried out. If he has a table of the multiplication facts taped to his book or desk and can refer to that while learning the new long division procedure, he can be on equal footing with his class in learning the new process. If he does not have that support, he will be stuck at the initial step of multiplication and will not be able to practice the skill set of long division.

Given the long division problem 428 divided by 7, he might spend five minutes adding up a column of seven 6s to calculate by "adding up" that 7 x 6 = 42. By the time he is finished with that, the class will be onto the third step of 428 divided by 7, and he won't be able to catch up. For children with delay in short- or long-term memory development, it is appropriate to support them with calculators or math tables so they can progress in math concepts along with their class. As a general rule, your child should have the option of using a calculator when the main point of the problem is practicing a concept of using math to solve a complex word problem. Calculators can help your child with trial and error, saving time on the arithmetic he is still mastering due to memory delay, so he can focus on the concepts.

It is frustrating—and a math turn-off—for children to be held back by basic rote arithmetic when they are learning a new operation. If your child is still working on memorizing rote facts while learning a new idea, this will limit his opportunity to develop the conceptual understanding of the new idea. Calculators can assist in math achievement if your child has learning problems or a delay in memory development, especially when he has good logic and problem-solving abilities but is held back by computation errors. He might even excel, by virtue of his alternative learning strengths, because he might find creative alternatives to problem solving when he is not held back by his delay in computation.

Your observation and documentation of your child's mathematical development can help his teacher place him in appropriate math groupings and provide him with appropriately differentiated mathematical experiences. The best teachers use flexible groupings, continuously monitor students' developmental levels, and move them to more suitable math groups or activities as they progress in math development. However, in some classrooms, once a student is labeled in terms of math ability level, often based on a standardized test taken as far back as spring of the previous school year, there is little opportunity for placement group change. These are the classrooms where your input will be invaluable to your child's success in mathematics.

MATH VOCABULARY DIFFICULTIES

Some children have trouble understanding the meaning of the vocabulary of mathematics, such as "greater than," "less than," "equal," or "equation." Math language is different from reading comprehension. Unlike reading, the meaning of a math word or symbol cannot be inferred from the context. Your child has to know what each word or symbol means in order to understand the math problem. For instance, to solve 6 x (3 + 4) = ___ or, "Is 12 < 100?," your child must understand the meaning of several symbols.

Her Own Words

Encourage your child to describe new concepts or ideas in her own words. Math vocabulary is often confusing because more than one word can describe the same general concept, such as "divide" and "find the quotient," which are both used to describe the concept of division. It is best for your child to first use her own words when talking about numbers. Then when she is successful describing the math procedures she is working on in her own words, you can help her substitute the formal math vocabulary for her own terms. She will appreciate these new words because they are more precise than the longer sentences she has been using to explain concepts.

Math Word Games

If your child needs to look up common math words like "product," "quotient," or "numerator" while doing assignments, the problem may be that this new vocabulary is a burden to his working memory, exceeding its ability to hold information. Help your child become more automatic in his recall of the meaning of math vocabulary by playing word games either of you creates on puzzlemaker.com. You can also make funny sketches of the word "doing" something it represents. For example, since *quotient* means *the result of dividing two numbers*, your child can write the word *quotient* "divided" into two sections as "quo-tient." He can also speak the word "quotient" divided into syllables, emphasizing the "division" of the word into parts. He can even make the gesture of sawing the word "quotient" to relate the word to the kinesthetic experience of dividing a piece of wood with a saw.

AS Learners

- Even though (or perhaps because) your child may have difficulty putting math symbols and numbers into comprehensible language, he may be much better at verbal review than written practice.

Consider starting homework or test study with verbal practice before moving into written problems.

- Graphic organizers can help your child connect familiar words or pictures with mathematical symbols or complex vocabulary words.

VSK Learners

- Use flash cards to practice the connection of math symbols to words.
- Encourage your child to read math problems more than once, underlining, speaking aloud, or taking notes on the math vocabulary words.
- Visualize the movement of objects to match the math calculation and symbol your child is trying to remember. Suggest to your child, "When you see the addition sign, imagine numbers stacking up on top of each other as a reminder that this sign means 'to add.'"
- Use objects to build the story that is in a math calculation (two blocks and three blocks get together and make five blocks). Manipulating objects gives spatial reinforcement to the concept. Putting a story to moving the objects is also appealing to learners who like new information in sequences.
- Help your child find ways to relate math vocabulary to her own life or interests. A child who likes to build things with tools can relate to clockwise movement by thinking of the way she turns a screwdriver to put in a screw. A fun syn-*naps* for a child who likes to run or dance is to move around the outside of various objects such as a rug or table and say that *perimeter* means the distance around the object.

SHORT-TERM MEMORY PROBLEMS

The demand on short-term memory is higher in arithmetic than in other elementary school subjects, so a child who didn't seem to have memory problems before may suddenly have difficulty in math. This can sometimes be traced to an underdeveloped short-term or working memory. It may not be until mathematics instruction begins in elementary school that your child's short-term memory problems become evident. Poor grades on tests may be due to these memory problems, not a lack of comprehension. This is especially true if you work with your child and see that he understands the arithmetic you do together but he doesn't show that same success on tests.

If your child looks up at the board before writing down each number or word in a problem or sentence instead of looking once and copying the entire piece, his working memory may not hold the sensory data long enough for him to write down more than a small bit of information. Other classmates may be able to see the whole problem 3 + 5 = ? and copy it after only looking up once. Your child may also have difficulty remembering verbal instructions, especially in multiple step procedures, because her limited working memory decreases her brain's capacity to hold two or more components in mind while simultaneously working on or trying to understand the next bit of information.

If your child shows any of these signs, consider evaluating if she has a memory or comprehension problem. See if she needs to look at the problem in the book several times when she copies it down. Make a game out of having her repeat number sequences back to you. By age five, she should be able to repeat a string of four to five numbers back to you, with one more added per year until she can repeat seven numbers forward and three to four numbers in reverse. If she has a short-term memory problem, she'll have difficulty repeating these numbers back to you. She'll also have difficulty repeating word sequences. Also keep notes on how long it takes her to complete her textbook homework alone compared to the time it takes when you copy the arithmetic calculations from the textbook onto the homework page for her. Share this information with her teacher so proper accommodations can be made for her success in classwork and on tests.

Preview Lessons in Advance

Familiarity increases recall. Have your child preview the coming lesson by skimming ahead. This way, when he hears the new terms he will have had at least one initial exposure to them. Just hearing the somewhat familiar term or procedure will increase activation in his brain in a process called "priming."

VSK learners can write and AS learners can say the new terms, important concepts, or major themes that will be taught in the next day's math lesson. These are usually outlined with definitions in the beginning of each chapter. Even without understanding what the words mean, your child will have rudimentary relational memories that will be "primed" and ready to be retrieved when he hears them in class.

When students constantly say "I don't get it" during a math lesson, even before the teacher finishes explaining the concept, it is a clue that they have had problems with this type of learning in the past and have lost confidence. Previewing the lessons at home the day before, at first with you, and later independently, makes your child more familiar and less anxious with the material taught in the lesson. Eventually, the previewing becomes unnecessary for many children, as they lose their math anxiety and listen with filters wide open.

If your child has difficulty remembering or even taking notes on lessons taught in class, see if he can bring a small tape recorder or other recording device to class so the lectures are available for him to listen to at home. At home, he can add to his notes or use objects to manipulate the procedures as he listens to them.

Build Working Memory

Help build your child's working memory by playing memory games like Concentration. If her memory problem is very limiting, discuss your findings with her teacher and seek out opportunities for school or professional memory testing. This evaluation may be helpful in suggesting accommodations at school that will prevent her from becoming discouraged and alienated from math, and also allow her to receive memory training intervention.

LONG-TERM MEMORY PROBLEMS

Repetitive stimulation of certain neuronal circuits in the brain is necessary for maintaining long-term memory. One of the best ways to do this is by constructing new knowledge from existing information. New math information can be used for *analyzing, comparing, judging,* and *deducting* from existing information, which stimulates multiple memory storage areas throughout the brain. Your child will use and not lose mathematical memory. For example, when your child reviews learned material by solving well-designed word or story problems, she is *making judgments* about what question is being asked, *analyzing* the data provided in an *organized* format to determine what is needed to reach a solution, and *comparing* the math procedures she knows to *deduce* which might be useful.

If your child reviews math information through multisensory activities, the visual, tactile, auditory, and kinesthetic memory storage regions of his brain are activated. This is why learning and reviewing information with more than one sense increases your child's ability to remember what he learns. Similarly, when new concepts are reviewed by using the new information in an activity that is meaningful to your child, the memory storage circuits are reactivated. For example, if after learning how to calculate percentages in class your child sees an advertisement for 20 percent off a backpack he wants, he can use his new knowledge about percents in a personally meaningful activity to calculate the discounted price of the backpack. That memory will now be reinforced because of the real-world experience.

Cue Words

Some children have memory-cueing difficulties. Perhaps your child can remember *what* she learns in math but has difficulty knowing *when* to use the memory stores she has. She can retrieve the memory when it is specifically prompted, such as asking for the equation for the area of a rectangle or how to convert inches to millimeters. However, she doesn't recognize the cues to retrieve these memories when she isn't specifically told to use a procedure.

If this is true for your child, she doesn't need more review and drill of the procedures, but rather more practice finding and recognizing clues in questions and problems to help her identify which information to retrieve from memory storage. Her homework assignment usually includes a number of arithmetic calculations that provide word and symbol cues at the beginning of an assignment or as "mixed review" at the end. The instructions may say "find the sum of these numbers" and each problem will have a plus sign.

If your child is successful at doing the procedures when they are identified, but not at knowing which procedures to use without the cues, you can help her practice calculations in which she finds other problems that don't have both cues. She can practice just identifying the procedure that *would be done and saying why*, without actually solving each problem. She would still do the regular work but build the missing skill on the practice problems. For example, your child may be able to perform all operations successfully when she sees the operational sign or the specific word for the operation, such as the "multiplication" sign or the words "find the product." But she may need practice interpreting what procedure to retrieve from her memory when the question is not specific and uses words such as "How many apples will she have 'altogether'?"

Use a chart of cue words (found later in this chapter) to help your child practice and gain confidence in selecting the right procedure. When doing practice problems with you, encourage her to also use her learning strength to write down the cue she used and the symbol it stands for, such as "left over" with the "–" (minus sign). She might benefit by saying aloud what she is thinking (AS learners) or manipulating objects, such as tile separators, as she represents the problem tactilely (VSK learners). You can purchase inexpensive bags of tile separators at tile stores. These are shaped like plus signs and can be cut to become minus signs. Two minus signs glued together horizontally serve as equal signs.

"Dendrite Food"

During the night, after about six hours of sleep, serotonin is released in the brain to promote dendrite growth (dendrites are the branches on neurons that receive information from other neural cells and are essential to building neural networks of new memory storage). New information becomes embedded in a neural network by these newly grown dendrites, which improves the traffic flow of information in what the brain sees as a particularly busy highway. This results in long-term memory storage. "Dendrite food" is knowledge practice—it makes the neural network of memory stronger because more dendrites grow and connections are more efficient.

At the conclusion of each day's math lesson, I have my students build long-term memories by writing "dendrite food" notes in their math journals. They write for three to five minutes about what they learned in class that day. The personalization and mental manipulation of new information gives them greater ownership and memory. Help your child get in the habit of writing her own "dendrite food" notes when she gets home from class. She can put the concepts into her own words, create sample problems connecting the math to her interests or hobbies, or draw pictures or diagrams demonstrating the new math ideas. While your child enjoys a good night's sleep, her brain is not distracted by conscious response to sensory stimuli. During this sleep, the "dendrite food" pays off as the dendrites turn the day's learning into new branches to hold fast to the memory.

Creating this mental stimulation is one of the best opportunities for your child to know and connect the new material with her learning strength. She can use writing, talking, and moving objects to process the information in another neural circuit or strengthen the one that started to develop during class. Because choice is a positive brain stimulator, you can provide a list of choices so your child can select the "dendrite food recipe" or style she wants to feed her brain with to build math connections that night. Later, these dendrite food notes become study and review aids before tests.

Dendrite Food Recipes
- Write what today's lesson reminded you of, or how the math you learned fits with what you already know.
- Draw a picture, diagram, or graphic organizer of what you learned.
- How does something you learned today relate to something in your life?
- Write about something that made you wonder or that surprised you.
- What do you predict you will learn next in class?
- How could you (or someone in a profession) use this knowledge?
- Write about something you are confused about or found difficult.
- Write about what you understood today that you haven't understood before.
- Write about the part of the lesson that was most difficult for you and the part you enjoyed the most.

- What strategy did you use to solve a problem today?
- What is the one thing you'll remember about today's lesson?

AS learners

- AS learners may need to read their text or notes aloud or have these notes read to them to reinforce their auditory memories. When your child reads her notes (or you read them aloud to her), and then she repeats what she hears in her own words, the memory is enhanced with personal meaning. What she writes down in her own words will be great review material for test study.
- On nights when there is no math homework, make a plan with your child to do about twenty minutes of math review. During these sessions, go back to earlier chapters and start with the simple example problems. Place a piece of paper over the worked-out answer of the textbook example and ask your child to solve the problem. If he needs a hint, you can move the paper down just a bit so he can see the first step. Often, the memory will be recalled when he sees that one step, and he'll have the satisfaction of reaching the solution almost on his own.

VSK learners

- Review information visually at home by rewriting and expanding on the notes taken in class. Create visual reminders for review.
- Use diagrams and graphic organizers to add memory strength.

MEMORIZING "MUST-KNOW" MATH

Memorizing high-frequency words makes readers more successful because less working memory is used "sounding out" or slowing down for words that are in automatic memory. The same is true for high-frequency math facts. Utilizing your child's prior knowledge of math facts allows him to dedicate more working memory to processing the new information. Because rote memorization of math facts and procedures is not fun or creative—even if your child enjoys doing things with numbers or solving real-world problems—consider having him memorize those facts that give the most "bang for the buck." Some of these high-frequency facts and procedures include the following.

Symbols and Words

Children need to know the common math symbols before they can follow a procedure. Since many words are used to indicate the common procedures, especially in word or story problems, consider having your child keep an ongoing chart in his room or homework area where he adds new words that are represented by the multiply, divide, add, subtract, equal, and ratio signs. As this information becomes more automatic, less active working memory is needed to keep it in place while he works to solve longer and more complex math problems.

Common Cue Words

Addition: *add, plus, sum, plus, total, altogether, increased by, grew, gained, total of, combined, more than* (as in 3 *more than* 7 is 10)

Subtraction: *minus, take away, difference, less than, from, remove, subtract, gives away, sells, loses, fewer than, decreased by, difference between*

Multiplication: *product, times, doubled (tripled,* etc.), and some problems that give information about *one* and ask for *total amounts.* When dealing with multiplication of fractions, *of* usually means "to multiply."

Division: *quotient, percent of, per, ratio, division, separated into, cut into, divided by, shared equally by,* and problems that tell about *many* and ask about *one.*

Equals: *comes to, is,* and depending on the process, the words *product, sum, quotient,* and *product* can refer to "equals."

Multiplication Facts through 12

It's worth the time and effort to turn these facts from rote memory to long-term automatic memory so that subsequent mathematics (including division, factoring, solving algebraic equations, finding multiples, and calculating with fractions) can be done with attention to the process, instead of taking up working memory time and effort to first figure out the multiplication facts.

Procedures and Relationships

- Powers of ten and place value
- Relationships and conversions between fractions, decimals, and percents
- Measurement and conversion of measurement units such as inches to feet or feet to meters

AS learners

Musical instrument playing, rhythmic dance, and reading music are all forms of patterning that appear to increase math sequencing skills, such as counting by 2s or remembering the steps in a "must-know" procedure such as long division. Musical-rhythmic learners may enjoy the "Multiplication Rap with the Facts" CD during syn-*naps* (available from Teacher's Outlet www.abcteacher.com/catalog/ts-mmurwtf.shtml) as a fun and effective way to learn early number facts. AS learners also enjoy practicing with a cassette recording of math facts that has pauses before each answer. You can record your own or purchase these at sites listed in the Resources section of this book.

If your AS learner relates well to sequencing activities, he can use verbal, reading, or artistic skills to explain, write, and/or sketch the steps of nonmathematical procedures. For a syn-*naps* you child can make a peanut butter and jelly sandwich or build a snowman then describe/sketch/write the steps in the sequence he just performed. He can describe the sequence of events that took place in the school day, in a movie he saw, or in a story he heard or read. You can build sequencing skills with games, such as asking your child to try to name his classmates in the order in which they sit in their classroom. He can also put math information into patterns. For example, your child can learn the names of shapes with increasing numbers of sides after first arranging a triangle, square, pentagon, hexagon, etc. in order and saying their names as he points to them.

VSK learners

Flash cards are very useful for self study or when working together with errorless learning. The content on the cards can come from school notes, journals, or the math textbook. Especially useful flashcards are for number facts that your child got wrong on tests or homework. This activity can increase feelings of satisfaction when your child moves a card from the study pile into the success pile after getting the correct answer (written on the flip side). He'll see immediate positive feedback as the success pile grows larger.

However, one success does not mean mastery. Encourage your child to start each review session with *all* the cards and only move a card into the mastery pile after it has been successfully reviewed several times over two weeks, and again about two and four weeks later. The mastery pile should be reviewed again before final exams and during the summer, especially before the beginning of the new school year. Graphing your child's progress helps him recognize that his effort results in achievement. Record the success of your child on self-graded timed tests, flash card work, or with individualized worksheets you can print from websites, such as www.superkids.com/aweb/tools/math/.

Computer feedback can also be a tool to reinforce success. Look for programs that give positive as well as clear, corrective feedback. The positive feedback can be in the form of graphic illustrations of the amount of material mastered, auditory praise, pleasing sounds, or scored points. One activity my students like for the dreaded conversion of numbers from standard to metric form is a Ferris wheel computer simulation at www.walter-fendt.de/m11e/conversion.htm. Each correct answer "fills" a seat on the Ferris wheel, and when the seats are all filled, the wheel rotates around several times and carousel music is played. Also try the Math Fact Café website at www.mathfactcafe.com. The computer keeps track of the number of correct answers and after twenty problems are completed, it shows the problems with incorrect answers with the corrections made and highlighted. Samples are available on the website, but there is a charge for the software.

12

BUILDING MATH MASTERY: KEY TOPICS (ALL AGES)

Math instruction throughout elementary school is taught as a spiral. Most of the topics discussed in this chapter are introduced in lower elementary school and built upon when revisited each year at a more complex level. To reflect your child's classroom instruction, this chapter is arranged by math topics rather than by age or developmental level. Within each topic, activities are described in ascending difficulty, starting with those for younger children at the lowest levels of mathematical development and moving up to activities for children at higher levels of development.

ADDITION AND SUBTRACTION WITH OBJECTS

Number Sense and Above

Your child can build a conceptual understanding of addition and subtraction through the manipulation of objects. Use objects that have high appeal to your child (plastic dinosaurs, etc.), and place them into two groups of unequal number. Place the larger grouping on the left to develop the neural pattern your child will need later for subtracting from left to right. Line up the objects in each group or just keep them in piles. If your child is not yet at the early conceptual thinking development level, she will feel more comfortable starting with objects put into lines. Some children also benefit from the greater visual and tactile reinforcement of linking cubes or Legos before moving on to dinosaurs or marbles, so comparisons of equality or inequality are more evident.

Next, ask your child to add objects to the smaller group from the larger group until she counts the same number in both groups. Ask her to tell you what she did to make the groups become equal. Some children will say "I added some from the bigger group to the smaller group," while others will be more specific: "I added three to the smaller group." Children not yet familiar with the term "addition" might say, "I put some from the bigger group to the smaller group (or line)." Write down your child's words with any needed clarifications and read the sentence together. Return the groups to their original quantities and ask your child to draw a sketch of the two piles before and after the objects are moved and then describe what she is drawing.

After she practices and is successful at making the groups equal, she is ready to move into concept development of addition. This time, move two objects from one group to another and ask your child to describe what you just did. If she says, "You moved two marbles from one group to the other," encourage further comments. Ask her what happened to the first group when you took two marbles away. What happened to the second group when you moved the two marbles into it? Continue this activity with different number moves and gradually insert the word "add" for whatever words she uses for that process. If she says, "You added two more into that group," you can repeat back, "Yes, I put two into that group."

When she is successful using the word "add" to describe the process, ask her to tell you what happens to the number in the second group when you add two, then three, and then four objects from the first group. The goal is for her to recognize that "When you add two marbles to the second group " Then, "When you add three marbles to the second group, *it gets bigger by three.*"

Introducing Symbols

Next, substitute math symbols into the previous activity, starting with the plus sign. It is best to start with a plus sign cut out from paper or to use a tile separator, as described in Chapter 11. Take turns making groups of different small amounts, and then putting the plus sign between the groups. Say aloud what you have arranged, "I have three dinosaurs and I am adding two dinosaurs." Then combine the groups together and ask how many there are "altogether."

When your child reaches mastery in these verbal descriptions (which could require several days or more of practice), begin writing down the activity using numbers to match the objects. The arrangement of two dinosaurs, then a plus sign, and then three dinosaurs is written as 2 + 3. Have your child combine the groups, count the total, and report that there are now five dinosaurs altogether. Write the equal sign and the number "5" to complete the equation. After doing these activities with addition, you can repeat the process for subtraction.

Number Sense Extensions

It is especially memorable to children when they can use their new math concepts in their own lives. As a syn-*naps* you can arrange your child's favorite stuffed animals in a circle for a tea party and give each one two or three crackers. She can then add up the total of how many crackers were given out. You might ask her to predict how many more crackers she would need if one of her dolls joined the party, and after that practice, ask her to predict the number of crackers she would need if she added yet another doll. That would give her the opportunity to "add up" in her head and then see if she is correct when she actually adds the next doll, gives her two crackers, and counts up the new total. The game can be played in reverse when one of the dolls leaves the party, taking her crackers with her. Your child can then describe the change in the total number of crackers remaining after the two crackers have been taken away.

MULTIPLICATION

Early Conceptual Thinking and Above

Learning the multiplication tables is one of the "must-know" arithmetic foundations that let your child progress more confidently through higher math procedures, such as division and fractions. Start with building the concept that multiplication is really the same as adding the same number a certain number of times.

Instead of having your child practice her multiplication tables in order from 1 to 10, start with the ones she is most likely to be most successful with, such as the 1, 2, 5, and 10 tables. Then go back to the more difficult 3, 4, 6, 7, 8, 9, 11, 12 tables. Keep your child's spirits up as you progress to the later tables by showing him on a list or chart the "doubles" he already knows. If he knows his 5s, show him that he already knows 3 x 5 = 15 because in the 5-times table, he learned that 5 x 3 = 15.

After your child masters additional multiplication facts with flash cards, he can have the pleasure of crossing off the facts he knows on a chart. Remind him that the brain needs exercise, just like muscles, so he'll want to keep that neuron network strong by going back and reviewing the multiplication facts he got right last week. When these facts become automatic and you see your child solving problems without taking time out to calculate a multiplication fact, remind him that his efforts paid off and he is now using his mental muscle to solve the problem.

VSK learners may be challenged by memorization and be held back from their high math potential because they have not memorized their multiplication tables. Find out if your child can use a calculator or a multiplication table in class when he learns new conceptual processes that require solid memory of multiplication facts.

DIVISION

Number Sense and Above

Help your child develop early division skills by playing games or "sharing" activities. Start by asking your child how she would share ten crayons with five friends. You can set up five of her dolls or stuffed animals, take out ten crayons, and give her a chance to experience dividing the ten to the five animals. Ask her to explain what she is doing as she distributes the crayons. How many did each animal receive? Ask your child how many groups of crayons there will be if she takes twelve crayons and puts three in each group. Have her explore, try it, and describe her thinking.

Continue with this practice until she is successful multiple times. When ready, you can move to a higher concept of division by using pennies. How many ten-cent pencils can she buy with one hundred pennies?

Continue to other questions about the hundred pennies and things that cost other amounts without remainders. Later, you can discuss what the remainder means and what she could do with the remaining pennies. To keep the activity fun, pretend she is buying items she likes with the pennies.

ESTIMATION AND MEASUREMENT

Developing Number Sense and Above

While precise measurement is critical in many occupations and hobbies, it can be dull to learn in school—especially when children don't have hands-on learning experiences. Play a game with your child where you alternate turns talking about a job, hobby, or sport that uses measurement. Hearing the ways measurements are used increases your child's interest in the topic.

Beginning measurement activities can incorporate estimation games for a refreshing syn-*naps*. "How many of these measuring cups do you think you can fill from this clear jar of beans?" Your child can estimate, pour the beans into measuring cups, and count the number of whole cups filled without worrying about leftovers. After this practice, he may be ready to look at the number of ounces marked on measuring cups, count the number of ounces from all the full cups, and add that sum to the ounces from the partially filled remaining cup. Repeat the activity with liquids and with different size measuring cups up to gallon jugs, then down to smaller items such as number of teaspoons in a tablespoon. When possible, combine the day's measuring activity amount into a cooking or craft activity, so the concept will become more meaningful.

SOLIDS AND WEIGHT

Developing Number Sense and Above

Use Ziploc bags of the same size and have your child fill the bags with different items (beans, marbles, lemons, etc.) in quantities he is able to count. Help your child weigh the bags on a bathroom or kitchen scale until the bags all weigh 1 pound. He can then count the number of each item it takes to weigh one pound and make a chart about how there are 20 marbles in a pound, 5 lemons, or 40 kidney beans. He can even cover the answers with sticky notes and play the "guess-how-many-in-a-pound game" with siblings or friends using his chart. He is building the very important concept that size does not always match with quantity.

Number Sense and Above

After bagging her favorite fruit in the grocery store, ask your child to estimate the weight of the bag. Place it on the scale and have her read the weight. Then ask her to estimate how many more fruits are needed to bring the bag's weight up to 5 pounds, or how many to take away to reduce the weight to 4 pounds. Children at the higher conceptual thinking level may be able to estimate how much one apple costs if four apples in the bag weigh 1 pound and the cost is $1 a pound.

Early Conceptual Thinking

While waiting in line at the airport, pass the time by asking your child to estimate the weights of luggage belonging to people in front of him. Ask him to explain how he uses the results of the real weights he sees on the scale to adjust his estimation of the next bag.

ESTIMATION WITH LIQUIDS

Number Sense

For this activity and multisensory syn-*naps*, your child can select her favorite color and use food coloring to make a large pitcher filled with colored water. Ask her to pour enough into an 8-ounce cup to fill it. Then, have her pour the cup into a separate clear plastic bottle, such as a large 2-liter soda or water bottle, and observe how much of it is filled with the 8-ounce pour. She can then predict how many total cups she'll need to pour from the pitcher to fill the bottle and perform the activity to check her guess.

Early Conceptual Thinking

Ask your child how she might gather evidence to help her estimate how many cups of water are needed to fill a large empty bottle. Give her a head start by placing a pitcher filled with water next to an empty bottle.

She may discover another method, but if she does start pouring water from the pitcher into a cup and pouring the cup into the bottle, ask her to estimate how many cups total will be needed to fill the bottle. The difference now is that each time she adds another cup, you invite her to change her estimate and tell you why she does or does not change her prediction. If she makes notes about how many cups she pours, she will build her estimation, math communication, and number-sense skills.

Higher Conceptual Thinking

A more advanced version of this activity is fun when studying metric conversions with your child, especially if he is a VSK learner. He can look at the ounce markings on a measuring cup and pour cups into an empty juice or milk bottle. He will find it interesting to use the manipulation of water to figure out the relationship of cups and ounces to a liter, and count how many ounces from an 8-ounce measuring cup are needed to fill a 1-liter bottle. He can then try to pour a full liter bottle of water into a quart container to gain the visual and tactile experience of recognizing that a liter is a bit more than a quart.

You can follow these experiments up with real-life connections. Once your child has experimented with 8-ounce measuring cups and you are out shopping together, see if he can tell you which is a better buy in terms of cost and quantity of beverage: a six-pack of 12-ounce cans or a liter bottle that costs the same price.

MEASUREMENTS OF CIRCUMFERENCE

Higher Conceptual Thinking

Children at this level, especially VSK learners, will enjoy building estimation skills and practice using circumference in real-world situations. Select objects for estimating circumference. Your child can write down her estimate, measure the circumference, and compare the two numbers. After measuring several objects (marbles, oranges, balls of different sizes, plates, or small round tables), she can look at her list of estimates and measured circumferences and consider if there is a pattern or trend in her estimates. Is she over- or underestimating? How might she adjust her estimates to be more accurate? She can then apply her theory to more estimations. This activity can also be used to estimate and measure the perimeter of squares, rectangles, and even objects with more than four sides.

ADDITION AND SUBTRACTION WITH NEGATIVE INTEGERS

Higher Conceptual Thinking

Number lines can help children make sense out of the often confusing procedures of adding and subtracting with negative integers. Your child can relate to the concept of a number line by looking at a thermometer and seeing how it is a type of number line because negative numbers are similar to temperatures below zero. Help your child create a number line card to practice with on his desk, or for a VSK learner, create a number line on butcher block paper rolled out on the floor so he can move his body from number to number.

Begin with a positive number line that starts at zero. Going up the line, measure off spaces for positive numbers up to twenty. Your child can practice adding by moving a button (or if your number line is larger, moving herself) from a starting number and advancing forward the number of spaces being added. Then, she can look down to find the sum. After this initial practice, have her start on a number of her choice and guide her to move her button or body the number of units you specify without looking down at the final stopping point. Ask her to predict what number she is on.

To introduce negative numbers, have her work with you to create the negative part of the number line, from zero to negative twenty. Starting at zero, she can walk a specified number of spaces and look down to see that when she took four steps to the negative side of zero she was on negative four. Advance these activities according to your child's comfort level.

Thermometers and Ocean-Depth "Number Lines"

Your VSK learner will enjoy thinking about underwater depth as negative numbers. He can pretend he is a fish or scuba diver starting out at 5 feet below the surface and going down another 10 feet. How deep is he now? If your child is interested in weather, he can use a thermometer to think in terms of a temperature drop in relation to zero degrees. If it is currently 15 degrees above zero and the temperature drops another 25 degrees, what is the new temperature? You can purchase a large thermometer and conduct experiments using warm and ice water where your child can predict the approximate thermometer change as it is moved from one to the other.

As your child improves his predictions about what the temperature reading will be, challenge him to estimate how much it might drop for each ice cube he puts in the water. In the future, when your child is stuck on a test problem about adding or subtracting negative numbers, he can visualize or sketch the thermometer or deep-sea diver to bring the positive experiences with you and use the experience to process the math question. I've had students draw thermometers and underwater sketches as well as regular number lines on their test papers and improve their grades on this challenging mathematical topic.

METRIC CONVERSION

To practice metric conversion, individualize an example of a centimeter for your child's size and age. Provide her with a ruler and ask her to try different fingers to see which or how many fingertips fill a centimeter space on the ruler. Then practice finding the length of a decimeter. Usually a full-finger spread of a hand is about 10 centimeters or 1 decimeter, but she can find out by measuring her finger spread. If it is too short, she can spread the fingers of both hands, overlapping thumbs, and see if that is closer to 10 centimeters. Even better, see which part of her body she thinks of using to find a close match to a decimeter. Then, try finding the length of a meter. For some children, a meter can be the distance between their fingertips when their arms are spread out to the sides. Interactive Metric Conversion computer activities can be found at http://www.learner.org/interactives/metric/index.html

FRACTIONS

Most children never learn the reason why you carry numerators and denominators across when multiplying fractions, even though you can't carry numerators and denominators across when adding fractions. It is therefore understandable that the most common fraction adding-error results from adding the numerators and denominators without first changing the fractions so they have common denominators. It would not be unusual for your child to solve $^2/_3 + ^4/_5$ by adding the numerators $2 + 4 = 6$ and $3 + 5 = 8$ and concluding that $^2/_3 + ^4/_5 = ^6/_8$. As will be described later, these procedural errors are less likely when math rules (algorithms) are "discovered" through a child's natural inquiry instead of memorized without context. Another problem is that children are not motivated to estimate or check their answers when their classroom instruction, geared toward standardized tests, promotes the goal of finishing many problems quickly.

FRACTION SENSE ACTIVITIES

You can help remedy this gap in your child's mathematics education by encouraging her to discover the reasoning processes of mathematics. By talking about the reasons procedures and formulas work and manipulating objects to see that adding $^2/_3 + ^4/_5$ gives much more than $^6/_8$, you will help your child develop the habit of evaluating answers to see if they make sense. The time you spend helping your child see the math all around him, recognizing patterns that recur through different math topics, and evaluating what is logical based on this prior knowledge will build his fraction sense and expand his math comprehension. He will also be more successful on tests because his experiences with you teach him to use logic and patterns so he can look at his answers and see if they make sense.

Developing Number Sense

Because children are most familiar with the fraction $^1/_2$, as in, "Do you want half my sandwich?" or "Can I share half your crayons?" the unit is a strong base with which to start fraction explorations. After doing measurements, by comparing a half glass of water to a whole glass of water, half a cookie to a whole cookie, half a book (opening it to the middle) to a whole book, you can encourage your child to show you when she sees or hears fractions used in daily life. Ask questions about your child's day related to fractions. If he says, "There were lots of kids out sick today," ask, "Was half the class absent?" When he says, "Not that many," ask him to describe the amount of classmates missing. He might first give you a number, but encourage him to use words to describe amounts: "You said you didn't think half the class was absent. Do you think half of a half were absent?"

As your child develops stronger number sense, you can work together to make index cards that read $1/2$ and $1/4$. Your child can put these as labels on things around the house that are $1/4$ or $1/2$ full such as the dishwasher, dog water bowl, or a bottle of juice. He might enjoy changing these cards when the amounts in these items change.

Early Conceptual Thinking

From an interest in coins, you can move from dividing up pennies into groupings of $1/2$ to show that $1/2$ of $1/2$ of 100 pennies is a quarter. Start with 100 pennies so there are 25 pennies in the section designated as $1/4$. Then, bring out a quarter and begin a description of equivalency between 25 cents (one quarter of the 100 pennies) and the object called a quarter. Ask him why he thinks the quarter got its name. He may think it is because it represents $1/4$ of 100 pennies. Then, you can show him how many quarters are in a dollar and even cut apart a play-money dollar (or one you draw) into four pieces and put a quarter coin on each piece of the dollar.

It is likely that if your child enjoys playing with money, he will take off from there with questions about equivalency in fractions and other coins. If he likes sports and hears that a game is in the first quarter, there will be new meaning in that word. When he helps you prepare dinner and you ask for a quarter-cup of water, the word comes up again and fractions become part of everyday life. If he likes drawing and sorting/sequencing, he may open a new box of twenty crayons and with a little prompt from you start exploring them with respect to fractions, including what fraction of the crayons are in the blue category and what fraction are in the pink/red category.

Higher Conceptual Thinking

At some point after your child has used fraction words and even manipulated objects into fraction parts, you'll find it interesting to ask your child if there is a number that is more than one but less than two. If he is still at the early conceptual thinking level, even though he has worked with fractions, he is likely to say "no." If he is at or approaching higher conceptual thinking, he may say, "Yes, there are lots of numbers more than one and less than two. They are called fractions!" Don't you wish your parents had turned you on to fractions before your teacher introduced them to you in third grade?

When you help your child think of fractions in a variety of ways, such as the meaning of a half-moon, halfway to your driving destination on a map, half past three in the afternoon, and what a half-hour feels like when he is waiting for his favorite show to begin, he will have intrinsic motivation to figure things out with fractions. He will build an internal concept and pattern by which he will be able to reconstruct what fractions mean when he forgets a rule. That is truly giving your child the gift of math power.

Numerator/Denominator Confusion

When my students have difficulty remembering which is the numerator and which is the denominator, I start with a box of six whiteboard markers and give each table group their own similar box (you could do this at home with whiteboard markers, crayons, or even six-packs of juice). They count that there are six markers in the whole package and write a "6" on their individual whiteboards. I then take one marker out of the pack. I start by saying, "I have six markers in my box to start with." I point to the markers and the number "6" on the board. I take one marker out and write "1" on the board above the number "6." Now that the 1 and 6 are on the board, I draw a horizontal line between them and invite students to use those numbers to tell the story of what I did when I removed a marker from the package.

When you do this at home, you can guide your child to understand the concept that $^1/_6$ represents a fraction that shows what part of the six-pack of markers you removed.

Ask your child:

- "What do you think the '6' stands for?" (The number of markers in a whole box.)
- "What do you think the '1' stands for?" (The number of markers you took out.)

- "How could you read this mathematical code to show what fraction of the markers I removed from the box?" (Using the word "code" instead of "formula" helps keep interest high if you have played fun code-breaking games with your child before this fraction activity.) Next to the $1/6$, you can also write the words "one-sixth" and describe the meaning as "one of six parts."
- "How could you write a mathematical code for the markers remaining in this box that originally had six markers, now that one is out?" Emphasize the word "six" for something similar to errorless math, as your child will repeat the word "six" because you just said it. You can write it as the denominator and draw the line above it so there is only one place remaining for him to place the numerator as he counts the five remaining markers in the box.

From this point on, let your child's learning strength and interest lead the way into explorations of writing other numerators and denominators as you reinforce the concept. Once your child has the understanding of which number goes on top and which goes below in a fraction and can describe in his own words what the top number and bottom number represent, you can introduce the formal names of reduced and simplified. I then tell a story to help students later connect fractions to division, as in $2/4$ means 2 divided by 4, or $8/2$ means 8 divided by 2, so it can be reduced or simplified to 4.

Fraction Calculation Activities

Ask your child to do a variety of calculations with the same numbers. For example, "What numbers can you add together to get your birthday or today's date?" Your child might start with two numbers and then realize she can add three, four, or more numbers, and later include fractions or decimals to discover even more ways of getting a final answer of the 21st of July.

Another "aha" question for your child who is growing comfortable with fractions is to ask, "Is there a time you can multiply two numbers and get a product smaller than either number? If she says, "No, when you multiply numbers, they always get bigger," you have a teachable moment to introduce the multiplication of fractions, because when two fractions with the same sign (both positive or both negative) are multiplied, the product is always smaller than either fraction.

If your child does get the correct answer to this question, you can ask more abstract questions such as, "What would you rather have: half of a quarter of a pizza or a quarter of a half of a pizza?" When you phrase a question as if there is a single answer—when in fact both of the choices are correct—your child has an "aha" moment after he works out that $1/4 \times 1/2$ or $1/2 \times 1/4$ both equal $1/8$. He can confirm this by drawing a pie. Another option is to ask this question when you actually have a real pizza. Now there will be a multisensory memory filled with smells, tastes, visuals, and conversation that will last a lifetime.

You will be surprised how often you find fraction-action opportunities all around you when you are with your child. While filling up the car with gas, when you are at half a tank you can tell your child what your tank capacity is (usually 12–25 gallons) and see if she can predict how many gallons the pump will register when the half-full tank is filled. Your child can make predictions about mileage and gas cost to figure out what information he needs to collect (starting mileage at the time of fill-up, number of gallons in the tank, distance driven when the tank reaches the same level as when it was filled) to calculate your car's miles per gallon. He can then multiply that mileage fraction by the cost per gallon to discover how much it costs for you to drive him to soccer games in other towns.

If your child can read music, she will enjoy relating fractions to the length of notes on written music and then playing whole notes, half notes, quarter notes, and eighth notes as she thinks about the relation of those notes to fractions. She will soon recognize relationships, such as that two eighth notes are the same as a quarter note.

DECIMALS AND PERCENTS

Early Conceptual Thinking

Decimals are studied after fractions in the typical math curriculum. It may help your child if during or before the formal study of decimals in class you prepare her with activities that demonstrate what decimals mean. You can use everyday activities with money ($1.21 is not just one dollar and twenty-one cents, but can also be thought of as one dollar and twenty-one hundredths of a dollar). If she studies the metric system at school, decimal activities also correlate perfectly with the powers of ten upon which the metric system is based.

You can outline 10 x 10 box grids of 100 squares on graph paper of any size (free downloadable graph paper with different size grids is available at http://incompetech.com/graphpaper/). VSK learners may benefit by starting with wall chart-size graph paper. Your child will enjoy the movement as she colors squares on the large grid or moves objects such as magnetic squares or Post-its on the squares of the grid as an alternative to coloring them.

Decimal grid activities begin with exploring the 10 x 10 grid you outline on the graph paper. How many square boxes are in the whole grid? How many total square boxes are inside three grids you draw on a single page of graph paper? How many squares are in each column? (There are 10 vertical columns of 10 squares each.) How many rows are in the grid? (10 horizontal rows of 10 squares each.) Your child can answer with greater comprehension if you color in the squares in a column in one grid and in a row in another grid using different colors.

Decimals as Larger or Smaller

After investigating the previous decimal concepts, move ahead to comparing decimals for size value. Here it is useful to use different sized graph paper with both large and small grids that all have 100 squares, so your child sees that .12 or twelve hundredths on a large square grid represents the same decimal or relative quantity as .12 or twelve hundredths on a small square grid.

When your child has a clear understanding of grids, she can explain in her own words that regardless of the size of the squares in a 100-square grid, it is the number colored in that determines the decimal, not the area or size of the colored region. It is now time to introduce comparison of decimal size. Start with grids of the same size and color in a different number of squares in several grids on a page going from smaller to larger numbers of colored grids, such as 20, 30, and 40. Ask your child to describe each of the different grids with the different number of squares colored in ("10 out of 100 squares are red," etc.).

Ask your child to then pick a number, color in that number of squares, and describe that grid. Ask her to move to the next grid, color in more squares, and describe that grid. Next, she can draw a grid with fewer colored-in squares and repeat the process.

After enough practice, probably on another day, she will be ready for you to write just the decimals (such as .40 and .60) and have her tell you which is a large quantity and then support her prediction in any way she chooses. Most children will choose to color in boxes on grids and compare them, but if your child is an AS learner, she may be comfortable describing it verbally. VSK learners may want to go back to moving magnets or boxes on larger grids to represent the decimals you wrote.

Decimals as Mixed Numbers

The next progression is into mixed-number decimals, such as 1.6. Start by having your child color in 99 squares in a 100-square grid and tell you the decimal equivalent of those 99 squares (.99 and ninety-nine hundredths). Then, have her color in the remaining square using the same color and describe the number of colored squares compared to the total number of squares. After she says that 100 of the 100 are colored in or writes 100/100, she may wonder about how to write that answer as a decimal. Here is where your verbal description will be very important.

Consider saying, "You have colored in the whole grid. How many whole grids did you fill with color when you colored all the squares?" She will respond, "One whole grid," at which point you can ask her to write the number "1" and ask her if she could put a decimal sign someplace next to that number 1 that would not change its meaning or value. With guidance, when she does write 1 followed by a decimal point (1.), ask her to say the number again. She should just say "one," and you can ask her if she can add zeroes anyplace without changing the value of that number.

If she has trouble, draw another grid next to the one that is completely colored in and ask her how many squares are colored in. When she replies "zero" or "none," you can write the zero, then write and say, "OK, so you have one whole grid and zero additional boxes colored in on this uncolored grid." You can write 1 followed by the decimal and two zeroes so it appears as 1.00 and help her read that as "one and zero one-hundredths," or if she has advanced to the concept of tenths, you can write 1.0, and she might say "one and zero tenths." Just keep her saying the decimal as words and avoid using the word "point" for the decimal. She will now be prepared for decimal addition.

Decimal Addition

If your child has gotten this far in decimal concepts, she is well into the higher conceptual thinking stage of mathematical development, at least in regard to decimals. Try working with mixed decimals, such as 1.40, by coloring in two adjacent grids of 100 with the first grid fully colored and the second with 40 squares colored. Practice with as many of these as it takes for her to feel comfortable using words, fractions, decimals, and decimal words. Here are some variations to try:

- Switch the order of the two adjacent grids so the one with 40 colored squares is to the right of the one that is fully colored. This will help her realize that it does not matter which is in front or to the right because she is simply adding up the total number of colored squares.
- Increase the number of fully colored grids to two, three, or four, combined with a partially colored grid for larger decimals such as 4.6.
- Progress to adding decimals by having two partially colored 100-box grids next to each other, such as 40 colored boxes next to a grid with 10 colored boxes. Ask her to predict how many squares would be colored if the two grids were combined or if the colored squares on the second grid were "added on" to the first grid.
- After practicing combining or "adding up" these grids and without writing the decimal addition equations, ask, or, if needed, show your child how to write decimal additions to represent what she did with "counting up" and drawing the colored squares together on one grid. She will write .10 + .40 = .50 and then say this in words as, "Ten hundredths plus forty hundredths equals fifty hundredths."
- To make this activity more of a game and a brain-pleasing syn-*naps* involving your child's interests, you can switch at any time to

using different materials to color the squares such as cloth, paint, or ink stamps.

- When your child is very successful with addition, you can repeat the procedures that worked best for her learning strength and work with decimal subtraction.

Percent in the Real World

Children practice percents when they calculate the savings on something they want that is reduced by a 20% off sale or when they calculate the tip in a restaurant. Even your young child with fairly advanced math development can enjoy experiences with percents before studying them formally in school. He might have heard an older sibling's excitement for the 100% he received on a test, or disappointment for a 70%.

If your child knows that a 50% sale means prices are cut in half and predicts that because 10 is less than 50, a 10% sale doesn't give as much savings as a 50% sale, she can make comparisons when you are shopping in stores or reading ads in the newspaper about items in which she is interested, is saving for, or hopes to receive for her birthday.

Start by modeling awareness of percents by saying, "I notice that the art set you want was on sale last week for 20% off and now it is 50% off. What do you think that means?" One child may say, "It is even less expensive now." Another child may take it further and reason or deduce, "The savings are getting greater, the price is dropping. Maybe they are coming out with a new version and the store wants to sell the ones they have so they can make room for the new ones. I wonder if the price will drop even more or if they will sell out because of this new discount." You can ask, "How can we make that prediction?" and go on to ideas about comparison of prices in other stores or checking the manufacturer's website for promotions of possible new versions of the art set. You are helping her progress from percents to economics!

If your child has $20 and wants to purchase books from an online site that is having a "10% sale on all purchases," she might enjoy planning several ways of spending the entire amount at once. Add the motivation for placing the entire order at the same time by explaining that separate orders are charged for shipping each time, but single orders have only one shipping fee. You can challenge her to find three different sets of books she likes and calculate which one comes closest to $20. She can then make her selection from those three groups. Perhaps as an acknowledgment of her mathematical thinking, you can offer to pay for that single shipment.

Percent and Earning Interest

When your child receives a gift of money, use this teachable moment to discuss the concept that interest is paid on savings account deposits. Your child can check the newspaper to see different interest rates offered at different banks and credit unions and predict how much simple interest he'd earn in one year, two years, etc. When he uses percentages to calculate simple interest he might earn on a deposit, he may be more motivated to save some of the money he earns or receives as gifts.

RATIO, RATE, PROPORTION, AND SCALE

Early Conceptual Thinking

- To practice measurement and build an experiential awareness of scale and proportion, your child can cut out a magazine picture, comic square, or copy of a photograph to enlarge. Start with a simple example, such as drawing a basic picture of a snowman, on a 2 x 5 inch card. Help your child draw a line half way down the length and half way down the width. Use a similarly proportioned larger piece of cardboard or poster paper, such as 4 x 10 inches (double the length and width proportionately) for a first project, and perhaps moving to a 6 x 15-inch (triple the length and width) for a second enlargement of the same snowman. You can help as needed as he again draws lines dividing this larger paper into four sections.
- Together, calculate at what time you would need to leave the house to reach a destination at a specified time. Use rate, mileage (perhaps with a map measurement), and miles per hour to calculate the number of hours. Perhaps your child can also convert fractions of

hours to minutes for exact times. Add fun by using professional travel time terms such as "ETA" (estimated time of arrival).

"My Shadow" Activity

A big favorite for VSK learners or any child who is ready for an outdoor syn-*naps* on a sunny day is to use shadow measurements and ratios to calculate the heights of trees or other structures. Your child can start by measuring her height and the length of her shadow and converting the numbers so they are in inches or in feet with decimals. Next, she can measure the shadows of a tree, garden shed, street sign, or another object of interest (during a time of day when the sun is fairly high overhead so the shadows are not too long) and then calculate the length of these objects using the ratio of her own shadow to her height and the length of the object's shadow to calculate the height of the object itself. The formula is her shadow's length divided by her height equals the object's shadow length divided by X, where X represents the actual height of the object. She'll need to keep units of measurement equal and measure her shadow-to-height ratio each time she does the project, because different times of day at different times of year will make that ratio different.

CURRENCY CONVERSIONS

Converting one type of currency to another offers opportunities to work with ratio, proportion, and unit values (such as how much one item costs based on the total price of several identical items). To increase your child's interest in the project, you can discuss the currencies of countries from your family heritage, countries he'd like to visit, or countries where his favorite foods originated.

You can find current currency exchange rate charts in major weekly newspapers or on websites, such as www.x-rates.com. After your child practices converting easier quantities of money back and forth between the two currencies, he can make specific currency conversions based on the cost of items he'd like to purchase in the country of his choice. This can incorporate a cross-curricular connection to a country he is studying in social studies as he learns the products for which the country is known or the cost of doing special activities in that country, such as riding in a gondola in Venice, Italy. Personal interest can enhance this activity if he researches the price of an item he owns and loves, such as his skateboard or iPod, and investigates the price in the currency of its country of manufacture.

PROBABILITY AND SPORTS

Probability and statistics are topics that seem unrelated to children's lives. Even the definition of these mathematical activities seems remote to a child in elementary school. Children are told they need to use probability and statistics to analyze data to simulate events and test hypotheses, but young children are interested in real events, not the statistics that analyze rate of inflation or population growth. However, sports like baseball are full of probability and statistics. Batting averages are ratios, and probabilities and team statistics are discussed between young fans frequently. To engage your child in these upper elementary school topics, you can follow a favorite team and players together and use mathematics to compare all the runs, hits, errors, and ratios. Ask your child if she was the team's owner or manager, how would she use math strategies such as ratio, proportion, and probability to gather team statistics and better her team's success?

SHAPES, AREA, AND PERIMETER

Developing Number Sense

When studying shapes, make a game out of seeking them out wherever you go. Children enjoy hands-on experiences with geometric shapes. When you help them find geometric shapes in tile floors and buildings, they will be ahead of the curve when they can identify a hexagon, rhombus, trapezoid, parallelogram, triangle, square, and rectangle in school. One website that provides a fun syn-*naps* and practice for early shapes is www.bright-productions.com/kinderweb/tri.html.

Tessellations

Tessellations are shapes that fit together on all sides without any spaces between shapes. Tessellation designs combine art and math. Children can build their own geometric shapes that tessellate (fit together perfectly) following instructions at www.tessellations.org. Samples of fascinating tessellation art by M.C. Escher can be found in books or images.google.com, or check out tessellations by Makoto Nakamura at www.k4.dion.ne.jp/~mnaka/home.index.html. By creating tessellation designs, your child will further develop her conception of math as art and nature as math and art. A website for a syn-*naps* during homework brain breaks that allows children to move shapes to build tessellations is www.mathcats.com/explore/tessellationtown.html.

Perimeter

To introduce the concept of perimeter with real-world applications well suited for children at this level, ask questions: "If you wanted to build a Lego wall around this rug, how many Legos (or equal size blocks or buttons) would you use?" "If you wanted put a chicken wire fence around this part of the yard to keep animals out of a vegetable garden, how could you use this ball of twine to find out how much wire fencing to buy?"

After beginning these activities, you can start introducing the word "perimeter" instead of saying "distance around," and then your child can suggest things for which he would like to discover the perimeter. After using string, he can then measure the total string length with a measuring tape to find the perimeter in feet or inches. If he uses blocks or Legos and is ready to convert the amount of blocks to an actual length, help him discover a way to make that conversion, such as measuring a single block, counting the blocks, and adding them all together or multiplying the length of one block times the number of blocks used.

Area

Just as you started your child's interest in perimeter by asking how to figure out the distance around a rug or small garden plot, ask her how much material might be needed to cover a small flat piece of wood (such as a bathroom shelf) with decorative paper. Allow her to make suggestions and try them out.

When she is ready to explore the concept of area, invite your child to use a 12 x 12 inch square piece of cardboard or a box lid that is a true square foot. To increase her "investment" and interest in the activity, she can actually plan to make a decorative cover from cloth or adhesive paper for a surface in her room she'd like to cover. Predicting how many of the measuring squares will be needed to cover the surface will also make her more invested in the activity.

Ask her how she can use the square to find out the total number of squares needed to cover the surface. She might decide to start on one side and actually trace the square over and over and count up the total number of squares, or she might make a column of squares down one side (the length) and count the number of columns that there would be in total by counting or drawing squares needed to fill in the adjacent side (width). She might then say there would be six rows of five squares each and add up the number 5 six times, or multiply 6 x 5 to calculate that 30 squares would be needed.

13
MATH MOTIVATION STRATEGIES (ALL AGES)

This chapter suggests opportunities to connect your child to math in his daily life through interest-driven investigations and also offers suggestions for getting the most out of homework time.

To increase your child's motivation for *any* math activities, start with his interests. Look for opportunities away from formal study sessions to enjoy personally relevant math, real-life math, math games, and mental math opportunities. Discover questions to ponder together using the artist's palette of mathematics.

In school, when rote learning is emphasized, children deal with facts and skills in isolation. Separating information and skills from experience forces your child to depend on rote memory without the meaningful connections and mental manipulation needed to build long-term memory circuits. If the information has personal relevance, however, it will be handled differently in the brain. Reinforce your child's math memory at home, and the knowledge will be strengthened by personal relevance. It will not require as much drill and review to be retained in his permanent memory.

You'll find opportunities to build your child's appreciation of math throughout the day when you shop, read, play cards, use money, eat meals, toss a ball, and together investigate your child's areas of high interest. With your help, math jumps out of the textbook and into your child's senses, becoming beautifully patterned into her brain.

MENTAL MATH OPPORTUNITIES

The following mental math opportunities are fun and also help build number sense:

- Shopping: As you shop, have your child mentally estimate the running total of items placed in the cart (rounded up or down to the nearest dollar for each item). Ask her to tell you when you have approximately reached but not exceeded the $20 you brought with you for the groceries. *Prediction builds interest and motivation.*
- Reading: Say, "This book of bedtime stories was written in 1990. You were born in 2002. How many years before you were born was this book published?" *Relating to her birthday makes math personal.*
- Mealtime: You have a roast that cooks at ten minutes a pound. Ask your child at what time you should start the cooking if dinner will be served at 6:00 p.m. *When he sees that his use of math makes a difference in your decision making, math becomes a tool that bestows power.*
- Restaurants: Ask your child, "When I pay this restaurant bill of $15.50 with this twenty dollar bill, how much change do you think I'll get back?" *Prediction builds interest and motivation.*

MATH GAMES

Incorporate games involving numbers and math into playtime for a change-of-pace syn-*naps*. There are many types of games—from flash cards on the Internet for learning basic math facts to games involving money, time, and logic. Card games such as Go Fish, Crazy Eights, Gin Rummy, Solitaire, Hearts, and War all engage mathematical neural circuits. Board games such as Monopoly and Rummikub are math builders, as are dominoes, Battleship, and regular or 3-D tic-tac-toe. Certainly Sudoku and math puzzles get the neuron circuits buzzing. With such a variety of games and interactive math websites, there are many ways to suit your child's age and interests (as well as your own).

- 99: Players take turns rolling two dice and keeping a running sum of total points (depending on age and ability, this can be done with pencil and paper for computation practice or without for mental math practice). The goal is to score as many points as possible without going over 100. You each must roll both dice each time. Alternate who goes first, roll once, and pass the dice to your child. The game point goes to the player who gets closest to 100 without going over.

• Ball toss: Toss a ball back and forth and ask each other math "must-know" memory review questions. When your child answers your question correctly, he receives the ball and can ask you (or a sibling who is playing) a question about math or a topic of his choice, etc. The game adds the fun of physical movement to math fact practice.

• Student teacher: If your child enjoys role playing, she can become the teacher and use props, such as a whiteboard, blackboard, and objects, to teach the day's lesson or test review to you and her assembled stuffed animals.

• War card game: A deck of cards can be used for an Addition or Multiplication War game. The dealer passes out all the cards, but players don't look at their cards. Each player turns up two cards. In Addition War, the highest sum wins the hand. In Multiplication War, the highest product wins the hand. Play continues until one player has no more cards.

• Where to eat: Using a menu from a local restaurant (many are found in the restaurant section of the yellow pages or on the Internet), your child can decide what three meals she could order with a budget of $15.

• Computer simulations can provide multiple learning style and multisensory opportunities. The website www.coolmath-games.com offers free real-world simulations for all ages. The Lemonade Stand game on this website has my junior-high math students coming in during their recess. The goal of this game is to make as much profit as possible within thirty days with a lemonade stand. The child controls pricing, inventory, purchasing of supplies, and quality (they discover that too much ice is costly and dilutes flavor, but not enough ice is problematic on a warm day—hence the value of checking the weather prediction option the game offers). Commercial simulations, such as Zoo Tycoon, allow the player to invest capital and earnings in zoo exhibits and shops to earn profit.

MOTIVATION WITH REAL-LIFE ACTIVITIES

Look for opportunities to help your child see the math in her daily life: She can pour two cups into a pint measuring cup to make pancakes, count the number of plates she'll need to set the dinner table for the whole family plus Grandma and Grandpa, figure out at what time she thinks you should leave the house to drive the thirty minutes to arrive at her friend's house for her 2:00 p.m. birthday party, or use the clock to decide how much time will elapse before her favorite television show starts. She will see the value of learning the math that is offered to her in school because she'll be using math skills daily.

Encourage your child to play a game of telling you things that have to do with math and numbers as you go for a walk or a drive. Let him hear you use math to solve problems, such as whether you will have enough money for popcorn at the movies if you need to keep two dollars to pay for parking when you exit the mall. When driving in the car, talk about how numbers help you determine how fast you drive, the distance traveled, or mileage the car gets per gallon of gas, and have your child predict how long it will take to get home based on speed and miles to travel.

Expose your child to money in his early school years. If he keeps coins in a piggy bank with a removable opening, he'll enjoy counting them out in various patterns (different ways of putting coins into one-dollar amounts, counting the total dollars, or putting similar coins together and adding those sums). If he receives an allowance, encourage him keep track of the amount or start a bank account. Ask your daughter to decide if she would prefer to receive one dollar more allowance for each year of her age or start this week with a one-penny allowance that would double weekly. (Hope that she chooses the former, because you'll be paying out hundreds of thousands of dollars within several years if she does the math and chooses the doubling penny.)

Activities for Young Children (Ages 4–7)

Children enjoy games where they make guesses and improve accuracy as you provide hints. Select two boxes or cans of food that weigh 8 ounces and 16 ounces. Have your child hold each as you tell her their weights. Then, give her a food item in a package or can that is marked with the weight, and without looking at the weight, have her compare the feel of the weight to the feel of the 8- and 16-ounce samples. She can then estimate if the new item's weight is closer to 8 or 16 ounces. As she becomes more successful, she may want to predict a more specific weight. Encourage her to tell you why she thinks the new can weighs 10 ounces, and she might say, "It is a little heavier than the 8-ounce can or it is much lighter than the 16-ounce can, but not as light as the 8-ounce can." She will be building number sense by experiencing the relationships between numbers and real measurements and developing concepts of *more than* and *less than*.

To further the concepts of *more than* and *less than*, you can ask your child how much he thinks an item costs. The goal is not for him to know prices, but to develop the number sense that larger numbers represent greater amounts. If he predicts that a $3 box of cereal costs $1 and you say "more," he may say $2. You say "more" again and he will continue giving answers as you direct him with "more" or "less" until he estimates the correct dollar amount. When starting this activity with a child who is developing number sense, stay with single whole numbers in his counting range. He will feel the positive intrinsic reward when he sees that the marked price matches his final estimate, but you may want to explain that the numbers after the $3, as in $3.25, represent parts of a dollar or change. If he asks for more details, you can have a discussion about parts of a dollar and show him the coins that represent the change. However, if his math development is still at an early stage, he will probably be happy to play the game with the whole numbers.

You can point out geometric shapes in sidewalks, buildings, and signs even before your child is ready to learn the formal names for rectangles and triangles. After you show him a window that is a rectangle, ask him to find another similar shape. Take turns so he builds the awareness of shapes and asks you to find a shape similar to the triangular-shaped yield sign he finds.

A trip to the bank can be a syn-*naps* that promotes your child's questions and interest and leads to a discussion that raises math awareness in everyday life. Similarly, an office supply or hardware store is a place to explore tools of measurement and compare large volumes to small volumes for *more than* and *less than*. When your child develops his math concepts further, you'll find interesting opportunities to discuss percents, discounts, sales tax, and credit card finances. These math experiences outside of school and your home will appeal to your child and sustain his math motivation.

SELF-MOTIVATED EXPLORATION

A toddler doesn't need to wander all around the playground or store to receive sensory information. He could stay in one place and passively watch the things around him. But most youngsters are inquisitive and driven by curiosity to look under, around, and climb up whatever they can, and by doing so they experience more of the world. Curiosity and inquiry are among children's most powerful learning tools.

As a parent, you can use math inquiry to help your child maintain her natural curiosity as she continues to build her mental storehouses of information. The more focused awareness your child's brain experiences, the greater her ability to make accurate predictions based on new information. These form the foundations of expanded math numeracy and concept development.

If you spend some time observing children in public places, such as airports or museums, you'll find some who seem to sprint off in pursuit of something they see or hear across the room. Parents who follow close behind without blocking their children's explorations are reinforcing their curiosity and supporting the growth of inquiry in these fortunate children. Parents who discourage exploration limit this growth.

You can be the influence in your child's life that sustains her curiosity and encourages her to be a creative thinker. Your child can actively build her own understanding of her world as she interacts with you, her peers, teachers, and books, and explores objects and concepts because she enjoys learning. Inquiry in mathematics will build on your child's inherent curiosity about the ideas behind the drills and formulas. The more you do to encourage your child's inquiry in mathematics and other areas, the greater her enthusiasm for learning becomes.

REAL-WORLD INQUIRY PROJECTS

The following projects can be used in the way they are explained, but they will be most enjoyable if you modify them to correlate best with your child's interests and learning strengths. The activities are presented in ascending order, starting with those well suited for children who have developed number sense. They increase to suit children with high conceptual thinking development, usually in upper elementary school. Feel free to skim through some of the later inquiry activities even for your younger child, as you are likely to find ways to modify these for varying levels of math development.

Doors and Windows

You know your house or apartment well, but your five-, six-, or seven-year-old may not have thought about how your home was planned and constructed. This inquiry starts with a question that you think will turn on your child's natural curiosity. He then collects data that can be analyzed using mathematics and creative hypotheses.

Perhaps it is a rainy day and your son is looking longingly out the window. Or your daughter might comment on a door that is frequently stuck or squeaks when opened. Doors and windows are perfect to investigate because they are easy to find and count, and can turn into a variety of inquiries.

Start a conversation about doors or windows and see where it leads. You can prompt the discussion by asking how many doors he thinks are in your home or which rooms he thinks have the most doors or windows and which rooms the least. Ask him how he makes his predictions. Ask how he might investigate one or more of his door or window questions. Depending on his age and ability, he can gather his own data, or you can accompany him.

Your VSK learner might want to put sticky notes on each door and then go back and count, or start with an overview by making a sketch of the house and rooms before filling in details gathered when he investigates each room. If your child is a more methodical AS learner, she may choose to walk sequentially from one room to the next adjoining room gathering data before putting it together for analysis. See what your child wants to do or offer several options to choose from.

After the data is collected, ask your child how the information might be *represented* so he can *investigate* the numbers and look for clues or patterns about the number of doors or windows found in different rooms. If he then uses symbols or numbers on a graph to represent the number of doors in each room, he builds number sense and appreciation for how math makes his investigation simpler. If your child has come to think of math as boring or difficult, the recognition that it is simpler to represent a door as a number or a check mark in a column is an authentic experience of how math makes things easier. Consider helping him recognize this by asking why he is using numbers or check marks instead of drawing doors on his paper for every door in the house.

Interest, learning strength, and math developmental level will all influence how he wants to arrange his data. For example, he may use a bar graph, indicating the name of the room on a horizontal line and using buttons or measured inches to represent the number of doors or windows in each room. Other options include graphic organizers that are arranged by number of windows. He could draw a Venn diagram and use the overlapping parts of the two circles to write the names of the rooms with the most common number of windows. He could use the non-overlapping parts of the circles to write the names of rooms with less than that number in the left circle and the rooms with more than that common number in the right circle. An AS learner will enjoy explaining to family members what his data collection represents.

Frequently, the collection and arranging of the data will get your child thinking about what the information she collected might suggest. Why do some rooms have more doors or windows than other rooms? If your child likes the overview before details, as many VSK learners do, she may come up with several hypotheses before analyzing them individually. She might want another perspective and decide to gather more data by examining the doors and windows from outside the house or a neighbor's house. An AS learner may prefer looking at his early data from a few rooms and predicting how many doors or windows he'll find in other rooms he'll investigate. He can then evaluate his prediction by collecting more data from a few more rooms and see if his theory is correct or needs to be modified.

Activity Extensions

After the inquiry, encourage your child to summarize what he has learned, what surprised him, how his predictions matched his results, what more would he like to know, and what part of his investigation he enjoyed the most. Keeping his inquiry data and conclusions in a math log provides a wonderful opportunity for him to look back on his growth in mathematics over the years. He might share some of his inquiries with his class, friends, or relatives who visit, or guide a younger sibling in a similar investigation in a few years.

You can add positive reinforcement and additional memories to the investigation journal by including photos, typing or writing down summary comments he dictates, or allowing him to use a special fountain pen or gold marking pen to write in his journal. Other household items, such as electrical outlets, lamps, or tables, can also be compared from room to room.

Whales to Scale

To investigate proportion with a topic of high interest, your child will enjoy creating scale drawings of her favorite objects or animals. Children are usually still growing when they study proportion, so size changes relate to personal interest in their own size changes. Because whales are the largest living animals, they are a popular choice, but your child may choose boats, airplanes, dinosaurs, or famous mountains. A website for whale length is www.enchantedlearning.com/subjects/whales/activities/graphs/gr2.shtml.

Questions to guide the investigation:

- Would you like to have a whale in your room?
- How big can the biggest whale be?
- How can we show how long that whale would be compared to your height?

- How much of your wall space do you want to use to display a drawing of your whale?

After some discussion to generate ideas, you can help with specific questions as needed, such as:

- What type of whale will you draw?
- How long is your whale in feet?
- How long is the poster paper you will use?
- Which size (proportion) would be the best to use for your whale, drawing so he'll fit on your paper? Can you compare his length to and include that in the drawing?

Try some calculations. If your child suggests that for a 40-foot whale, she might use 2 inches of paper to represent every foot of the whale and every foot of her own height, how many inches would both drawings be? Will the whale drawing fit on the paper? If 80 inches is too long for the paper, what is another scale she could try? If she predicts that 1 inch to 1 foot would work because 40 inches would fit on her paper, help her decide how many inches she would use to represent her 4-foot height.

AS learners might enjoy listening to whale song music while doing the activity or singing songs about the sea during a syn-*naps*. She may want to write a poem or analogy about her discovery: "A gray whale can be made so small that next to a very little me, we both fit on my wall." She might want to draw other whales to scale in sequence, largest to smallest.

VSK learners will have fun and give their brains a syn-*naps* by looking at videos and websites of different types of whales and selecting interesting characteristics by which they want to sort and select whales after getting the overview. Perhaps they'd like to graph whales that vary in color, by the foods they eat, by their habitat, or by the types of whales that migrate closest to your coastline or to a coastline he once visited. Instead of just drawing whales to scale, VSK learners might want to use clay to model them in proportion to each other. The website http://library.thinkquest.org/3926/size.html offers other interesting whale facts and gives examples of whale measurements from orca to blue whales.

Activity Extensions
Predict how many people of your child's height lying head to foot would it take to be the same length as a whale. Have him predict an answer, trace and cut out a copy of the representation he drew of his height, and count how many times he needs to place his cutout to reach the length of the whale. How close was his prediction? Discuss the relative scale of human beings to other large animals, such as elephants, or to mammals smaller than humans.

Wall Street on Your Street

Money is a high interest item for most children from the time you play games and math activities with coins to the more advanced use of dollars and cents in percents and decimals for children at higher levels of math development. Prime your child's interest in the math of the stock market by relating finances to his other interests, such as finding the stock-market code for companies that manufacture some of his favorite possessions (sneakers, skateboard, computer, iPod).

Your VSK child can also watch a bit of the business news with footage from the stock-exchange floor with all of its high energy, or read about the accomplishments of people recently chosen to ring the opening or closing bell. History buffs will enjoy reading the history of Wall Street, especially when they are learning about the 1929 stock market crash.

Your AS learner who enjoys words will be intrigued by the origin of the terms "bear" and "bull" market. Websites with Wall Street history and activities include http://pbskids.org/bigapplehistory/parent-steachers/business_lesson7.html and www.atozinvestments.com/more-wall-street-history.html.

Once your child is interested, show him how to "read" the stock-market section of the newspaper or one of the many websites, such as http://finance.yahoo.com, where he can find the past performance and current activity of stock. Suggest that he find about five to ten companies that make or do things that connect with his interests. He can read about these companies on the Internet and use their previous stock performance and daily national or international news events or trends to predict whether the company's stocks may go up or down in value. For example, ask him how a positive review of a new game from a software magazine he likes could influence the value of the stock.

After making his stock selections, have him start with a specified amount of money and decide how to invest it among his five stocks. You can increase the "buy-in" if, for example, you tell him that he will start with $5,000 in stock-market money represented by $5 real money. Explain to an older child that just as $5 is .001 percent (one-thousandth of a percent) of $5,000, he will get to keep .001 percent of his final profit.

Depending on his math development level, various notations can be made in his official stock market portfolio (a journal with information he collects about his companies and data he collects daily from a website or newspaper pertaining to their business activities and stock prices). He can incorporate graphs, percent change, and actual change in value of the number of shares he owns, a running total of his profits, losses, and net worth each day. (A printed-out chart is available from the Yahoo site.)

As his investment data grows, ask him why he thinks values of his stocks went up or down and what changes he predicts next. You can include the option of selling one of his stocks and shifting the money to another stock he investigates if he predicts a change in the coming week based on information he gathers.

MATH HOMEWORK MOTIVATION

Not all children will need all of these suggestions. Consider reading through these ideas and checking the ones that you'd like to try with your child. If he develops different homework problems later, you can return to this list and see what new strategy to add.

"That's Not How My Teacher Does It!"

Perhaps the homework that causes the most parent-child frustration and tension is math homework. You might feel strongly that you can explain something in a way your child will understand that is not exactly like the explanation her teacher used—and you may be right! However, children (including my own) seem to think that if they don't do calculations the way their teacher showed them, their work will be incorrect. The refrain, "That's not the way my teacher said to do it" is an all-too-common response, even when children are the ones who ask for parental help with homework.

As a teacher, I try to improve the situation by encouraging students and parents to work together to use and discover new and different ways of solving problems. I explain that creative, different ways of solving problems is one of the joys of math and one reason why mathematical thinking is such a valuable skill set, regardless of future career plans. Students seem to be more open to exploring the different approaches suggested by their parents when they know I support their collaboration. I reinforce the different approaches they learn from their parents by encouraging my students to demonstrate the alternative strategies they learn to the class. If your child wants your help but is hesitant because you don't do the calculations "the teacher's way," consider asking her teacher what his or her policy is about parent help and alternative approaches. If the teacher is open to this, you might suggest that he or she explain that to the students.

Homework That Seems Pointless

Low motivation becomes an issue when teachers don't explain the value or purpose of homework assignments. Math homework should reinforce classroom learning as your child applies her newly acquired skills and knowledge, or provide background she will use in the next day's math lesson. When your child knows how homework will allow her to investigate topics more fully with respect to her interests, learning strengths, and level of mathematical development (such as with differentiated homework assignments based her student math development level), she will be more motivated to do the assignment.

When math homework is consistent with these goals, your child is more likely to consider the work reasonable and put in the effort because she understands the value of doing so. Your knowledge of your child's interests will allow you to help her see the personal value of math practice and skill-building homework relative to her goals and interests. Unfortunately, much homework is drill without differentiation for students who already have mastery, or it is too confusing for children who did not successfully comprehend the lessons needed to succeed with the homework. Repeating the same mistakes on homework that your child made in class just reinforces incorrect mathematical thinking. You can help your child with these problems by strengthening her understanding of new concepts using strategies suited to her learning strengths.

Being Your Child's Math Consultant

A parent can play many roles when helping a child solve math homework problems. You can serve as your child's consultant, companion, strategist, and supporter. Just knowing that your time and attention is focused on your child builds her motivation for doing an activity that she knows will keep you near and interested. (Unfortunately, this is often why tantrums work for kids who want attention.) With math problem solving, studying, and homework, the sense that you are in close proximity and ready to support her when needed as a consultant or strategist builds your child's math homework confidence and motivation.

Your child can develop a sense of how to use you as a consultant when you offer to discuss possible options once she has read and reread the question and looked at the examples in the book. Before offering suggestions, ask your child to explain what she thinks she is asked to do in the math calculation or problem. Especially if she is an AS learner, she may find that when she reads the instructions aloud and then says them in her own words, she understands the problem and how to solve it.

Because you want your child to be an independent learner and develop the confidence that comes from knowing she has faced challenging, confusing, and frustrating math problems and succeeded, you serve her best as a consultant and supportive companion. She might feel supported just doing her homework in the same room in which you are doing your own work (as long as you are doing something that can be interrupted, such as preparing a simple meal, sketching, organizing cabinets, paying bills, looking through catalogs, reading a magazine, or folding laundry).

Your child may understand a concept by simplifying the problem. Once he creates and solves the simple version, he can apply the strategy or procedure to the problem at hand. If the problem is $5/7$ x $4/11$ he can substitute simpler fractions to refresh his memory of how to multiply fractions. Once he writes $1/3$ x $2/5$ and gets the answer of $2/15$, he's likely to recall the procedure. After success at this "simplification" strategy with you, he'll find it very useful in class and on tests.

If your child frequently worries that his answers are incorrect and wants you to check his homework, you help him most by showing him where he made errors and encouraging him to discuss his reasoning or confusion. Perhaps he can look at the last similar problem he successfully solved and compare what he did on that problem to what he left out or did incorrectly on the troublesome problem. If he can make corrections at that point on his own, great. If he can't do so independently, he can make a note next to the problem and let his teacher see specifically where he needs further explanations.

MOTIVATION TO SOLVE WORD PROBLEMS

Regardless of your child's learning strength, if he is like most students, the word problems he has done in his math textbooks have not been particularly interesting or relate to his life or interests. Many children approach word problems with stress or expect to be frustrated because they take more time than simple calculations and the words are more confusing than dealing with numbers.

Start your child's exposure to word problems before they are part of his regular math homework, and he'll be more comfortable when these problems are taught in school. When something happens during the day that provides an opportunity to use math to find a solution, consider turning it into a word problem. For example, have him figure out how many mini-muffins you need to bake for his class of twenty students so they will each receive two muffins.

To make real-life problems become more like the word problems your child will read in her textbooks, consider writing them down. At first, you might tell your child the problem verbally before you write it down. After she hears you describe the problem, encourage her to put it into her own words for you to write down. Using this written problem, you can work together to discuss the math needed to find a solution. Later, she can actually use self-constructed word problem formats when she wants to calculate the best cell phone plan for the family or a budget for her allowance.

The goal is for your child to see math as a way to solve real problems, analyze data, and communicate information. If she is introduced to word problems in authentic settings and sees how you and other people she admires use math to solve problems expressed as words, she will understand the value of the ones she is required to solve in class. These textbook problems may not apply to her life, but she will recognize that working on them is reasonable because she will have experienced real-world problems in the same format.

Your child may have difficulty with word problems even if he is good at math calculations. If his first introduction to this type of math is in a class that doesn't include learning strength differentiation, or if he has not yet developed one of the information-processing skills needed to solve word problems, he will face some challenges. You can help him in partnership with his teacher or independently at home by looking for the causes of his difficulties.

Solving word problems requires persistence and risk taking. Any difficulty your child has with any aspect of mathematics or arithmetic is likely to be magnified with word problems. Is he confused by the vocabulary or sentence structure, or by determining what the problem is asking him to do? Is it hard for him to decide which information is important, and which words and numbers are included in the word problem but not needed to find the solution? Can he understand what the problem is asking him to do, but is unable to remember which of the math procedures he knows can help him solve the problem? Does organizing information clearly on paper challenge him? Does he know how to make notes so he doesn't have to keep facts or numbers in working memory while doing more complex procedures and calculations?

If you feel that your child knows the math, but can't understand what the question is asking or how to process the information, consider making a list of the possible issues. As you work with your child on word problems she finds confusing, jot down some notes that describe her difficulty and possibly link it to one of the categories described in the preceding paragraph. Write down the math problem number and textbook page for future reference. Look for patterns that point to her area of difficulty that you can bring to her teacher's attention, along with the observation notes you prepare.

RACER Strategy

Most children can increase their success at word problems by applying a system to all such problems. RACER is an acronym I created for math problem approaches for my math students. You can use RACER to help your child follow a plan when approaching word problems: **R**ead, **A**sk (yourself), **C**alculate, **E**stimate, and **R**epeat.

1. **Read** the problem completely without writing anything down (AS learners may prefer to read it aloud quietly). After the first reading, go back and select the information you think will help you solve the problem. Underline or make a list of this information. Some VSK learners are distracted by lots of words and can approach the problem more clearly when they cross out information that they determine is not essential to solving the problem. When reading the problem, it may help your child to look for cue *words* that are directions to add, subtract, multiply, or divide, at noted in Chapter 11.

2. **Ask** yourself what you are asked to find and what procedures or operations you need to do to answer the question. What information do you need to answer the question?
Once you translate words into the symbols of math, such as plus, minus, and equal signs, write these symbols above the words so they don't have to be held in your working memory. (Depending on your child's age and learning strength, you can explain that when he writes down these symbols, he frees up more *work*ing memory to do the *work* of solving the problem.)

3. **Calculate** the math needed to reach a solution.

4. **Estimate** the answer and see if your calculated answer is logical. VSK learners who do best with a global overview first might prefer

to estimate an answer before solving the problem and then check back to see if their calculated answer is close to the estimated answer.

5. **Repeat** or resolve the problem with your answer to see if your solution fits the question that you were asked.

What Are Your Child's Best Strategies?

As a parent, you have the advantage of using your child's learning strengths and discovering which problem-solving strategies are most effective for him. With that information, you can help your child remember his own "superpower strategies" to focus his brain's strength on solving problems. You'll find out what works best by trying the following strategies at home and observing and noting which work best.

Simplify: Take the same problem, but substitute simple whole numbers in place of the numbers in the problem and see if that makes it clear to your child which procedure to use. For example: A farmer has a 6.5-acre parcel of land and wants to give $1/3$ of it to his son. How many acres will he give to his son? This problem has decimals and fractions that can be changed to whole numbers in a simplified version: A farmer has a 6-acre parcel of land and wants to give half of it to his son. How many acres will he give to his son? After recognizing that the problem in simplified form is asking what is $1/2$ of 6, your child can put back the original numbers and calculate $1/3$ x 6.5 because he knows the cue word "of" usually means "multiply" when fractions are involved.

Pattern Recognition: VSK learners are particularly responsive to patterns, but all children learn and recognize information through pattern matching of new data with stored information. Your child can develop the habit of strengthening his mind's natural pattern-seeking response by asking himself what the problem reminds him of that he has seen or done before.

Chart or Diagram: All learners should try to create a diagram or chart to model a problem they are stuck on and see if that simplifies or clarifies what information is provided and what information they need to find. VSK learners may add sketches to their charts depicting what is happening in the problem, and AS learners may choose to use a more formal graphic organizer.

Visualize or Rewrite: AS learners may find it useful to tell themselves the problem in their own words and perhaps write it down in those new words. VSK learners can visualize the problem before drawing a diagram or chart.

Child-to-Child Advice

When I asked my seventh-grade math students what advice they would give to parents or to younger students to help them with word problems, they offered insightful suggestions. I share their expertise with you as you take on the challenge of helping your child with word problems specifically, and with mathematics in general. Here are their suggestions:

What are some of your best word-problem strategies?

- *Take good notes, and check my notes to see if we did similar problems in class.*
- *Don't rush; take my time.*
- *Draw diagrams.*
- *Read the chapter before doing the problems.*
- *Organization is life saving.*
- *Make a picture of it in my mind.*
- *Check my work.*
- *Read the whole problem before jumping into it.*

What are the best things your parents did to help you with word problems?

- *They were patient.*
- *They said positive things that motivated me to keep trying.*
- *They related the problems to something interesting.*
- *They taught me to write out my plan before starting to solve the problem.*
- *My parents help me best because they really knew how my mind works.*

GOAL SETTING

Ask your child to tell you his goals and dreams without limiting himself to what he thinks is realistic or possible for him to attain. Write these goals on a wall chart, and when he needs motivation to persevere, help him understand that learning the math today might help him achieve or be successful at one of his goals later. Using these visions of the future as personal connections to what he is learning will add a positive expectancy to the way he relates to his studies. This positive attitude will actually change his brain neurochemistry—with dopamine release increasing his brain's likelihood of remembering the new learning.

Share your optimism with validating comments, such as, "I see in you a child who will do (one of his goals or dreams) some day." He will personalize your confidence in him and build his own optimism. In a wonderful cycle, his responsiveness and increased engagement to the activity will in turn motivate you to persevere, because you also have the intrinsic satisfaction of success as his learning guide. This cycle continues. Optimism influences learning success, which increases optimism and more learning.

If your child's interest lends itself to advanced or independent work in any area where practice will result in greater mastery (such as sports, playing an instrument, or matching states and capitals), you can encourage him to recognize the result of his practice. Each time he experiences greater success through practice, he'll feel more capable and self-confident. He'll begin to recognize that practice and repetition yield tangible results. With these confidence-builders, he will feel capable of setting goals in math and putting in the extra work because he has experienced the intrinsic satisfaction of practicing to achieve goals.

14

TEST PREPARATION STRATEGIES: MATH (ALL AGES)

Prediction activities help your child learn what to study for a math test. Encourage your child to predict what information from his text, homework, and notes will most likely be on the test. He should try to check the accuracy of his predictions and judgment by writing them down before the test and later comparing what he predicts to the actual test questions. Prediction builds motivation by increasing personal connection with the outcome. Children want to see if their predictions were correct, so your child will be authentically interested in going back and looking at his test predictions. This will be an opportunity to review both the missed material and the accuracy of his predictions. When he builds prediction skills, he'll build study efficiency.

As with all tests, preparation builds confidence and success. Most children don't enjoy studying for tests, and many put it off until the night before. As a result, information is kept in memory only long enough to take the test, but not long enough to become retained in long-term memory.

You can help your child plan a successful study schedule and then use personalized strategies and shared activities to turn study times into productive, brain-friendly skill- and concept-building sessions. Using prediction, visualization, and test fortification, test preparation becomes productive for the long run—far beyond test day.

STRATEGY REVIEW

Help your child look back at an ongoing list she keeps about her learning strengths and the strategies that have helped her succeed on math tests in the past. During the unit overview, you can reduce anxiety and build self-assurance (open her brain's filters and increase memory retrieval) by identifying strategies she has used before that support her learning style strengths and that are likely to be useful on this test.

After determining which strategies will be most useful, help her sustain her memory of and confidence in the strategy by using it on some practice problems. She can try doing the odd-numbered problems in her text, which usually have the answers in the back, or go to the website offered by her math textbook's publisher that pairs with her book to find worked-out solutions to some of the homework problems.

Regarding these strategies, your child will be more responsive if you "ask, don't tell." In other words, ask him which strategies on his list he thinks will be best, and ask him to show you examples from the chapter where the strategy will apply. See if you can guide him to patterns in his math test errors, such as not writing down steps of a problem so he loses track of a negative or positive sign, or not circling the plus and minus signs before doing the problems so he confuses which procedure to do and adds when he should subtract.

VISUALIZATION

Discuss with your child what test day will look, sound, and feel like. Help her visualize walking into the room with a positive attitude, feeling refreshed from a good night's sleep, nourished by a good breakfast, and confident because she studied the facts and developed a test-taking plan. She can extend the visualization by listening closely to the verbal directions her teacher gives before the test instead of rushing into the test, and by asking for explanations of any confusing instructions.

Just as memory formation requires information to pass through the brain's emotional filter in the amygdala, retrieving memories needed for test answers also requires that the stored information pass through these same filters. If test stress shuts down the filters and puts your child in the fight/flight/freeze mode, her brain will be in the *reactive* nonthinking state. Test success requires her brain to be in the *reflective* state, so she can use her highest thinking networks to connect her patterns of stored knowledge with the new input—the test question.

Practice visualization with your child where she pictures something that makes her feel very good so she wants to keep that thought. When she practices this positive visualization successfully with as many senses as possible, she will have the capacity to self-calm when test anxiety shuts down her memory retrieval. She will be able to settle herself into the reflective, instead of the helpless reactive, state.

TEST FORTIFICATION

Once instructions are clear to her, during the test your child might benefit from writing down (in the margins or at the top of the answer paper) all the important formulas or procedures she thinks will be needed for test success, such as 10 millimeters equal 1 centimeter or 4 quarts equal 1 gallon. She might also write down any mnemonics or memory-prompting poems or sketches she uses to remember steps in a process. Writing these down before even looking at the test will decrease her anxiety and take the pressure off her working memory. She won't have to recall these formulas each time she solves another problem and will have more of her brain power to focus on the process itself.

Just before I give the first test of the year, I implement a strategy I learned from a master teacher, Bob Tierney. I lower stress by lightening the mood. I hand out a Skittles candy to each child and tell the class they are brain pills to make them smarter. When a child ultimately says, "These are just candy," I comment, "See? They are working already." Positive expectancy changes brain neurochemistry and increases dopamine release. Whatever you think will raise your child's spirits before he leaves the house on test day will raise his test focus.

Remind your child about the activities he uses at home to restore his brain chemicals and suggest that even thirty-second mini–brain breaks during the test will help restore neurotransmitters. He might stop, drink some water, take a deep breath, look at something pleasurable out the window, and visualize his success.

Just as your child may benefit by writing down memory prompts before the test, she may also find it useful to write her best strategy reminders in the margins before starting the test. One of my top math students always wrote on top, "Did I check my answers?" Other suggested reminders my students use include: "Did I copy the problems correctly? Remember to put units in my answer? Use the right operation? Put my answers in the right places?"

AFTER THE TEST IS RETURNED

Many children look at their test grades first, ask their friends what grades they received, then stuff the test in their backpack or binder without looking at any teacher comments or the problems they got right and wrong. You can help your child by going over the problems when tests are returned. Start by acknowledging the problems he got right and asking which strategies he used that helped him. He can then add this information to his strategy list. Next, check his predictions as described as part of test preparation and encourage him to be proud of his successful predictions.

Next, read the teacher's comments and discuss them. When moving on to test errors, encourage your child not to see them as failures, but rather as opportunities to learn. Remind her that this is one of many math tests she'll take throughout her school years and just the beginning of the mathematics she'll use throughout her life. By making the error and correcting it now, she'll be changing the course of her own future for years to come, because she may avoid making that type of mistake in the future. That is a powerful and encouraging message.

PART IV:

Social Studies and Science

15
IGNITING INTEREST IN SCIENCE AND SOCIAL STUDIES (ALL AGES)

PROBLEMS WITH SCIENCE AND HISTORY IN OUR SCHOOLS

There is no greater loss to your child resulting from the teach-to-the-test, rote-fact instruction than that which is taking place in science and social studies. Your child is not experiencing science through experiments, discovery, demonstrations, and field trips. Similarly, instead of understanding history and geography through engaging activities that teach your child about various perspectives and how to use critical analysis skills, he is probably memorizing dates and names without context and meaning.

I asked my daughter, who successfully graduated high school last year after thirteen years in the current public school system, if she could tell me the causes of any of the wars in history, or even put into chronological sequence the wars fought on American soil. I asked her the purpose of the metabolism of glucose in animal cells and why plant cells that carry out photosynthesis. Her grades from K–12 were fine, and college at the University of California is going well for her, but she could not answer my questions. She knew lots of facts, but she had a limited sense of the scope, reasons, and concepts of these important subjects.

I wish I'd known earlier what I know now about helping children develop authentic understanding *of* science and social studies instead of just memorizing facts *about* these subjects.

Your child is learning how to take science and history tests based on these facts, but she may not be learning how to evaluate data, make deductions or predictions, and solve problems. In addition, with more emphasis placed on math and literacy tests, science and history are losing class hours, and large blocks of time are rarely available in elementary school for investigations, experimentation, or open-ended class discussions. These activities are necessary so that children can link personally with the subject matter and see the interconnectedness of history and science with their lives and the world they live in. The loss of creative thinking and opportunities for analysis, exploration, and discovery learning is reducing our children's interest, as well as proficiency, in these subjects.

Fortunately, I can pass on to you what I learned too late for my own child, so your child will not miss out on the awesome concepts of science and the deep understanding of history that can enrich his daily life. You can raise the bar for what he gets out of these subjects by doing what only a parent can do best—building bridges of interest and learning strengths that motivate your child to persevere through these challenging subjects to reach self-valued goals. Children need the opportunity to experience real success by achieving challenges they believe are significant. When they are motivated by confidence, rather than fear, and learn to equate their effort with goal progress, they pay more attention, are likely to believe in their abilities, and achieve their highest potential. In the following chapters, you will find activities, inquiries, and games that you can use to give your child something positive on which to focus. With your help, your child will go beyond memorizing facts to develop a sense of science and history that will become the foundation for future learning in all subjects and in life.

SCIENCE, HISTORY, EVERYWHERE

One of the first things you can do in order to open up the worlds of science and history is to create an atmosphere of discussion and learning in which your child *wants* to participate. And when you show sincere interest in his questions and opinions, you open doors that are closing in his classrooms.

Here are some ideas to get you thinking:

- When your child expresses interest about future careers, point out how success in those careers benefits from strong background knowledge in history or science and the logical, inductive, deductive, and relational thinking skills that these studies build. Invite friends for dinner who use these thinking skills and knowledge in their interesting work. Encourage your dinner guests to share their early frustrations and challenges, as well as their success stories, to help inspire your child, because such inspiration may not happen in the classroom.

- Share your appreciation of science- and social studies–related activities. Comment about the physics of leverage when you move heavy boxes with a dolly. Reveal your interest in history by reading aloud from the morning paper about a new archeological discovery. Explain what you find interesting, and ask your child's opinion. Follow up on any questions he asks and acknowledge the importance of his questions by looking for information about which he inquires in books or on the Internet. Whatever you do to sustain his curiosity and wonder will increase his connection to science and history classes at school.

- When you are with your child, look for science and social studies in the real world. Help him make the connection that these school subjects can provide tools he can use to understand and discover what is happening around him. Before your child starts a school unit about the ocean, for example, you might keep an eye out for ocean-related information. If you see a picture of an ocean on a billboard, ask him something like this: "I wonder what the world would be like without oceans?" or "What would you miss if there were no oceans?" or "What is your favorite ocean animal, and how do you think it could change to adapt to life on dry land?"

- If your child uses words in your discussions that could be replaced by more scientific terms, consider the opportunity to increase his scientific vocabulary. You might respond to his comments by repeating part of his statements back to him, substituting the scientific word for the one he used without drawing attention to it as a correction. Simply substitute the scientific term in your conversation. If he asks,

"I wonder what would become of the crabs and lobsters if there were no oceans?" you could respond, "Do you think those *crustaceans* could adapt to life on dry land?"

CONNECTING YOUR CHILD TO SCHOOL UNITS OF STUDY (ALL AGES)

The following are some general principles you can use to plan and carry out brain-friendly history and science activities. These principles activate prior knowledge, connect with personal interests, and relate school topics to the real world, all of which will promote your child's interest, motivation, and long-term memory. Each time you help your child recall and link her past experiences to new information, you help her build stronger long-term relational memories and increase her school success and enjoyment.

Prior Knowledge Activation

KWL

KWL are the first letters of "Know–Want–Learned," a strategy first mentioned in Chapter 6. Here's how to use it: Create a three-column chart. Fill in the first two columns with what your child already **K**nows and **W**ants to know, and fill in the third column later with what he **L**earns.

K: Ask your child what he already *Knows* about the science or social studies topic, and add to the list as he thinks of things he remembers during the course of the unit.

W: Ask your child to suggest questions about what he *Wants* to know about the topic.

L: After your discussions, investigations, and his classroom experiences, add your child's comments about what he **L**earned to the chart.

Interviews

Enjoy playing interview games to help your child remember information he already knows that connects him to the topics he is currently (or will soon be) studying in school. Take this situation: You know your family traveled to the Grand Canyon when your daughter was five, but she may not recall the trip very well. Play a fun game in which you act as a television interviewer and she is the guest on your show, and ask her questions to prompt her brain to activate those memories in a fun context.

Personalize

Personalizing new information activates prior knowledge and increases the brain's internal scanning of its stored memory categories and patterns that relate to the topic. When your child starts a new unit, you can explore ways he will want to "enter" the topic through interest-related motivation. Talk to him about his ideas first. For example, you may already have found websites and books that enrich the history or science topics, but start by seeing what your child suggests. Your child builds ownership of learning when he takes an active role. When he sees the relevance and potential uses of what he is learning, he becomes an involved participant instead of a passive recipient of information without context—information that he can't connect with his brain's networks of previously stored patterns of personal knowledge and experiences.

You can also personalize the information by making the topic relevant and meaningful to where you live. If you live near the cornfields and your child is studying seeds, for example, he will be more engaged if you use a familiar corn seed to plant at home. If you live in Alaska, connecting pollution studies to the Exxon Valdez oil spill disaster via old newspaper stories or conversations with tourist bureaus or wildlife preservationists helps your child relate personally to the topic.

Wondering

You can also use "I wonder" or "What do you think might…?" comments to start personalized conversations about the topic he's studying as you take a walk for a syn-*naps*. Prevent the activity from feeling too much like homework through your phrasing and tone of voice and by avoiding direct questions. For example, instead of asking directly about the topic he's studying, offer up some sincere curiosities you have. This will help your child feel comfortable discussing the information he remembers, and can prompt a thoughtful guess. With you, unlike at school, he will not fear consequences of an incorrect answer. You might say, "I wonder what might be the lightest bird?" "What do you think could be the largest planet?" or "How heavy do you think it might be compared to the earth?" or "What do you think is the longest river in the world?"

You can prepare your questions by skimming through the current chapter in your child's text or the one his class will study next. You don't need to know or say the answers even if you do know them. Your child will learn more from your modeling of what you do when you are curious about something than if you just tell him an answer. And if you don't know the answers, you can set an example. When he sees you go to the dictionary, textbook, or Internet for information, he will recognize those as **re**_sources_—not _sources_ of boring homework assignments. He also learns more interesting sidelights about topics that may have been omitted from the school curriculum because they are not answers to standardized test questions. It is often these side stories that make a topic interesting and inspiring and clarify the relationship between the specific topic and the big picture in science or social studies.

You can also ask hypothetical questions to stimulate his thinking: "If you could have dinner with (fill in the name of a historical person or scientist) what would you ask him/her?" "What would you tell the person (if he/she is long dead) about how things have changed in their field?" "What would you tell the person that he or she could have used back when making the political decisions or conducting the scientific experiments about which you are learning?"

AS learners may be pulled into this kind of "wondering" by starting with something that you read aloud and they visualize. Again, phrase your suggestion as a game, not an assignment. After reading a passage from his text or a topic-related source, say something like, "Have you ever imagined yourself as someone else? I used to imagine I was an astronaut walking on the moon." Or "What do you see when you imagine yourself as _____?" (Fill in the name of an historical figure or scientist whose research your child is studying in school.)

VSK learners will enjoy looking at pictures in a book or on the Internet related to a school topic as a bridge to the academic subject. During a syn-_naps_, your child can tell you her thoughts about what she imagines is taking place in the picture or what may have happened to the person or animal or in the scene just before the picture was painted or photograph was taken.

These wonderings about pictures can also include movement as your child mimics some part of the picture, portraying the person, place, or animal.

As with AS learners, your VSK child may need you to start off the "wonderings" game by describing what you see in the picture and what it makes you wonder about.

Entice through Interest

Information passes through the limbic system into long-term memory quickly and successfully when it is associated with positive emotional experiences. Your child will reach states of excited interest and emotional comfort when her topics of study at school are connected with things or places in which she is already interested.

This is also a way to get kids into subjects about which they may have negative feelings. Cross-curricular (also called thematic or interdisciplinary) investigations provide your child with opportunities to start with his interests and expand into areas that correspond to the units in school that may not be of high interest. With this strategy, your child's learning strength or interest will pull him into an area of lesser interest through exploration; problem solving; and discovery games, activities, and investigations. If art is included in a social studies topic, for example, your young artist can be more motivated to relate to the history. Making posters of cave paintings or Native American art could be a way of connecting artistic or VSK learners to the study of that historical period or geographic region. This positive introduction to the topic will be accompanied by a more optimistic belief in her potential to understand the unit. Even if she has not had positive past experiences in history, she will be empowered by engaging in an art project for this lesson. Her brain filters won't shut down during the lessons and reading, so her memory and comprehension will increase. This will lead to confidence, interest, competence, and then to higher achievement in the subject.

Here's another example: If your child loves mathematics, lure him into history by having him plan for a fictional wagon train trip across the country during the Westward Expansion movement. He can be the head of the wagon train party and can use mathematics to plan the quantities of supplies needed and the different rates of travel based on various terrains or weather conditions. Your child will be pulled into the pleasures of history through the mathematics of travel. And if your child isn't interested in either math or history but loves adventure, the frontier exploration element may pull him in.

Your Child, the Expert

If your child has a particular topic of high interest, and you encourage him to develop that interest into expertise, you'll both be surprised at how being an authority can connect him to topics of school study across different subject areas. If he knows boats, he will be called upon to help classmates when they want to know what kind of boat is best for the diagram they need to make for their explorer project. If he knows a lot about bats, he'll be the go-to guy when his scout troop camps near a bat cave on an overnight. He will have the confidence-building experience of what it feels like to know more about something than anyone around, including his teachers and parents.

Real-World Connections

Real-world connections can make any exploration more personal and brain-friendly. Try this spin on opening up the real world: Consider people you know whom you might visit at their places of work or whom you might invite for dinner to expand the real-world meaning of a topic. For example, if your child likes reading and writing, a theme such as communication could connect her to a related topic in science (sound, the senses, machines) or social studies (historical research, Westward Expansion and the telegraph or Pony Express, communication through history, propaganda, use of codes during wartime).

People who could enliven the theme of communication would include newspaper reporters, book editors, authors, radio or television professionals, post office workers, foreign language translators, computer programmers, sign language instructors, poets, 911 emergency communication workers, singers, songwriters, and code analysts (cryptographers). You'll be surprised at how your friends' professions and hobbies relate to your child's thematic studies when you consider the many ways that topics, such as communication, health, or transportation, connect to the real-world activities of people you know. You might consider pooling resources with friends by trading off short-term mentoring of each other's children on subjects they are studying in school of which you have special knowledge, experience, or interest.

Using Learning Strengths to Make Subjects Come Alive

Social studies and science success for children who are weak in or not interested in these areas can be achieved by connecting them to the topic through their learning strengths in addition to their interests. Planning an activity to engage your child's learning strength before she starts challenging units of study in school builds her self-confidence, motivation, and success.

AS learners enjoy audio books about their science or social studies topics, as well as discussions or projects with sequential instructions so your child can follow the plan. She will relate well to the sequences in history or the processes in a science investigation through timelines and discussing her ideas with you.

Even though AS learners respond well to auditory input, they may not have the memory development to remember the information they enjoy listening to. Your child can create useful study aids by writing notes, creating graphic organizers, or tape recording his verbal summaries of what he learned in school that day. When he explains his notes or graphic organizers to you or a younger sibling, the audio processing stimulates the building of relational memories of the day's lessons and reading.

Another useful audio tool is the Garage Band software on Macintosh computers. Your child can use the software to create a news podcast or even a dramatized dialogue or interview in which he is the expert you interview about the topic of your radio show.

Making a recording before the formal unit begins in school allows your child to focus on his personal interest or connect his prior knowledge to the unit. If the topic is states of matter (gas, liquid, or solid), for example, and he likes hot air balloons, he can act as the reporter from the annual New Mexico Balloon Festival and describe the sequence of activity as he looks through a book or website about the festivities. He can explore the type of gas that becomes the "air" in these hot air balloons as he makes his audio recording or podcast. These early activities will engage your child's learning strength before he starts the challenging unit of study and increase his interest, motivation, and success.

VSK learners often see possibilities and relationships others do not. At home, you can give your child the chance to follow these ideas with games, activities, inquiries, and discussions so she will create memory patterns that incorporate the new information into long-term memory.

Your VSK learner may enjoy taking things apart and reassembling them; playing games; following maps; visiting museums; building models; conducting experiments; watching historical or nature television shows/videos; doing Internet explorations; examining or creating photos, drawings, posters, models, and collages; and participating in science projects that go beyond "cookbook" predictability. Your VSK learner can also use a he is the expert you interview about the topic of your radio show camera to take photographs of things that fall into a category she is learning about in science (solids, liquids, gases), geography (igneous, metamorphic, and sedimentary rock), or history (objects that represent each of the rights in the Bill of Rights).

He can be more connected to class lessons when he uses Internet exploration, library books, and his ability to see the big picture by relating school lessons to his perceptions of the world around him. He may enjoy map drawing; creating graphic organizers of cycles in science; or connecting with a historical period through its art, clothing, and artifacts. You can encourage your child to immerse himself in a time period, country, or scientific topic of study by helping him decorate his room with items reflecting that culture or country, such as travel posters, maps, and photographs or topic-related science posters, plants, or pictures of microscopic enlargement of cells downloaded from the Internet.

Physical activities connected to school subjects are enjoyable for most VSK children. They can be syn-*naps* activities that add new brain references for storage of the information. In science, your child can move like a planet around a beach-ball sun or an electron around an atom's nucleus. When studying the differences between solids, gases, and liquids, he can move objects, such as marbles, to represent the space increasing between atoms from dense solids, to less-dense liquids, and least-dense gases.

Games, sports, cooking, woodwork, sewing, arts, and crafts bring history alive for VSK learners by activating their sense of touch and movement and turning on their learning strengths. Your child can cook a recipe from the historical period, sew a costume for a doll from the period of study, and use the doll as a prop in a recreation of specific historical events or daily life during that period. She can search the Internet with you for the games played during that period. My class celebrated "Colony Day" by working in groups or individually to learn a game, such as tug-of-war, played by children during Colonial times and then teaching the game to classmates.

Because his mind relates to concepts and abstractions, your VSK learner may need help memorizing specific information on which he will be tested, such as dates, animal kingdom classifications, or names of battles. Your child may have a wonderful overview of the causes and conflicts that led up to a war, the battle strategies that were most successful, and the people who influenced the course of events, giving him the knowledge to make future political decisions, but he may need you to help him connect these to the details of the rote facts he needs to know for the test.

Share Learning-Strength Information with Your Child and Your Child's Teacher

When you observe which learning activities work best for your child, consider writing notes about instances when you see him using a strategy that suits his learning strength. At a convenient time after the activity, ask him how he felt about the learning activity you shared and see if he is open to a discussion about why he thinks it worked for him.

Learning should feel good, and helping him be aware of the good feelings adds emotional power to the knowledge and reinforces the neural network. There is no need to respond or interpret for him by saying things like, "So, you do learn better when the television is off or when you make diagrams from your notes." That is the "I-told-you-so" message that is a turn-off and robs your child of ownership of self-knowledge.

If you see a pattern in your notes over time, consider showing him your notes or having a chat where he can add his thoughts, draw his own conclusions, and take ownership of his learning strategy. Through this guided self-discovery of his learning strengths and best strategies, your child will feel more in control of his learning and move toward the goal of being a self-directed, independent learner.

If you see that your child is more responsive to learning history by making diagrams and graphic organizers instead of taking notes in outline form, consider showing evidence of his preferred strategy and your observation notes to his teacher and find out if your son can continue with this variation of note taking as long as he shows the expected progress on learning assessments. If your daughter can explain complex scientific concepts to you clearly and precisely, with accurate scientific vocabulary, but has a hard time writing the information down during timed tests, perhaps explaining this to her teacher will result in an accommodation. It may be possible for her to write as much as she can during the test time and demonstrate her knowledge of the remaining questions orally during break or lunch period that day.

ELEMENTS OF A SUCCESSFUL SCIENCE AND SOCIAL STUDIES ACTIVITY

In the next two chapters, you'll find specific ideas for home enrichment or improvement in science and social studies, but first I'd like you to consider the following neuro-*logical* characteristics of successful home-to-school bridges. Activities in which your child sees for herself the connections between what she learns in school and her own experiences greatly increase the chances of remembering what she learns. This is possible with all academic subjects; opportunities for science and history activities are literally all around you.

Multisensory Activities

When your child experiences subject matter information through multiple senses, the information is stored in several different memory banks and is more easily retrieved. Multisensory activities include games, humor, art, movement, play, music, letter writing, problem solving, and other opportunities to incorporate factual knowledge with your enjoyable times together.

An example of a multisensory activity is the simulation of a historic battle. The preparation for the simulation involves understanding and discussing the reasons for the battle, who was involved, where it took place, and what strategies were used. Through this preparation for an activity he knows he will enjoy, your child learns the facts he needs for class. As he arranges action figures, acts out the role of a soldier on the front lines, or makes plans as a general for the coming battle, the facts become memories.

For a science topic, such as magnetism, multisensory activities can include exploration of a variety of magnets and various substances, followed by the option of making notes in a graphic organizer, drawing sketches, or summarizing hypotheses orally. Investigations can cross over from science to geography if she uses a compass and learns about the difference between true north and the magnetic North Pole, and how compasses work. Magnetism also becomes relevant to your child's real world when looking at MRI (magnetic resonance imaging) scans available on Internet sites. Compelling images of human anatomy, mummies, painting authentication, and examination of ancient artifacts show exciting modern scientific uses of magnetism.

Games

The effectiveness of games is enhanced when your child helps design them. As a change-of-pace syn-*naps*, try helping your child modify a game he enjoys by relating it to science or social studies. For example, modify the mystery game Clue by turning facts about states being studied or scientific processes (water cycle, metamorphosis, properties of electric circuits) into clues. Modify the names of the streets on a Monopoly game to the names of places he is studying in social studies. A game can be a great springboard for a learning session, or a way to resume a session with positive feelings after a syn-*naps*.

Games can also build patterning skills and improve sequencing ability for all children and are particularly helpful for VSK learners who need practice following procedural steps and remembering sequences. Learning magic tricks, building Lego constructions following increasingly complex instructions, and playing matching games like Concentration using a deck of cards all build memory and patterning skills. Encourage your child to teach you a new game. This sharing of expertise and explaining instructions in a sequence builds confidence and helps your child feel more comfortable speaking up in class discussions.

Preschool games that are consistent with practicing procedures or patterning for science and social studies include LeapFrog, Dora the Explorer, Educational Insights Smart Games like North Pole Camouflage Game, and Geoboards. Early-elementary games include the more advanced LeapFrog games, Blokus Strategy board game, SET game, and Tangrams.

Just a few of the many excellent upper-elementary games include Oceanopoly, Brain Quest Around the World Game, Where in the World, MoneyWise Kids, Dino-Opoly, Learning Resources Planet Quest, Risk, Scientific Explorer's Disgusting Science: A Kit of the Science of Revolting Things, Snap Circuits, Questionary, the Making Inferences game, and games described in *Changing Pace: Outdoor Games for Experiential Learning* by Carmine M. Consalvo.

Humor

Laughter releases dopamine and endorphins, and the associated feelings of pleasure and increased positive emotional memory helps learned material hook into the brain. For example, when using visualization to remember new scientific vocabulary or the names of explorers, encourage your child to visualize a funny, bizarre image, such as "Ma**gell**an with lots of ***gel in*** his hair."

MOVEMENT

Movement involves multiple memory systems for better recall. VSK learners especially love it, but all children can benefit from movement. In science, your child can move through the water cycle like flowing water, evaporating steam, and precipitating snow or rain. She can wiggle parts of her body as you name parts of a plant (roots, stem, leaves, flower) or parts of an ant (head, thorax, abdomen). In geography, your child can enjoy a syn-*naps* by searching for household objects that have the country of manufacture on them, such as clothes, electronics, packaged ethnic foods, or toys. She can then locate the country on a wall map of the world and mark the country with a pushpin.

Conversations for Authentic Learning

Your child will experience greater levels of understanding when he talks, explains, and debates with you, instead of passively listening to a lecture or reading a text. Studies repeatedly correlate children's academic success, health, and avoidance of drugs and excessive alcohol with families who regularly eat dinner together. A University of Michigan study found family time together, even more than time spent studying, was the highest predictor of academic success and low behavioral problems in children ages three to twelve. So why not combine family dinners and conversations for learning?

Making a sudden switch from casual family dinners to discussion-centered dinners will seem unnatural and unappealing. Transitioning to more academic discussions can start with themed dinners or dinners in fun locations. A picnic on the living room floor with candles or a theme dinner where everyone wears a hat brings positive emotions to dinnertimes and starts the transition to discussion-centered dinners. Plastic tablecloths and wet-erase pens can engage your younger child in drawing about a school topic he discusses or describes.

When you are ready for a more academic tradition, try playing "Who Am I?" In this game, each person gets the name of a famous person pinned to his or her back. Family members see the name, but the wearer does not. Each person can ask questions to figure out who he or she is, such as, "Did I invent anything?" The game continues until all family members "identify" their characters.

A word of caution: As you gradually promote more academic discussions at mealtime or during car drives and walks, don't let the conversation veer into a practice quiz or an interrogation session about school. Instead of asking, "How was your day?" try to engage your child in conversation that relates what she learned to something personal. "I saw that you are studying the chapter about pollution. Is there anything we can do in our home or neighborhood that would help the environment?" is more likely to get a response than "What did you study?" and may even lead to a family activity.

Topics for Conversations

Your daily newspaper or weekly news magazine probably contains articles you can relate to a school history or science unit. Consider selecting a short article to read or summarize at dinner to promote conversation. Other sources of topics are "this day in history" facts found at historychannel.com/thisday. From these conversational prompts, family members can offer opinions and your child can make real use of the background material he reads in his text or hears in school when he contributes that knowledge to the conversation.

Thinking Out Loud

As you get into the habit of thinking and reasoning out loud, you will see your child use that same strategy as she builds her reasoning skills. Listening to her think out loud will also give you more insights into how she learns best.

The thinking aloud process can start during informal activities before you incorporate it into learning sessions related to school units. When you walk the dog together, your son may wonder, "Why does this one tree drop its leaves before the others?" "How do the construction planners know which asphalt is the best for our cold, snowy winters?" Soon you can do these think-aloud formats to encourage deeper thinking about school topics.

As you enjoy some of the following activities with your child to increase her connection with and knowledge about her science or social studies unit, you'll find that you spend less time nagging and more time enjoying the process of learning new things together.

16
SOCIAL STUDIES BEYOND THE CLASSROOM (ALL AGES)

You can usually find out from your child's textbooks or teacher what social studies unit her class will study next. With that information, consider which of the activities in this chapter might build her interest, curiosity, connection, and success regarding the topic she is about to study in school. The following activities are especially suitable for building knowledge and interest in social studies classes.

HEAR ALL ABOUT IT

AS learners

Read aloud newspaper stories together to find the five Ws (who, what, where, why, when), so your child will know what to include in his stories. A great syn-*naps* can be to examine newspapers from other countries, such as from the country your child is studying. (To find newspapers of the world, visit www.newspaperlinks.com/home.cfm.)

To increase your child's interest in the activity, you can preset your word-processing program to format documents in newspaper or news bulletin form, which allows your child to include digital pictures or ones he draws or copies from books.

- Create a book jacket or report cover that depicts information about the social studies topic (or scientist/science topic) your child hears and reads about.

- Sequential learners will enjoy creating PowerPoint presentations of historical or geographical images and facts.
- Make an audio recording about a time in history currently being studied, including radio or television reporter–styled stories, interviews, or commercials about the available goods of the time.

CREATE ART

VSK learners

Most children enjoy a variety of art activities, so art is often a successful "pull-in" to stimulate interest in a new topic at school. Consider any of the following suggestions as a potential bridge when your child can use a boost to support him through the coming unit of study.

- Create a mobile with aspects of the social studies topic. Add to it every day or so during a syn-*naps*.
- Build a model of the ancient ruin or geographical terrain using papier-mâché, sugar cubes, clay, or plaster of Paris.
- Make travel posters with original artwork or pictures from the Internet. Travel posters do not have to be limited to different countries. My students enjoy making posters advertising colonies, such as "Come to Jamestown, the Best Settlement in the New World." In science, travel posters can be modified to include "Come Visit an Atom" or "Travel the Circulatory System" or "Come to Jupiter, It's Out of This World." Your child can add details to the poster as the unit progresses.

READING BEYOND TEXTBOOKS

If your child enjoys reading but can't get excited about her textbooks, children's literature can open the door to the world of history. By reading historical fiction and biographies/autobiographies of the people who lived in or influenced the historical times she is studying, she can work her way into the topic. Suggestions for grade-level and topic-appropriate historical fiction are available from sources such as your child's teacher, school librarian, or community library or bookstore. Once your child finds an author whose books she enjoys, help her explore amazon.com or barnesandnoble.com, where she'll find additional recommendations for other books by the author or under the category, "Readers who enjoyed this book also liked…"

AS learners tend to prefer books that follow a clear sequence in time and may be "pulled into" a book if you read it aloud or take turns reading. If the book stimulated her curiosity about the time period, perhaps because it included children her age, encourage her to wonder aloud about her questions. She then might want to find out more about how school children then were similar to and different from children who are the same age today.

VSK learners are likely to prefer books with more illustrations or those that are more action-oriented. After your child reads a historical fiction book she enjoys, you might ask her what she thought was fact and what was fiction. If famous historical characters are in the book, she'll probably realize that casual dialogue is fictionalized. See if you can use her enjoyment of the book to promote her curiosity about finding out what information in the book was fact and what was fiction. If she is interested, you can suggest that you investigate together by looking at history texts or art books and visiting museums and websites.

DEVELOP HOBBIES AND INTERESTS

Many children develop interests in history or geography from the hobbies they already enjoy.

AS learners often find connections to history through hobbies, such as building model ships, weaving, cooking with historical recipes, and even learning the sequential development of dog, cat, or horse breeds.

VSK learners often find connections to history through hobbies, such as rock, stamp, and coin collecting. Other hobbies you can expose your VSK child to include sports or Olympic history, fashion, art history, and horticulture.

Each of these hobbies has connections to other parts of the world and earlier historical times that bridge to school units of study.

BE PART OF HISTORY

AS learners

Letter Exchange

If your child enjoys writing, she might like to compose a letter to you in which you play the role of a famous person in history or science. You can find appropriate factual information for your responses on Internet sites like www.askforkids.com. This activity could evolve into a letter exchange between you and your child, and sometimes she could act as the famous person. In those exchanges, you would write letters to her about your opinions and questions related to her character's role in history. In order to answer your letters, she would seek information from her textbook and class notes and pay more attention in class. These letter exchanges can be turned into reports assigned for class, and some teachers may be open to having the letter exchange serve as an alternative for the report format assignment.

Book It

Your child can plan, organize, illustrate (using drawings or digital images), write, or narrate a book for younger children about the school topic. This can be as simple or complex of a book as your child likes. If she selects a grade level for which to write her book, consider if any of your friends or relatives has children in that grade who might enjoy reading and commenting.

VSK learners

Pen Pals

Pen pals are a great way for your child to make real-world connections with children his own age in other states or countries he studies. Websites for pen pals include www.pen-pal.com/history.php (Internet pen pals) and www.ipfusa.com (letter-writing pen pals).

What if You Were There?

Your child may enjoy writing, drawing, creating a scrapbook, acting, or talking about how she may have experienced a time and place in history. Have her pretend she was in a profession that coincides with her real interests, such as a journalist, business consultant, architect, city planner, politician, environmentalist, teacher, artist, athlete, or even a wedding planner. A similar activity is for your child to pretend (with or without costume) that she is a major historical figure who responds in her own way to the conflicts, dilemmas, disasters, threats, or discoveries that her historical figure would have faced. Encourage her to explain whether her decisions are the same or different than those made by her character in history, and why.

THEME DAY!

A historical era or country theme of the day can be planned at home by connecting one day's meals, music, artwork, and games to a historical period or country, perhaps even including costumes. You can also read stories from that culture or country, watch a travel video, and play a popular game of that time or culture.

AS learners can plan for the day by interviewing senior citizens who lived through more recent historical times. Encourage your child to ask about their experiences during the Depression; World War II or subsequent wars; water shortages; or the impact of innovations like commercial flying, television, and computers on their lives.

VSK learners can incorporate dramatizations and simulations in the theme day. History can become visual and tactile when your child uses puppets, dolls, action figures, and stuffed or plastic animals to set up historical events and play them out. These dramatizations do not need elaborate planning, but they will motivate your child to read his books or notes so he can plan the action of the dramatization.

SIMULATIONS AND VIRTUAL TRAVEL

AS learners enjoy the planning, organizing, and sequencing provided by computer game simulations. Events such as the Oregon Trail movement, Lewis and Clark's expedition, and wagon-train travels during Westward

Expansion are available commercially, but you can also re-create these experiences for your child with props, diagrams, and discussions. She can use the facts from her text and notes to plan what she would need, what route to take, what dangers might occur, or what resources might be available along the way. The activity is enjoyable because your child gets to choose, plan, and make decisions.

Simulations can incorporate ideas suited to your child's interests and abilities.

1. Prepare a list of things and people your child wants to see, taste, explore, photograph, or experience on his virtual visit.
2. Find useful books and websites, such as www.field-guides.com, www.tramline.com, http://oops.bizland.com/vtours.htm, and www.nasa.gov.
3. The inquiry takes on personal meaning when your AS learner investigates, plans, and organizes ways to make the most of his virtual visit. What are the agricultural crops, fish, and animals native to the country that provide the ingredients for the foods he loves? How does the country's climate and geography influence these native resources?
4. What is the music like, and where can he go to hear performances? What are the country's exports and imports—especially related to his interests, or where you live if your city produces items exported to the place he is virtually visiting? The WorldWatcher website (www.worldwatcher.northwestern.edu) offers geographic visualization and data analysis programs best suited for students in upper-elementary school or above.
5. Travel plans: How far away from home is this new place, and what are the different ways of traveling there and the benefits of each (time, cost, convenience, most scenic routes of travel)? What are a few phrases of the language to help him get around? He can create a travel plan, budget, and itineraries of what to do and see in logical order based on location using maps and earth.google.com or maps.google.com.

6. When the planning is complete, he can take the whole family on his virtual tour, perhaps using a few phrases of the language and teaching you a few customs.

VSK learners enjoy Internet travel simulations, which can be powerful opportunities to personalize history and geography and to help your child build those long-term relational memories. She can virtually visit any place and time in history. It is easiest to start these adventures with an Internet visit to a present-day country or state your child is studying in school. For example, if the unit is the countries of Western Europe in the present day, your child might select the country with his favorite soccer team, favorite foods, or family heritage. He would then do the Internet exploration to virtually experience aspects of interest related to the location. Your child may enjoy keeping a record of her virtual trips in journals, PowerPoint presentations, pictorial travel books, or from the perspective of a photojournalist.

This simulation can follow the steps listed here or incorporate other ideas while eliminating suggestions that aren't suited to your child's interests or abilities.

1. Prepare a graphic organizer or brainstorm together about the people your child wants to see and what he wants to visit, eat, explore, photograph, or do on his virtual visit.
2. Find useful books and websites such as www.field-guides.com, www.tramline.com, http://oops.bizland.com/vtours.htm, and nasa.gov.
3. Which of your child's favorite activities or interests connect with the country? When is the best time of year to visit to see his team play soccer or to see the migration of the birds or whales that interest him? What unusual animals might he find, and where can he see them in their natural habitats (this can connect to a cross-curricular investigation of animal habitats, their needs, and adaptations)?
4. What natural and manmade things should he plan to see in addition to his main attraction? What museums or cultural events might be related to his interests?

5. Your child can take the whole family on his virtual tour, perhaps using the websites he used, his journal, or a PowerPoint presentation to show you the places he visited, people he met, animals he saw, sporting events he attended, and meals he ate.

6. You can celebrate his virtual return by going to a restaurant that serves that country's food or preparing a meal together that he "ate" on his simulated trip.

ANALYSIS OF HISTORY

Even your first or second grader can begin to analyze perspective, opinion, or bias related to history. Learning to evaluate the accuracy of different sources of historical information and developing his own opinion about the events he hears about in school is an extremely valuable tool.

Before children are motivated to investigate for bias of perspective, it helps if you show them examples of bias in writing. For example, going to Internet sites that claim that a cow can really jump over the moon will demonstrate to your child that anyone can claim information is true on the Internet, even when science and primary sources prove otherwise. Once your child sees dramatic examples of distorted historical perspectives on such websites, you can offer examples of more subtle misrepresentations of history to demonstrate the importance of distinguishing fact from opinion.

A great source of perspective bias can be found in outdated school textbooks from used bookstores or even in storage at your child's secondary school. History textbooks used in schools as recently as twenty-five years ago emphasize the ignorant, evil Indians who killed innocent settlers for no reason other than their savage natures. These textbooks written by non-Indians are eye-opening when children recognize the evident prejudice in these books compared to primary source materials that are now available on the Internet and in libraries.

Continue to engage your child's interest in recognizing the difference between fact and *opinion stated as fact* by reading together different descriptions of a current news, sports, or entertainment event in which he is interested. These comparisons are even more meaningful if your child can see the event or film or hear the music before reading the critics' responses.

Once your child realizes that opinion and perspectives influence the writing and interpreting of history, you can build his skills of understanding events from the perspective of others. This builds his empathy and ability to relate successfully with people who don't share his perspectives.

AS Learners Analyze History with In-Depth Explorations

Thanks to the library and Internet, AS learners who enjoy delving into areas of interest in greater depth have access to firsthand written accounts, diaries, letters, newspaper articles, photographs, audio and video news clips, and other documents of historical events. Children can look at the same sources historians use to form their interpretations of history. The Library of Congress website (www.loc.gov) offers a bounty of such documents and even features recordings you can download.

Starting with a personal interest, such as baseball, your child can find the original baseball programs from the days of Babe Ruth and read different columnists' opinions about his physical abilities and social behaviors. From there, your child might become interested in the political climate of the time and what events were taking place that may have influenced how people felt about Babe Ruth. Then, he can express his own opinion about Babe Ruth's character and decide if that changes his regard for the athlete's performance in his sport.

VSK Learners Analyze History as They See, Touch, and Move

The most powerful memories of social studies come from multisensory experiences, such as taking tours of a city hall or courthouse; attending local government meetings; visiting local historical sites, museums, and monuments; taking trips to places of historical prominence in states formed from the original thirteen colonies; and touring federal government agencies and buildings where history is memorialized (such as the Lincoln Memorial) and where history is being created (as on the floor of Congress).

Other places where your children can connect with social studies include the archives of a newspaper office, courthouse, or post office;

ethnic restaurants; old cemeteries; and public events sponsored by historical preservation or reenactment organizations.

If you are traveling by car to more distant historical sites, history and geography can be found en route by looking at different license plates and finding the state on a map of the United States. Your child can mark your driving route on his map before the trip and prepare a few surprising facts to share about the states as you drive through them. He can even bring his compass to relate to his study of magnetism and mapping.

Your child will enjoy these experiences best—especially visits to museums—if you encourage him to select which exhibits or parts of the building to explore first. Let him set the pace and choose which plaques or descriptive posters to read or have you read. This type of exploration will allow him to follow his interests and learning strengths to experience the museum or site in the way most enjoyable to him. You will also learn more about new potential areas of interest and learning strengths by observing where he goes and how he relates to what he sees.

17

SCIENCE BEYOND THE CLASSROOM (ALL AGES)

Schools today offer very little of the hands-on discovery science that allows children to experience the pleasure of designing experiments to solve real-world, personally meaningful problems. Instead, science has become much like vocabulary, with lists of terms to memorize, and math, with formulas or procedures to practice over and over.

But as we've covered in this book, there are activities you can do at home to connect your children's interests and learning strengths to what they're learning in school, even in increasingly dry science classes. Without your help, your children may not appreciate their powers of observation or the wonders of their natural world. You are the person who can reveal to your child the thinking and experiences that led ordinary people who were once children like her to use scientific knowledge to discover how to launch rockets to the moon or analyze all the genes that make up a human being.

Science is propelled by curiosity, and children are naturally curious. The best thing you can do to help your child develop interest in the science around him and taught in his classroom is to encourage his curiosity. When your child asks questions, guide him to the resources or explorations that will provide answers. When you join in the inquiry with your child, you are honoring her questions with your interest and bolstering her motivation by sharing her quest for knowledge.

OBSERVATION

AS learners

When you're outside with your child, sit down in silence for a few minutes and ask your child to notice all the sounds he hears during that time while you do the same thing. You can then compare observations. If he doesn't hear the same bird or breeze you did, he may want to try again. That is wonderful, because it indicates he is interested in building his observational powers.

VSK learners

Take an object from nature (a leaf, shell, or rock) and hide it under a playful tablecloth. Your child might first feel the object through the tablecloth, describe what it feels like, and predict what it might be. She can then pull off the cover and enjoy drawing or writing everything she observes about the object. She might then want to go to the place where you got the object, explore the area, and make observations about what she sees, hears, smells, and touches.

PLAY AND COOK SCIENCE

AS learners

- At mealtime, discuss, predict, and investigate where a food comes from and how it got from farm or ranch to your table. Ask your child: "If we wanted to reduce fossil-fuel emissions by only eating food from a 100-mile radius of our home, what foods could we have for three meals on one day?"
- Play syn-*naps* guessing games like animal/vegetable/mineral (element or compound) with the ingredients in the meal (for example, water [H_2O] and salt, or sodium chloride [$NaCl$], are compounds made from elements).
- Your preschool child may be too young to measure ingredients for cooking, but she'll enjoy comparing quantities with measuring cups, measuring spoons, and kitchen funnels. *The Science Chef: 100 Fun Food Experiments and Recipes for Kids*, by Joan D'Amico and Karen

Drummond, offers easy-to-perform cooking projects with scientific explanations for questions, such as why onions make you cry.

VSK learners

- While slicing carrots for a salad, show your child the bowl you'll use for the dish or a picture of the item from a recipe book. Then, show him an average-size carrot and invite observation and prediction about how many carrots he would need to slice to fill the cup of sliced carrots called for in the recipe. An older child can then slice the carrots and see if his prediction was accurate. You can slice the number or carrots predicted by your younger child to see the accuracy of his prediction.
- While preparing a meal with your child, try a demonstration of relative temperature to reveal the multisensory aspects of science. Have your child wear a mitt potholder or glove for a few minutes on one hand and predict what he expects the water will feel like on each hand when he puts both hands into a bowl containing room-temperature water. Try it again after he holds a bag of frozen peas in one hand.
- *Exploring Matter with Toys*, by Mickey Sarquis, invites children to learn about matter and their senses using items from your kitchen or around the house. As your child pours liquids or rice from one container to another, she'll gain visual, tactile, and kinesthetic experiences with relative quantities as her brain is refreshed by a syn-*naps*.

PREDICTION TO HYPOTHESIS

Your elementary-school child may not know the words "prediction" or "hypothesis," but you can gradually substitute these words in your sentences as you play guessing games together. Predictions followed by comparisons build the experience of making deductions based on observations. When forming a hypothesis (a tentative explanation for a phenomenon that will be evaluated by further investigation) or a possible rule to improve subsequent predictions, your child is engaged in the scientific process.

AS learners

Science Fiction

If your child enjoys hearing or reading stories about imaginary space travel or beings from other worlds, science fiction can build a bridge to the science he learns at school. Help your child select some science-fiction books (for you to read or to read aloud together) that start in the realm of imagination and fiction and include some accurate scientific theory and facts. A great source of these books comes from scientists who also write science fiction, such as physicist Stephen Hawking and Lucy Hawking, who wrote *George's Secret Key to the Universe*. Another example is the *Einstein Anderson, Science Detective* series, by Seymour Simon, for children in upper-elementary school, which demonstrates the inquiry-discovery excitement of science.

Mixture and Solution Predictions

Upper-elementary school children are ready to consider the differences between mixtures and solutions. (Liquid mixtures usually separate into layers until shaken. Solutions are chemically bonded so they do not separate into their original elements.) After making predictions for liquids your child knows (or you name) that are found in your kitchen, your child will enjoy predicting which are mixtures and which are solutions. She can then test her predictions by seeing which items are in fact separated into layers and become mixed when shaken. This can be followed by her creating a diagram or a sequence of sketches of her investigation.

VSK learners

Estimation Activities

The estimation activities described in the mathematics chapters are one type of prediction. You can also use small boxes of cereal with different colored pieces, such as Trix, to predict how many will be in each box total and how many of each color. If your child eats a small box of the same cereal for five days, he can make a chart or keep count of the total number of pieces and of each color to see if there is a pattern he can use to predict what he expects to find on day six.

Taste can be added to the scientific exploration. Can he taste the difference between two different colors when he sees the colors before tasting them? Can he then name the color when he tastes six pieces of different colors in random order with his eyes closed?

Experiment with items with more distinctive flavor differences, such as jelly beans. Can he name the color or flavor without seeing the jelly bean first? If so, can he name the color or flavor if he eats it with his eyes closed and nose held? (People with anosmia, the absence of a sense of smell, cannot distinguish most different food flavors because much of our brains' interpretation of taste comes from olfactory, or smell, input.)

Science and Sports Predictions

On a rainy or snowy day when your young sports-lover is stuck indoors, she can make predictions, deductions, and hypotheses about the characteristics of different balls. Gather an assortment of balls, perhaps several of each type—one new and one old, or with different amounts of inflation. She can consider possible investigations, such as which balls bounce higher or the greatest number of times. How high does she need to hold a ball from the floor to have it bounce exactly three times? How does this height compare between high- and low-inflated balls of the same type or among different types of balls? Similar comparisons can be made by measuring the distance a ball travels after it rolls down a homemade ramp, such as a shelf removed from a bookcase.

PLANT WORLD ACTIVITIES

AS learners

As your child walks through a park, have him collect leaves that have fallen from various trees to examine further at home. Using a book that identifies different types of trees, your child can write or dictate some observations about each type of tree, including details about the leaf. For a syn-*naps* activity, the leaf can be pressed between the pages of a thick book and later covered in cellophane and taped to a notebook—your child's personal tree-science journal.

If your child likes poetry, she can write similes to complete the following sentence: "A fern is like_____because_____." For example,

"A fern is like a feather because it has little parts coming off a bigger part, and the little parts look similar but they are different sizes, just like birds have different-sized feathers."

What about the water for the garden? You can investigate together the use of gray water for plant irrigation, and which plants are most drought-tolerant. Are the streams or rivers near your home, especially uphill from your home, polluted? Can the pollutants leach out into the ground water and seep into your soil? (Consider an activity for your upper-elementary-school child where he purifies water by evaporation and condensation, available at http://www.epa.gov/OGWDW/kids/activity_grades_4–8_waterpurification.html.)

VSK learners

Your child can select several packets of seeds, and together, you can read the packet's recommendations for spacing when planting. Then, your child can predict and experiment with different spacings and later compare the quantity and quality of the flowers, berries, or vegetables in the different spacings.

Other garden experiments include investigating which plants or natural ingredients, such as salt or baking soda, can be planted or sprinkled around the perimeter of a garden patch to decrease unwanted insects. What insects, such as ladybugs, can keep down the population of harmful insects? Search the Internet with your child for suggestions on how to grow the biggest pumpkin—perhaps to enter in the county fair—and have him make predictions as to which variety he thinks will be best; then, plant and grow his pumpkins.

PLACES TO VISIT

Science is involved in many local business and community facilities. Follow your child's interests and learning-style preferences to demonstrate the science connections in certified organic markets, airports, fire stations, nursing homes, veterinary offices, pharmacies, wildlife rescue centers, pet stores, planetariums, aquariums, nature preserves, botanical gardens, nurseries, zoos, farms, dairies, ranches, fish hatcheries, cave tours, and national parks with ranger tours.

YOUR CHILD LEADS THE WAY IN SCIENCE INQUIRIES

The best way for the *information to become knowledge* is for children to *construct* the knowledge. In order to promote that mental manipulation (executive function) and intrinsic satisfaction (dopamine-pleasure), encourage your child to discover his own answers.

When we give answers, we deprive children of the positive emotional boost they get when they discover things themselves. To help your child find his own answers, you can ask leading questions, relate her question to information she already understands, or plan an experiment. Your child will take pride in her questions and construct the strong neural networks that come from meaningful, pleasurable learning experiences.

Observe for areas of high interest when your child selects television shows, videos, library books, and places to visit. These will be clues for topics to incorporate in science investigations.

Let your child lead you on a path of inquiry about the phenomenon around her that she is interested in. If you make notes about science or history questions she asks when you are on the go, you can keep these notes and find themes that seem to interest her most. Young children may not know that they are interested in rocks as a category for investigation, but if you bring out the questions your child has asked about rocks, she'll be impressed by the attention you have paid to her questions. This will increase her enthusiasm when you suggest a real scientific inquiry.

Creating Investigations

It is exciting when your child is interested in investigating an idea to the degree that she wants to put time and effort into the discovering the science involved. At the beginning, she will need help defining the question she wants to answer. There will be a paring-down process for young children who often want to find out a great deal of information on topics such as how do cars drive, planes fly, or mountains form. Here is another opportunity to give the question back to your child. Instead of telling your child that her question is too complicated to investigate with an experiment, ask her what experiment might answer her question.

AS learners are likely to realize that big questions need to be broken down into sequential questions to be solved piece by piece. Once she has her question, she can start by using her prior knowledge and information-gathering experience to plan her investigation. Help her evaluate prior knowledge and what she needs to find out. You can do this with a brainstorming conversation where she lists (or dictates) anything that comes to her mind about the topic.

An AS learner might enjoy books that give sequential instructions for investigations. *Scientists Ask Questions*, by Ginger Garrett (lower elementary), and *Science Around the Year,* by Janice VanCleave (upper elementary), are good resources. Your child may want to start by using her organizational skills to consider how much time each part of the planning, activities, and experiments might require. You can create a plan together to consider how information can be collected, organized, and monitored for progress, such as dictating into a recorder or drawing a timeline of events. Your child may enjoy taking digital photos at different stages of her investigations and putting them into a journal or scientist log that she decorates especially for the investigation.

At the conclusion, revisit your child's original question. What did we learn? What ideas did you get for future investigations? How can you now apply the knowledge you gained?

VSK learners often prefer staying with the big question and enjoy thinking about other big questions related to the first one. Your child may have so many ideas to investigate that it is difficult for him to stick with one and break it down into an investigation he can handle. That's fine, because as his imagination reaches out, he'll gain momentum he'll later be able to apply. If you try to stop all his branching ideas, he may be frustrated and not want to play and investigate with you. You can help him build his organizational skills without squashing his imagination by making notes of all of his questions and ideas before suggesting that he selects one to focus on first.

When he is ready, he can choose the first idea he wants to investigate. You can help him use charts, graphic organizers, and diagrams to organize his ideas into categories to plan his inquiry.

A VSK learner might enjoy researching a variety of resources, such as videos, websites, specialists (your friends), community resources, museums, upcoming television specials, or software programs. He can first make a general list and then create a graphic organizer that connects specific resources to specific aspects of the investigation you are planning together.

How will the final compiled data and conclusions be displayed? Will he want to include large wall-sized posters, photos and descriptions of observations, graphs, or for an older child, a PowerPoint presentation?

At the conclusion, encourage your child to share her discoveries with others through a demonstration or presentation to the family or class. If your child is older, she may want to enter a competition. A culminating activity or presentation will confirm the importance and value of what your child accomplished and will increase her memories of what she learned.

Topics to Investigate

Most of your scientific investigations will be prompted by your child's curiosity and questions. If you want to suggest topics of inquiry to correlate with his current unit of study in science class, children's science books and educational websites (such as those listed in this chapter) offer subject-related questions you can propose to stimulate his interest. (You can read sections of biographies of scientists, such as the *Great Minds of Science* series, during a syn-*naps* to promote interest in the people behind the science. Included are associated experiments to try at home.)

Early Elementary School and Preschool Science Inquiry Topics (Ages 4–8)
- What is the smallest living thing? The largest?
- How does a seed know to grow up through the soil instead of down or sideways?
- Does name-brand cereal taste different than the store brand?
- Does a puppy gain the same number of pounds every week until it is full grown?
- How can we predict weather?

- Why do some whales, butterflies, and birds migrate great distances?
- Where do the stars go during the day?
- How does a caterpillar turn into a butterfly? (Kits are available for your child to observe this process and then release the monarch butterfly.)

Upper Elementary School Science Inquiry Topics (Ages 9–12)

- Is it true that cows have seven stomachs? How does a cow's digestive system differ from a human stomach, and why does that make sense based on what the cow has to eat?
- What do owls eat? (Kits are available with owl pellets [droppings] in which your child will find the tiny bones or bits of fur from the rodents eaten by the owl.)
- How do things change with the seasons, such as trees, animal colors or fur thickness, snow and rain levels, or neighborhood birds? Your child can take digital photos of things in nature during different seasons and make comparisons over the course of a year.
- How do different animals use camouflage to protect themselves or be more successful hunters?
- What rocks and minerals can we find in our town? What categories can we use to sort them?
- Create a timeline of the development of an invention from primitive to modern (motorized vehicles, computers, motion pictures). Include what advances in science and scientific tools contributed along the way to help the development progress.
- What are things we use in daily life that were discovered as researchers worked on other projects (e.g., what has space technology and engineering contributed to things we benefit from in our homes and lives)?

18

STRENGTHEN STUDY SKILLS IN SCIENCE AND SOCIAL STUDIES (AGES 8–12)

Although the emphasis in elementary school is on reading and mathematics, these subjects become tools when your child studies science and social studies. Science often requires mastery of topics from mathematics, and social studies is often dependent on successful reading skills. Both subjects at times call upon writing, analysis, and organizational skills. Your child cannot achieve her highest potential in either science or social studies without well-developed study skills, including note taking, learning subject-specific vocabulary, reading complex text, writing reports, and studying for tests requiring both memorization and essay writing.

This chapter bridges the neural circuits your child is building in the critical areas of reading and math to connect with the higher thinking tasks required for success in science and social studies. It is time to give the prefrontal lobe its workout and build your child's powers of critical judgment, data analysis, information evaluation, synthesis, prioritization, goal setting, long-term planning, decision making, reasoning, and creative problem solving. In Chapters 19 and 20, you'll go beyond study skills to find tips on report writing and test taking.

TAKING NOTES

This can be your child's first opportunity to mentally manipulate new information by putting it into his own words.

Problems

Almost every one of the brain's executive functions is needed for good note taking. In science and history, notes are taken during lectures, class discussions, textbook reading, video viewing, experiments, observations, and as part of report writing and test review. In order to write good notes, your child needs to develop skills of organization, prioritizing, and deciding what information is important enough to write down, and what can be eliminated. He needs experience organizing information into clear, useful notes that will cue his brain to remember more than what is written on the page. Many teachers expect students to listen and understand their lectures while also organizing that information. If your child is expected to write good-quality notes at the same time new information keeps coming at him, it can be challenging to do these two important things simultaneously and do them both well.

Solutions

Paired Note Taking

If your child has trouble deciding which parts of a text or lecture are important to write down as notes, you can practice *paired note taking* starting with a topic in which she is interested. The practice will build her experience with and confidence in note taking. Start with a magazine or newspaper article your child selects about a topic she's interested in—one that is at her independent reading level. As you read it together (silently or aloud) you should "think aloud" your thoughts about the words or phrases you select to write down as notes. This is a good time to show her abbreviations that decrease note-taking time and suggest that she fully spell out important names, places, and unfamiliar words that are important new vocabulary for the topic.

When your child is ready, perhaps for the second half of the article, she can tell you what she thinks is important enough to write down. You can help her describe her reasons for how she selected the "noteworthy" facts, and guide her to notes she should include or point out ones she included that weren't necessary. After she is comfortable selecting notes verbally, she can take her own notes while you take yours. She can then compare your notes to hers. It is ideal if she wants to talk about things she left out that you included. The discussion will help her better understand how to decide which information is "noteworthy." However, if she is not inclined to talk about the comparison, by seeing your notes and hearing you think aloud, she'll begin to recognize things she can do to improve her note taking.

The next step is to hone her note-taking skills during lectures in class. Read aloud again something of high interest, this time without giving her a copy of the article. Show her by emphasizing with your voice what is important. This builds her ability to listen for cues as to what notes to write down when her teacher speaks. Demonstrate actions that speakers use to show which information is particularly important. Watching for gestures, voice changes, and pauses helps her recognize when her teacher says something noteworthy.

When she is comfortable with her progress in taking appropriate notes about topics of interest, you can progress to reading aloud articles about social studies or science so she can practice subject-specific note taking. This building up of listening and evaluating skills will be invaluable to your child as she moves along in school grades, especially if she is a VSK learner who has a harder time absorbing information given through verbal lectures. If difficulty with note taking persists, your child may find it helpful to tape record the lesson and take notes from the recording later.

Note Taking/Note Making
If your child does not understand the notes she takes in class once she reads them later, she can benefit from *note taking/note making.* In this strategy, she lists important facts on one side of a divided page and her thoughts on the other side next to the fact that prompted her thought. (She can prepare in advance by having notepaper already divided with a vertical line before class.)

The note-making part of taking notes is your child's chance to jot down her thoughts about what she hears. This increases her personal connection to what she hears and her comprehension and memory, which is especially useful for VSK learners, who face the greatest challenge in turning a teacher's words into comprehensive notes. To build efficiency in her note making, work with your child to develop a shorthand set of abbreviations or symbols that represent what kind of note-making comment she is including. The most useful items to include in note making are her questions about the information in the notes, what the new information reminds her of from a previous lesson (relational memory), what she wants to know more about, what she already knows about the topic (prior knowledge), what she thinks is very important about this part of the notes, and what confuses her. She could use a different letter or symbol for each of these note-making responses, such as *R* for reminds me of something; *?* for "I don't understand this part," etc.

Clues for What to Write in Notes

Help your child learn how to listen and watch for clues that information in the lecture, discussion, or demonstration is important. Cues for importance include changes in the teacher's vocal emphasis, as well as specific word cues, such as, "This is the important part," "This will be on the test," and "Write this down," or summary statements, such as, "In conclusion," "In summary," and "What you now see is that…"

Other cues for importance include writing on the chalkboard/whiteboard, the teacher's use of a different color chalk/dry erase pen to emphasize data written on the board, repeated phrases or names, or information given after the teacher pauses to be sure all students are listening.

To help a younger child recognize these cues, explain to him that he needs to be like a detective looking through all the crime scene information to search for the valuable clues. Ask your child what he notices the teacher does when something in the lesson is very important. After listening to and listing your child's observations, ask specific questions to see which of the cues described in the preceding paragraphs he might have missed in his list. Perhaps the teacher does pause before saying something that should be included in his notes, but until you pointed it out, he didn't realize that was happening.

Note Reformatting

Help your child get in the habit of going over all notes taken during the school day. Organizing the notes into a more brain-friendly format for his learning strength will be described later, but for now it's important to know that this first note review should take place as soon as possible after the lesson, so he can fill in any information he recalls from the lecture that he didn't write down. He can also use the comments he wrote in the note-making side of the page to direct his reading or questions in class the next day. The goal is for him to find the answers to questions or things he didn't understand in the lecture.

If something he originally wrote still seems confusing, he can reread the text to clarify or check with a classmate or the teacher. If he uses symbols or different colors for the different categories in his note making, this "first-look" activity can be more efficient, because his codes direct him instantly to his note-making questions about the confusing parts of the lesson so he can get clarification.

Organizing Notes

The best way for your child to prepare for the day's homework, textbook reading, and the next day's class is for him to not only review but to also revise his notes each day. The process will increase his memory of the information. Another benefit of note revision is test preparation. His daily revision of notes into a style best suited to his learning strength means he'll be organized to study for the test. His notes will be structured in a way that allows him to identify which information is most important and how topics interrelate.

For example, if your VSK learner creates a graphic organizer for the day's notes, he can add to the organizer as the lessons progress and topics branch off into related topics. This same ongoing, growing graphic organizer can also be made into a wall chart with lots of room to grow branches for adding information.

AS learners may prefer putting their notes into traditional outlines. This is the note style of using Roman numerals for main categories, capital letters for secondary categories, standard numbers for sections under the capital letters, and lowercase letters for details under the numbers. These notes can automatically be created by most word-processing computer programs, such as Microsoft Word. The Blackboard Backpack website explains different types of note-taking formats and offers tutorials with samples (http://backpack.blackboard.com/NoteTakingTutorial.aspx). Interactive templates for traditional Cornell notes can be found online at http://interactives.mped.org/view_interactive.aspx?id=722&title=.

BUILDING SUBJECT-SPECIFIC VOCABULARY

Subject-specific, technical vocabulary in science and history poses another challenge for many children. There are more vocabulary words learned in a high-school science course than in a year of middle school foreign language study, and that high quantity of new vocabulary holds true for elementary-school science and history. Studying science, world history, or geography includes learning the new technical vocabulary at the same time your child must learn new facts and concepts.

One strategy mentioned in Chapter 15 is for you to substitute the subject-specific vocabulary term for a less precise word your child uses in conversation. For example, if he says, "I think it will rain or snow tomorrow," you can respond, "I think you are right. We are in for some kind of precipitation." No formal lesson is necessary, unless he asks you to explain. Simply repeating his phrase with the more technical word increases his exposure to and familiarity with the new vocabulary term. Here are some other strategies:

Acting Out the Words

Acting out the words is a strategy described earlier, in Chapter 4. For example, if the words from a science vocabulary list discuss the water cycle, think about including the words "condensation" and "precipitation" in a chant as you do a rain dance during a syn-*naps* with your daughter. You two can act as the water molecules in a cloud and start across the room from each other. Then as you get closer, reflecting the cloud getting denser, you can say, "We are in *condensation*, I think it is time we became *precipitation*," at which point you both become rain drops and run off in the same direction, perhaps out into the yard with water guns or to grab a hose and water the plants.

Personalizing Vocabulary Words

Personalizing vocabulary words and using multisensory experiences to connect the new word with as many senses as possible builds stronger memory circuits. Here's a science example: After learning the definition of an "electron," your child can visualize an electron orbiting the nucleus of an atom, mimic the buzz of electricity as it whizzes by, or feel a tingling associated with the electron's negative charge by rubbing a balloon against his arms and feeling the hairs move. If he then draws a sketch of his visualization and verbally communicates it to you or writes about it in his own words, multiple brain pathways are stimulated to carry the new information into long-term memory.

Multiple Word Meanings

When your child encounters a science or social studies term that has multiple meanings, you have a great opportunity to help her build multisensory memories of the word.

The word "reaction," for example, is likely to come up when your child learns about photosynthesis, in which chemical reactions convert sunlight to energy. You can build a visual and kinesthetic memory with your child by demonstrating a simple chemical reaction. If you drop an Alka Seltzer tablet into a glass of water, the "reaction" of bubbles is the release of carbon dioxide.

To build auditory and visual memories of other types of "reactions," you can put on a mask, walk into the room where your child is reading, and say, "What's up?" in a different voice. He'll experience an emotional "reaction" of surprise. Other ideas include watching water steam when it boils (a thermochemical "reaction") and hearing your dog bark when the doorbell rings (yet another "reaction").

To mentally manipulate the multisensory memories your child now has to the word "reaction," she can draw pictures or create a graphic organizer of the different types of reactions. A Venn diagram can visually represent the comparisons and contrasts between the different types of reactions—what the reactions had in common (something changed, moved, happened) and what was different (changes caused by different things: heat, surprise, chemicals coming together).

STRATEGIES FOR UNDERSTANDING TEXTBOOKS

Science and social studies textbooks are unlike any of the math or literature books your child reads in early elementary school. Even second-grade science and history books require that children read successfully, have some background knowledge of the specialized vocabulary, and know how to understand captions on diagrams or photographs embedded in the text.

Your child's strengths and interests will determine what challenges him in reading these textbooks. To get your child off to a strong start, take time to read a chapter she is scheduled to read before she reads it.

If your child is a AS learner and enjoys the orderly sequence of subchapters within chapters, you can show him those pages as an enjoyable preview to the chapter. If he likes a global, big-picture opening (VSK), look for an interesting or curious passage from the chapter or a wonderful quote from a historic person in the chapter. If you read that passage aloud before he starts his reading, he will be more interested in doing the reading. If you know (or find on the Internet) a fun fact about the science or history topic in the chapter, you can share that fact with him before he starts the reading as another way to increase his motivation.

Parallel Reading

Parallel reading is a way to learn about the science or historical period together by reading about the same topic with your child. You might read historical fiction about the period or a biography of a scientist who pioneered discoveries about which he is learning in class. Each of your books would be at your own reading levels, but because the topics overlap, you can share what you learn to build his interest in the school unit. You will also be showing him that you value the topic because you are choosing to read about it.

Personal Goals Increase Memory

A recent study of elementary-school children divided students into four test groups. Each child was each given the same one-page story to read. The children in the first group were told to just read the story. The second group was told they would answer questions about the story. Group three received the instruction that after reading the story, they would be expected to tell it back to the teacher. Group four was told that after reading the story, they would individually tell the story from memory to a student a grade behind them.

After each student in all four groups read the story, he or she was given the identical test. The students in group one had the lowest comprehension scores, and the scores increased in each group compared to the one before. The children who were told they would retell the story to a student a grade behind them scored highest.

This and similar studies reveal that when children read with a purpose or specific goal, they retain more of what they read.

Suggestions for helping your child find purpose in reading her textbooks:
- Review the chapter and section headings and convert them to questions that relate to your child's interests or past experiences. This way, she will look forward to finding something interesting when she reads. For example, a subtitle indicating "The Great Depression" might be related to, "Do you remember what your grandfather told you about his childhood during the Great Depression? Times were so terrible, but somehow the economy improved. After you read this chapter, will you let me know what you think helped people like Grandpa get back to the way of life he enjoyed before his family suffered the poverty of the Depression?"
- Ideas for finding personal connection to the text can often be found in questions at the end of textbook chapters. These are often not assigned as homework because they call for more opinion and less memorization of facts. Yet these questions can build your child's curiosity and higher-level thinking skills. Look for questions that ask children to compare something about their lives to some thing, time, place, or person in the chapter. Ask your child the question before he starts his reading, listen to any ideas he has, and tell him he'll find the answer in the chapter.
- Familiarity with important vocabulary words, formulas, and other facts necessary for comprehension make the reading less frustrating.

It is disruptive to the flow of reading when children need to frequently stop and look up the meaning of new terms. When your child knows the new terms before she begins reading, she can think about the information in the text instead of being confused and frustrated by words she doesn't understand. Perhaps you can help her find a system of having her notes or a chart nearby with this background material. Encourage her to add new terms, dates, or facts to the chart as she reads. The final result will be a great test study aid.

- To help your child take notes on a chapter or gain an idea about what information is most important, review a chapter together pointing out clues that can guide him. He'll learn that highlighted, large, bold, italicized, or underlined words and phrases are cues for importance.

- In social studies, consider connecting the textbook reading to primary source material from the Internet, such as journal entries or letters written during the historical period.

- Previewing the pictures, charts, sidebars, or diagrams before reading the chapter will help VSK learners get a global picture of what they are about to read. Your child will then be able to connect the details in the reading with the big idea of the chapter. Reading the summary or conclusions at the end of a chapter before beginning the chapter can also give a helpful big-picture overview to motivate reading.

- Perhaps your child can "interact" with the text by using colored highlighters (VSK learners often enjoy using vivid colors to underline specific categories of information such as red for dates, blue for people, and green for scientific facts or formulas). If your child can't write in a school textbook, he can use sticky notes of different colors to indicate information he thinks is important or interesting. Placing these sticky notes will help him stay more connected to the reading and help him find the important material to review for tests.

- Include syn-*naps* during your child's reading time so he can replenish his brain's neurotransmitters periodically and return to the reading refreshed and alert. During these brain breaks, he can investigate the topic through an area of his interest, such as looking up which modern inventions came through the use of the chemical, biological, or physical processes about which he is learning.

Websites provided in many science and social studies textbooks include helpful interest-connecting Internet resources. AS learners who enjoy listening to music may enjoy listening to music from the historical period or country being studied during a syn-*naps*. VSK learners may be ready for some movement during their syn-*naps*, such as acting out a fact, person, or event from the chapter as you guess who or what he is.

KWL Activities Build Reading Connections and Interest

Because prediction and curiosity stimulate the brain to look for answers, you can use KWL activities to motivate your child's interest in what she is about to read. As described earlier, the KWL chart includes three lists for your child to fill in: the *what I **K**now* and *what I **W**ant to know* lists are started before she begins the reading, and the *what I **L**earned* column is filled in as she reads, gains knowledge, and finds answers to her questions. When you help your child create and add to these lists, you are helping her stimulate prior knowledge and connect the new information with memory patterns already in her brain. You are helping her create strong memories that last beyond the test.

Graphic Organizers Consolidate Reading Memories

We've discussed graphic organizers several times in this book, but their usefulness in learning is incredible. Even while your child is reading with questions and goals in mind, she can further increase her long-term memory of what she reads by using graphic organizers. These diagrams help her look for things in her reading that remind her of things she already knows. When these previously stored memories are linked on the graphic organizer to the new information, her brain is creating memory patterns that mentally organize what she reads. She is now transforming new facts into knowledge. As your child adds to her graphic organizer, she is sorting new data into logical and personally meaningful categories. She is also gaining the memory-building experiences of thinking actively about the information as she recognizes similarities and differences, compares/contrasts, organizes, and characterizes the new data.

Science Graphic Organizer Examples
- Cycles in science: water cycle, lifecycle of butterfly or frog, food chain.
- Rocks and minerals: categories, uses, and how and where to study them or see them.
- The senses: Boxes or circles are titled with the name of the sense and the body part that does the sensing. In each of those boxes, your child draws or writes examples of things he can taste, smell, see, touch, and hear.
- Parts of a whole diagram can represent the layers of the earth with characteristics of each layer. Parts of a cell can be matched with their functions, and parts that work together can be drawn with connecting lines to show interrelationships.
- Characteristics of a group compared to another group: mammals to amphibians, saltwater to freshwater fish, and rocks to minerals.
- Timelines of experiments, geological periods of the earth (the earth's geological past is organized into various units according to major geological or paleontological events which took place in each period such as mass extinctions), the development of a modern "tool" (computer, airplane, disease treatment) from primitive to current day, and what other things grew out of the research along the way.
- Cause and effect of natural phenomenon: earthquake, volcano, monsoons, and tides.

Social Studies Graphic Organizer Examples
- Compare the different Native American tribes: their lifestyles, locations, sources of food, tools, living arrangements (hogans, rock dwellings, cave dwellings, portable homes, teepees), and celebrations.
- Show the cause and effect of a major event such as a war, the Industrial Revolution, or the Age of Exploration.
- Characteristics of historical time periods can be represented as top categories using boxes along a horizontal line for three periods, such as the Dark Ages, Middle Ages, and Renaissance. Below each of these,

list changes that took place in various aspects of society, the arts, religion practices, travel, trade, or communication during each period.

• Compare two regions on earth and when/how they were changed by various events: inventions, drought-related famine, crop-destroying insect infestation, impact of invaders or explorers, disease epidemics, or great leaders.

• Draw a timeline throughout the school year for historical events as they are studied. If your child makes a timeline of the topics studied in American history in grade five, he can bring it out when American history is again the social studies curriculum in middle school. He can also share his timeline with a younger sibling when the sibling enters fifth grade.

19

LONG-TERM REPORT AND PROJECT PLANNING IN SCIENCE AND HISTORY (AGES 8–12)

We've just covered homework organization and study skills, but in science and social studies classes, there are more also complex assignments, such as reports and projects. Science or social studies reports are usually the first reports children write in school that are not book reports. These are almost always the first reports that involve data collection from multiple sources. Helping your child develop his abilities in researching, long-term planning, and managing time serves him well beyond schoolwork and builds lifelong habits of successful organization and planning.

CHOOSING A TOPIC

The best plan for success is for your child to select a topic of high interest, so the investigation and information gathering will be a positive experience. Teach your child how to select topics that are broad enough that information will be accessible in books and websites, but also narrow enough that he can find a focus and not be overwhelmed by too much information.

To help your child make report choices that motivate him through interest and past experiences, consider the example of selecting which state he might choose for a school report. If he likes rock and roll music, consider Ohio, home of the Rock and Roll Hall of Fame. A baseball fan may be interested in New York for the Baseball Hall of Fame in Cooperstown. The Ben and Jerry's factory in Vermont can tempt ice-cream lovers. If you visited Delaware on your family trip or his grandparents live in Florida, those states might appeal. Butterfly lovers can follow their interest to California, where the monarch butterflies make migration stops, filling the trees in places like Santa Barbara. Youngsters who can't get enough of airplanes might want to choose North Carolina, because the historic flights of the Wright Brothers took place in Kitty Hawk.

TIME MANAGEMENT

Your child can start developing her time-management skills by creating a schedule as you help her predict the amount of time needed for each stage of the report. As she progresses and finds she over- or underestimated time needs, she is building her planning skills for future projects. A sample report plan or timeline could include schedules for segments such as research (books, magazines, Internet, interviews, primary sources), followed by writing an outline of major topics to investigate, then time to gather notes from her sources for these topics. The next parts of the plan could be writing a rough draft and then editing it (it helps for children to read their work aloud to discover any grammatical errors that could be missed with just visual reading). She can then add diagrams (charts, maps, cover design) and finally a bibliography. (A helpful bibliography instruction website is http://citationmachine.net.)

AS learners enjoy building progressively to a goal. As your child sees progress each step along the way, her motivation is sustained. When you help her set intermediate goals for long-term projects, the process becomes less intimidating. Each time she completes one of the goals, she will feel successful and inspired to continue.

VSK learners who prefer to see the global big picture may benefit from looking at the whole process, starting with the end product in mind. Encourage your child to describe what his ideal final report would look like and what he could learn from his study of the topic. Backwards planning—from a successful ending to the beginning—can be motivating and help him get started. He can even write a final paragraph using the list of things he hopes to learn and write a sentence about them that might turn into his report conclusion. Seeing that conclusion in writing will keep his focus on the goal and help him avoid too many tangents. Tangents can be great because they indicate interest, but if they get in the way of progress, you can suggest that he keep a list of all the side topics he wants to investigate and follow through on these after the formal assignment is completed.

AS Problem: Missing the Big Picture

Sequential learners are often strong at gathering lots of facts, but have difficulty relating the facts to each other or to larger topics. For example, your child may gather lots of notes from different books but may have a hard time knowing which facts belong together or judging which are important and which are less so.

Solution

Because sequencing and ordering is often a strength of AS learners, help your child apply those skills to sorting his report information. He can read each fact or write it on an index card and think of one word that describes what it is about. He can then write that word on the back of each card. After he is finished collecting data cards, he makes a list of all the single words on the card backs and sorts out the words that logically go together. You can help him find a "bigger-picture" word that incorporates the individual words he wrote.

For example, if the report is about the cotton industry in the early 1800s, he might have single-word captioned cards, such as *flax, seeds, cotton gin, picking cotton, plantations, slave trade, linen,* and *clothing*. After reviewing the questions he is answering with the essay, he can go back to the cards and place each one into the appropriate stack on a chart where he has written for the name of each large category: *farming of cotton, slavery, goods manufactured with cotton*. This process allows him to use card sorting to complete the big picture from the separate parts.

VSK Problem: Missing Details

Big-picture thinkers may tune out fine details. Their strong conceptual understanding of the topic may exceed their ability to handle the details of report writing. Your child may write with great perspective and creativity, but fail to include all the specific information and answer all the questions required.

Solution

Your child may have difficulty formulating his ideas into well-organized thoughts. To help bridge the gap between what he is thinking and what he can write, your child can draw a series of pictures on index cards, with or without words, depicting the ideas for his report. These can be physically moved when he wants to make changes. The pictures become brain prompts so he can use the drawings when he is ready to write the words.

He can start the big-idea planning or writing, perhaps by writing the introduction and conclusion paragraphs first. After writing his ideas into lists and then structuring them into graphic organizers, he can revisit the larger ideas and questions. He will keep his thoughts and ideas together and the structure will be set, so he can fill in supporting material and relevant details. Through this process, his wonderful big-picture thinking will not be discouraged.

ALTERNATIVE REPORTS

If your child is not yet at the stage where she can dig in and write the kind of report assigned to her, there may be alternatives. Many reports are assigned that have students collect isolated information on index cards, put the cards in a teacher-directed order, and fill in the sections with material virtually copied from a website or book. Children are told they must put the information into their own words, so they often think changing the order of words in a sentence is enough to fulfill the requirement. This doesn't allow them to really make the knowledge their own (not to mention the plagiarism problems).

You can help your child become interested and invested in the report if he sees it as an opportunity to answer a question that is meaningful to him. Help him recall experiences when history came alive for him and prompted his curiosity. Help him wonder aloud about historical events he would have liked to experience. He will then see the report process as a chance to experience that part of history on a personal level.

Incorporating your child's learning strength into the report process may mean planning an alternative to the formal report. This alternative might well be acceptable to his teacher, but even if it is not acceptable as a final product, his poem, comic strip, play, video, reenactment, historical fiction story, or newspaper article can be his motivation to do the data collection and background research for the actual report. He can also write journal entries or letters from the perspective of someone living through the time who is describing his experiences to a friend. Because he likes a particular form of expressing information, this alternative will motivate his desire to find out more about his topic. He can then write the required formal report more easily because he has already done the background work when he researched his report alternative.

EXTENDING AND ENRICHING REPORTS

Extending and enriching reports may appeal to your child if she is already skilled in regular report writing and benefits from more stimulating challenges. After writing the required report, or while doing the regular writing, she can consider some secondary investigations. Here are some ideas that extend a hypothetical report on New World explorers:

- How have the tools of navigation, shipbuilding, or communication that your explorer used changed over the last five hundred years? What technological advances do you think are possible in the next hundred years in ocean travel above and below the sea?
- Write a story for a younger child about the person she is writing about for her school report and include illustrations.
- Spend a family evening or part of a weekend day *as* the person you researched or someone who lived during that historic time. Tell your child, "We'll ask you questions, or you can tell us about your life as if you are a time traveler from the past spending time with our family. I'll help you make a costume or design a prop so you'll feel more authentic. You can tell us about the things you saw, heard, tasted, enjoyed, and dreamed back in your time in history and ask us about the unfamiliar objects you find in our house. We'll have fun trying to explain a television set to you if there were no photographs during your time in history."

• Considering what you learned about your explorer, how would you take that knowledge and relate it to a mission you were going to lead to explore life on a habitable, previously unexplored planet?
• Create a map of your explorer's travels, marking the places to which your explorer traveled. Include a map key to explain your distances, directions, color coding, and symbols. You can use your skills of ratio and proportion to make your map to scale.

In these extended investigations, your children will have opportunities to use more critical thinking and get more enjoyment and brain stimulation from the report or project that has been assigned.

20

BRAIN-FRIENDLY STRATEGIES FOR TEST PREPARATION (ALL AGES)

Just as is the case for note taking, homework, and report preparation, test preparation in science and social studies is a job for the prefrontal lobe's executive functions. These strategies may seem more appropriate for older children, but I have used them with children from second grade and up and have found that even younger children can think ahead, plan, and use these higher-level thinking strategies to reach their goals.

When your child intentionally selects strategies and realizes that his choices and effort helped him succeed, his confidence increases and he becomes more able to delay immediate gratification to reach long-term goals. When you help your child see that he has the ability to achieve the success he seeks by using his executive functions of organizing, prioritization, judgment, and analysis, you are helping him strengthen his ultimate study skills.

These executive functions are strengthened by brain-friendly strategies that promote motivation, positive attitudes, and personal connections. Each time your child uses executive functions to evaluate information, he not only strengthens his test-taking success, but also grows in the thinking skills that will increase his judgment to make the important decisions he will face in the years ahead.

FRONTAL-LOBE EXECUTIVE FUNCTIONS: THE ULTIMATE STUDY SKILLS

When you consider the processing and decision making that goes into deciding what, when, and how much to study, it turns out that that the frontal lobe's executive functions of *organizing, judging, analyzing, prioritizing*, and *selecting the most useful strategies* are the essence of efficient studying. As you help your child relate her school classes to her interests and help her discover and practice the study strategies most compatible with her learning strengths, she becomes more and more successful at processing and storing critical information for tests and, more importantly, for future use.

As you read through these executive-function study strategies, consider which seem best suited for your child. When some are particularly successful, help him recognize what was effective so he can apply the strategy on his own in new situations.

Organize

Identifying "big ideas," or themes that connect chunks of information together, helps all children build stronger memories of the material. When children are faced with lots of facts to learn and haven't had much experience in class discovering or investigating the information, it can be difficult for their brains to know which fact relates to which. To help your child build relational long-term memories, encourage him to sort the facts, dates, names, places, and new subject-related vocabulary into categories and to describe (AS) or make diagrams (VSK) of how the pieces fit together.

Prioritize

Study plans include determining when to begin studying in advance of a test, which material is highest priority and should be reviewed the most frequently, and what information in your child's notes or text is more or less likely to be on the test (prediction). Creating study plans builds the executive function of prioritizing skills to make the most efficient and effective use of study time.

If your child is able to prioritize, she can strategize her approach to test taking as well as studying for tests. She can answer the questions she knows first and come back to the harder ones later. If she realizes that she is successful and accurate with this approach, she will use this knowledge to repeat the strategy again on subsequent tests.

Judgment

This executive function includes self-checking strategies, such as self-editing by reading aloud, checking over answers to see if all parts of a multipart question were covered, planning for the most effective use of time during a test, and looking for clues in subsequent questions.

Your child can develop judgment by learning to stop at planned intervals during a test to check in with himself and ask the question, "Am I staying focused, or letting my mind wander?" Consider practicing a self-checking strategy with your child during a study session by flipping over a note card that asks, "Am I focused?" every ten minutes or so when he is studying or doing homework. At first, he might think it is silly or annoying, but soon he'll internalize the self-checking strategy and recognize that his studying or test taking is more efficient because he reclaims his focus.

Analysis

You can guide your child to increase her awareness of her study and test-taking strengths and weaknesses. She can then use this analysis to guide her future decisions. If you encourage her to keep track of the types of mistakes she most commonly makes on tests (not reading the question completely, or not checking her work), she will learn from this analysis.

SAMPLE STUDY QUESTIONS FOR SCIENCE AND HISTORY TEST REVIEW

There are enough similarities between science and social studies that the following list, divided by age groups, can be modified to suit most units of study in these subjects. Even if you don't know the material your child is studying, the questions that encourage your child to explain main ideas to you will motivate her to look up information that she now realizes she should know. Asking these types of questions throughout the unit of study helps your child keep up with the material, so she doesn't have to cram for a test.

Lower Elementary (K–3)

- What happened before this event *(before the butterfly came out of the cocoon)* or to cause the event *(so many people traveled to California in 1849)?*
- What occurs, or occurred, when → *(you heat water to 212 degrees, seasons change, the Pilgrims didn't have enough food)?*
- What do you think is the most important thing about → *(Thanksgiving, caring for animals)?*

Upper Elementary (Grades 4–6)

- Is this event or phenomenon similar to something you learned about before?
- How does this information compare or contrast with what you know about that similar event, person, or phenomenon? *(How does this chapter in geography about the layers of the earth compare with what you learned last month about the layers of your skin or the layers of bark around a tree trunk?)*
- Are (were) there different opinions about this event *(the extinction of dinosaurs)?*
- What is the difference between → *(the three branches of government, amphibians and reptiles, igneous and sedimentary rocks)?*
- How do you think your life would be different if → *(your great-grandparents did not immigrate to this country, if antibiotics had not been discovered, if the polar ice caps melted rapidly)?*

GENERAL TEST-PREP STRATEGIES

You can start playing games when your child is young that later turn into excellent test study activities. For example, guessing games like 20 Questions build analysis and memory skills. Putting sticky notes on all red things in a room sets up pattern recognition, and making up songs using a variety of animals teaches your child how to use songs to remember information.

Games, Songs, and Stories

When it comes time to study for real tests, you can transition the 20 Questions game into *"guess which person in history or what country I am by asking me questions."* Just as you created different verses of "Old McDonald Had a Farm" by adding different animals, you can work together to make songs or raps to remember parts of a plant or capitals of states. Take turns adding parts to narrative stories to help your child recall a sequence in history (the order in which the first colonies became states; the Bill of Rights; and a scientific process, such as the water cycle, photosynthesis, or digestion).

Sticky Notes

Sticky notes once placed on red things can now be placed on items that are opaque or transparent, natural or manufactured, or organic or inorganic to coincide with your child's science studies. Timelines that were once used to count down the days until a birthday can now be used to organize events in history or scientific developments. Use sticky notes to cover information to be memorized on a map or on a chart of a scientific process. After stating his answer, your son pulls back the sticky note. If his answer is correct, the sticky note stays off that day and his motivation increases as there are fewer and fewer sticky notes. In addition, the visual and physical components of the activity add to his multisensory memories. Every few days leading up to the test, replace some of the sticky notes with those of another color (so he knows he was already successful with the answers) and have him review to be sure that *practice makes permanent!*

Interviews

When reviewing a topic for a test, suggest that your child act as the interviewer and perhaps prepare note cards with questions to ask you. You might increase her enthusiasm if you record the interview with a video camera on a tripod or a tape recorder. She can review her notes to prepare good questions. You can watch samples of good interview shows on television (about topics she likes on MTV, the Disney Channel, or ESPN) so she sees how good interviewers are prepared with knowledge-able questions about the interview topic or interviewee. Explain that when television interviewers are skillful, they have read the book of the author they interview, listened to the CD of the recording artist, or watched games played by the athlete.

Help her see how interviewers ask specific questions that only someone who read the book or watched the game would ask. Point out how in response to these knowledgeable questions, the interviewee responds more enthusiastically. Encourage your child to include specific informa-tion on her question cards so she can be a knowledgeable interviewer like the ones she admires on television. This card preparation motivates her to review her notes and textbook.

Prediction

Helping your child learn what to study for tests through prediction relates to the power of prediction to increase the brain's attention. After making a prediction, the brain seeks out information about which the prediction was made. Prediction builds your child's motivation to see if he was right. When studying for tests, prediction is even used uncon-sciously, as children decide what is important to study because they think it will be on the test.

Help your child recall if the teacher provided any verbal or written instructions about what will be covered on the test and what types of ques-tions the test will include (short answer, essay). As described in Chapter 7 for math test prediction, have her predict what information from her notes and text reading she believes will most likely be on the test.

Textbooks offer clues that identify important information. If she makes a list of her predictions or uses sticky notes to mark them in her textbook, you can look together after the test is returned to see which predictions were correct and what strategy she used to make those correct predictions (so she will remember to use it again).

Event Memories for Powerful Retention

Event memories are tied to sensory-charged events with positive emotional intensity. Event memories, which are also called flashbulb memories, usually stimulate more senses and relate to the experiential education motto that we learn 40 percent of what we hear; 60 percent of what we hear and see; and 80 percent of what we hear, see, and do. A memorable multisensory event during test review will cause the incoming information to travel quickly through the brain's filters, and the good feelings linked to the event in the amygdala will strengthen the memory.

To help your children remember difficult information, consider ways to link the information to a special, memorable moment with laughter or a surprise, such as uncovering a paper with a secret code that spells out the scientific word. If your child is studying about electricity or electrons, you can create an event memory while he is occupied in another room enjoying a syn-*naps*. If you rub inflated balloons against your clothing and touch them to the walls of his room, they will adhere without tape because of the static electricity. After he takes a break outside or a snack in the kitchen, ask him to get something you need from his room. He'll be delighted by the surprise of the balloons and enjoy discovering how he can also create "electricity" rubbing the balloons against his shirt.

Other test-study activities include strategies previously described to build relational and long-term memories, such as creating analogies, visualizations, and sorting mixed-order index cards with data or occurrences into the correct order of the scientific process or historic events.

THE BEST TEST-STUDY STRATEGIES FOR YOUR CHILD'S LEARNING STRENGTH

Test-studying strategies can be matched to suit your child's learning strengths. The idea is for your child to discover what study strategies engage her brain through her learning strengths and apply these strategies to make her studying and test taking successful. You help set a positive emotional tone for greater passage of information into memory when your child feels good. You can help her recall past successes, identify which strategies were useful, and by your positive attitude and encouragement, avoid signs of frustration she might sometimes feel.

Draw Pictures and Diagrams as Visual Text Cues

VSK learners benefit from reviewing their underlined words, phrases, and sentences in their notes or textbooks. Your child will also find it helpful to go through the text reviewing the bold type, pictures, diagrams, sidebar information, and tables.

Your child can make a diagram or charts to represent the historical or scientific facts. Once he makes a diagram, consider making photocopies of it before he puts the words or labels on. These copies can become practice sheets so your child first *says* what the label should be and, *if correct*, he writes it down with correct spelling. To make the experience more stimulating for your child, have him use a special pen, such as a gold or silver marker. When he names the label correctly, he can fill in the space with the special pen.

During car rides or other on-the-go times, see how many facts about the topic (mammals, states, dinosaurs, simple machines, planets) your child can name.

AS learners can verbalize the information portrayed in their textbook highlights. Your child might enjoy teaching the information to her dolls or even her pet hamster using the sequences she finds useful in her notes or following the bold subtitles in her textbook.

Analogies

Analogies increase relational memory and therefore are also great study aids, because they show how two sets of ideas or concepts are related: "The Mayflower is to the Pilgrims as the Pinta, Nina, and Santa Maria are to Columbus and his crew." "Henry Ford is to automobiles as Thomas Edison is to telephones." Analogies are well suited for AS learners. During study time, you can cover any one of the four parts of the analogy with a sticky note and your child can predict the name or word that is hidden.

Visualize

Encouraging your child to visualize and describe or sketch his visualizations of the historic events or scientific processes adds multisensory brain stimulation that enriches the impact of the knowledge for VSK learners. Just as athletes may visualize a move before they execute it, you can encourage your child to visualize the biological process or historic event. He might even create models, mobiles, or note card sort orders to interact kinesthetically with the new information.

Suggest that your AS child visualize the scene in history or science as you read it aloud to him and remind him to practice similar visualization as he reads aloud his notes to himself. An AS learner will enjoy visualization of sequences, such as the passage of a cookie through the digestive system, the pathway of blood cell through the circulatory system, the regions traveled along the Lewis and Clark expedition, or a ship route in the 1800s leaving from Boston, sailing down below South America, and then going back up to California.

Music/Audible

If your child is an AS learner who relates well to music, she might enjoy a review format and syn-*naps* in which you play a song she likes, and each time you stop, she gives you a fact she recalls from her studying. Test study and review sessions for AS learners could also include listening to recordings of lectures or of them reading aloud from their textbooks and notes. Your AS learner will also benefit from hearing the material read out loud directly. She can read the material aloud to herself or you can read it to her. Studying with a classmate is also great for your AS learner who will hear a peer—someone she relates to—speak with her about the topic and thus will retain information more easily.

MEMORIZING STRATEGIES FOR TESTS

When your child needs to memorize information, help him find the strategy that appeals to his learning strengths. Strategies already described for remembering facts include using the facts to create rhymes; changing the words of familiar songs to include the facts; drawing illustrations; visualizing; dramatizing; using flash cards (including the errorless learning strategy with flash cards previously described in the reading and math chapters); having your child teach the information to family members; and creating analogies, acronyms, and mnemonics.

"Pleasantness"

This strategy is useful for memorizing lists of single words that do not have to be remembered in specific order, such as types of bodies of water, causes of a historical event, or examples of reptiles. Your child simply arranges the list of words in a personally meaningful order. My students are amazed when I show them how useful the idea of "pleasantness" is. I demonstrate the strategy by using half the class as the control group and the other half as the experimental group. The group that uses this strategy usually remembers 25 percent more words than the control group. I suggest a demonstration to show your children how effective this strategy is, so they are more likely to use it.

The strategy is to arrange the list that follows in order of "pleasantness." There is a positive benefit to having no "correct" way to list the words, because pleasantness is a matter of opinion. In addition, the very idea of "pleasant" is relaxing, especially for children with test stress or who feel frustrated about doing any memorization.

Experiment with the strategy starts by preparing two lists of about ten words each (less for younger children). The words themselves are not important. The lists I use are:

Piano	Story
Ball	Rainbow
Smoke	Window
Kitchen	Toaster
Legs	Flower
Sky	Spoon
Telephone	Cloud
Fruit	Basket
Car	Tent
Raisin	Magazine

Have your child copy the first list from your written list. She then turns the paper over and writes the words she remembers in any order. When she is finished, she compares her remembered list with the original and counts the number remembered correctly. She next copies the second list, but this time, she places the words in order of "pleasantness" before turning the paper over and writing the words she remembers in any order. She then checks the number of words she remembered correctly. It is quite likely that she will remember more words after listing them by "pleasantness."

As a result of this demonstration, she will be motivated to use the strategy of listing words she must memorize in order of pleasantness. She can continue with the arrangement in order of "pleasantness" or any other positive way of listing the words, with the best, happiest, and most pleasant at the top.

Make Memorization Manageable

To lower the barrier, not the bar, encourage your child to plan in advance and not leave the memorization until the night before the test.

This strategy allows your child to work to his potential without getting discouraged with the material. If your child needs to memorize all the presidents of the United States for the next school day, most would shrug off the assignment as impossible. However, if your child memorizes only the first five presidents for the next day, and continues this pattern until all of the presidents have been memorized, you have lowered the barriers to learning all of the U.S. presidents.

Internet Fact Practice

Interactive Internet websites for fact review are available for science and social studies facts. For example, your child can practice country identification and facts about the country, such as rivers, capitals, and mountains, at www.ilike2learn.com.

ESSAY TEST PREPARATION

Even though your child has had experience writing essays and papers in English class, the more conceptual essays required on many tests in science and social studies call for additional skills. For these essay questions, it is often necessary to include not only facts, but also an analysis, such as the comparison of two or more historical events or scientific properties.

To build your child's essay-writing skills, start with discussions that promote the combination of facts. Using casual conversations at first, help your child describe the facts of any topic of interest and ask him to offer his opinions, based on the facts, to describe possible relationships, similarities, and differences of opinion about the topic (anything from designated hitters in baseball to the best way to build a model plane). Encourage him to clearly distinguish between what he says that is factual and what is personal opinion, and you do the same.

Phrase your questions such that they call for longer, more thoughtful responses instead of single answers or true/false responses. Because you'll have a give-and-take conversation about his topic of interest and expertise, you can ask questions such as, "What do you think was the best baseball team ever?" and your child will start with an opinion. Then, you can simply ask why he thinks so and encourage him to use facts to back up his opinion. Through give and take, you are welcome to add facts of your own to demonstrate how facts are used to support opinions.

Soon, he'll be ready to move on to the questions found at the end of textbook chapters or questions you design that are within his challenge level and relate to parts of the science or history unit that he knows best. Chapter and section headings can also be formulated into essay questions. If the chapter heading is "The Land and Sea Trade Routes from Europe to the Far East in the 1500s," for example, you can ask him to tell you, "What were the major trade routes to the Far East? What were the problems with the land routes? What were the first attempts to reach the Far East by sea? What were the advantages and disadvantages of the two types of travel?" If his memory improves with writing or sketching, he can draw diagrams, timelines, maps, or sketches to further imprint the long-term recall of the verbal answers he tells you.

Depending on his learning strength, you can suggest ways to plan or organize the facts to include in the essay using lists, graphic organizers, metaphors, analogies, or diagrams. When he is successful at this part of the process, you can ask him to make comparisons and connections between two topics in the unit of study and add to his notes or diagrams.

Gradually, you can make the process more formal and ask more complex questions that resemble the essay questions he will be asked to write about on his tests. You can even ask his teacher for examples of questions from previous years to use as practice. AS learners might prefer to organize answers in sequential ways, while VSK learners might prefer to start out right away with verbal answers, inserting facts with their opinions.

AS learners and children who prefer a strategic, analytical approach are likely to start by making a list of the facts and ideas they have for responding to the essay question and then organizing these into subtopics, as well as separating fact from opinion. Some children may then want to change the lists into outline form before they start writing. Global-thinking VSK learners may start with graphic organizers or diagrams that show their "big idea" first and then add branches that correspond to the specifics of the essay question.

If remembering facts challenges your child, or he has difficulty organizing facts into a sequential outline, he might begin the process of writing down all the facts he recalls about the topic before he organizes them according to the specifics of the essay question. Seeing his list will make him more comfortable with writing the essay, because he has the facts in front of him. This strategy also helps your child if the writing process, such as opening sentences and transition sentences between paragraphs, challenges him. After listing the facts, he can work backwards, put the facts for each part of the essay response into clusters, order the clusters, and then develop opening sentences that present the main idea of the information he listed to include in each paragraph.

If your child responds to essay questions with a flood of ideas, he may feel best if he allows himself to write out these random ideas. He probably knows these tangents are not appropriate for the essay, but he may be so curious that he doesn't want to forget each fascinating idea. If he writes them down, he'll know he can follow up with them later, after the test. Just by writing down these tangents, he'll feel better and can proceed with the proper focus of the essay.

If your child is a fast thinker and becomes frustrated with practice sessions in which you ask him to write out his answers in essay form, consider typing his words as he speaks them. This will free him from anxiety about punctuation and spelling and allow him to focus on the facts, ideas, and presentation.

You can then work together to read over these dictations and find the best parts. Analyze why these sections are especially good, and point out that it's because they separate fact from opinion and use facts from the chapter to support opinion. Most likely, they are also the sections that clearly respond to the instructions, such as comparing and giving examples of two different historical events or scientific concepts. Once he has the confidence-building experience of seeing and hearing his successful work, you can go back over the essay with him and see how he thinks he might make the other sections as good as his best sections.

You can then move on to editing the final essay together using a list you collaborate on that includes all the qualities of a good essay. The list might include:

- Does the opening paragraph describe what questions the essay will answer and how the information will be presented?
- Are the first sentences of each paragraph clearly presented, so the reader knows what facts will be found in the paragraph?
- Does the paragraph then go on to include enough supporting factual information to back up the first sentence?
- Is there clear presentation of what information is factual and what is opinion?
- Does the final essay answer all the questions?
- Does the closing paragraph pull everything together and match well with the "promises" of the opening paragraph?

Using this building-block approach to essay writing, your child will have experience of organizing his thoughts and creating an essay he knows will satisfy the requirements. The essay will no longer be intimidating, because he has practiced the skills and found the best way to use his learning strengths to succeed.

The whole process is driven by acknowledging success and extending best strategies to strengthen weaker areas. This preparation will build his confidence and increase the pleasure he feels because you are giving him your full attention by first starting the experience as a conversation, then typing his spoken words, and ultimately acknowledging his successful ideas. Any time you devote to listening to your child's ideas, writing them down, and discussing them reinforces his efforts and prompts him to continue to strive to do his best.

For the final essay-test preparation, it is helpful to simulate the real test situation at home. This time, he'll write an essay himself using the strategies you've practiced with him. You can select or ask his teacher to provide sample essay test questions. With the positive memories of the discussion-dictation sessions with you and confidence built by practicing the "real thing" at home before the test, he'll approach the exam essay with familiarity and confidence instead of confusion and anxiety.

AFTER THE TEST IS RETURNED

When the test is over, there are great opportunities to learn from the test and plan for future tests. Through a process of thinking about thinking, or *metacognition*, each test experience can provide insights into how to be successful on future tests.

Work together to list the study and test-taking strategies your child found most helpful and which predictions about the test were accurate. As with any process that might cause your child to feel criticized or defensive, focus first on positive predictions and strategies before considering what he can change to be even better next time. Just as with analysis of practice essays, you can go over a list of test evaluation questions after the test is returned. These questions (which can be revisited with each subsequent test) can include:

- Did you start with the questions you knew and then go back to finish the ones you skipped?
- Did you find answers to some questions from information included in other test questions?
- Did you write the facts you wanted to remember on a list at the top of your test or on scrap paper before even reading the test questions so you wouldn't forget them because you saw a test question that stressed you out?
- Did you read over your essay to see if you followed the steps for checking the practice essays we did together at home?

- Did you study the right material for the test? If not, what needed more study—your class notes or your textbook reading?
- Did you plan your time for each part of the test, based on the point value of the parts before starting the test?
- Did you reread questions to be sure you understood everything you were asked to do and followed all instructions?
- What did you do well that you want to do again next time?
- What could you do differently, such as underlining key words in instructions and rereading them before answering the questions?

PUTTING TESTS IN PERSPECTIVE

With so much emphasis placed on tests in school, you as a parent need to be the source of perspective so your child doesn't judge herself by the single parameter of a test grade. Even in the most test-focused classes, teachers use other criteria to determine students' final grades, such as class participation, group work, homework, reports, presentations, and projects. Before the test, remind your child of her academic strengths, such as memory of facts, great writing ability, successful report writing, projects, and previous tests on which she did well. Let her know that you respect the work she did preparing for the test and that she has a right to be proud of herself for what she did know, even if it wasn't included in the test questions. Remind her that you love her for who she is and that you admire her kindness, patience, generosity, motivation, perseverance, or whatever else about your child that you truly respect and admire.

A single low test score may be a source of great distress to some children. Help your child understand that he is much more than a test score, and tests are not the best measure of how well he knows the material and how much information he learned in the unit he reviewed well. Remind him of the successful review sessions you had together that proved he knew the subject thoroughly. Explain that some tests are poorly designed and test for what students *don't* know, rather than giving them the opportunity to demonstrate what they *did* learn.

Share examples of gifted professionals in athletics, science, and the arts who sometimes have a bad day or perform many experiments before they develop a scientific discovery that they can prove to be correct. Mention actors who are wonderful in many movies and then disappointing in another, only to come back with a great performance in the next one. Share your memories about what it was like for you to receive a low test grade and how upset you were until sometime later, when you changed your study habits or connected better with the topic, and your test grades improved. Most importantly, let your child know that you know how wonderful he is in so many ways, and that you would never change your love and respect for him based on a grade on a piece of paper.

CONCLUSION

Brain research, when applied to learning, helps you energize and enliven your child's mind. As his learning coach and homework consultant, you will help him build life skills, such as improved memory, focus, organizing, and goal setting. Using the brain-friendly strategies best suited for your child's learning strengths, he will build aptitude and confidence in all school subjects and become a lifelong learner who can apply what he studies to real-world applications.

When you help your child grow in skills, strategies, and higher levels of thinking, he becomes increasingly engaged in learning in and out of school. His self-confidence grows, and he is more resilient when he encounters obstacles and frustrations. He knows he can accomplish anything he sets his mind to because he has done just that with you. Positive expectancy changes brain neurochemistry, which increases your child's brain growth and development.

When you help your child build a better brain, you are not only demonstrating techniques that will serve her throughout her school years and beyond, you are growing your own dendrites, strengthening your own memory, and expanding your interests and knowledge. The engagement and responsiveness you see as you continue to partner with your child will motivate you to persevere, because you'll feel the intrinsic satisfaction of success.

It's truly the win-win opportunity of a lifetime!

I AM GRATEFUL TO YOU

As a mother, physician, and teacher, I am grateful you have taken the time to read this book and use some of its activities, games, and strategies to help your child reach her full potential as a student and citizen. The guidance your child receives from you will change the rest of her life. Because of your support, encouragement, and the tools you provide for her success, her happiness, curiosity, resilience, and wisdom will grow, as will your shared experiences, appreciation, and enjoyment of times together.

GLOSSARY

AS learner: Children with this learning strength demonstrate sensitivity to sounds, structured patterns, logic, order, sequence, and words. Proficiencies include several (but usually not all) of the following: organizational abilities, logical deduction and concept building (parts-to-whole construction of knowledge), evaluating patterns and connections in information they hear, memory sensitivity to spoken and written language, vocabulary, and foreign-language aptitude.

Brain mapping: Using electroencephalographic (EEG) response over time, brain mapping measures electrical activity representing brain activation along neural pathways. This technique allows scientists to track which parts of the brain are active when a person is processing information at various stages of information intake, patterning, storing, and retrieval. The levels of activation in particular brain regions are associated with the intensity of information processing.

Decoding sensory input: Any new information or learning must enter the brain through one or more of the senses (hearing, seeing/visualizing, touching, tasting, smelling, and emotionally feeling). First, the information is decoded by the sense-specific sensory receptors in the body. From there, the information travels through the nerves in the skin, specific sense organs, or internal organs to the spinal cord and up *through the reticular activating system* to the specialized part of the brain that interprets (decodes) the input from the particular senses.

Dendrite food: A nickname for an activity in which children summarize new information in their own words and record these notes. The name "dendrite food" refers to the fact that when new learning is physically established in the brain, it is accompanied by the growth of more connections between nerve cells called dendrites.

Dendrites: Branched protoplasmic extensions that sprout from the arms (axons) or the cell bodies of neurons. Dendrites conduct electrical impulses toward neighboring neurons. A single nerve may possess many dendrites. Dendrites increase in size and number in response to learned skills, experience, and information storage. New dendrites grow as branches from frequently activated neurons. Proteins called "neurotrophins," such as nerve growth factor, stimulate this dendrite growth.

Dopamine: A neurotransmitter most associated with attention, decision making, memory, executive function, and pleasure-associated learning. Dopamine release on neuroimaging has been found to increase in response to intrinsic sense of accomplishment and positive experiences. Scans reveal greater dopamine release while subjects are playing, being read to, laughing, exercising, and participating in high-interest activities.

Endorphins: Peptide hormones that bind to opiate receptors found mainly in the brain. When endorphins activate these receptors, the effect may naturally mimic the opiate (narcotic) effect of reducing the sensation of pain and increasing pleasant emotions. Increased endorphin release is associated with pleasurable activity and exercise.

Event memories (or flashbulb memories): Memories tied to specific emotionally or physically charged events (strong sensory input). Memory theory suggests that memory-provoking or dramatic events can be linked to academic information to increase the emotional significance of the information and thereby increase its memory storage. Recalling the associated emotionally significant event with which academic information is connected (such as by positive surprise) may prompt subsequent recollection of the academic material when the event that occurred during the learning is recalled.

Executive function: Cognitive processing of information that takes place in areas of the prefrontal cortex that exercise conscious control over one's emotions and thoughts. This control allows for patterned information to be used for organizing, analyzing, sorting, connecting, planning, prioritizing, sequencing, self-monitoring, self-correcting, assessment, abstracting, problem solving, attention focusing, and linking information to appropriate actions.

Flashbulb memories: *See Event memories.*

Frontal lobes: With respect to learning, the prefrontal cortexes of the frontal lobes contain centers of executive function that organize and arrange information and coordinate higher thinking and the focusing of attention.

Functional brain imaging (neuroimaging): The use of techniques, such as PET scans and fMRI imaging, to demonstrate the structure, function, or biochemical status of the brain. *Structural* imaging (x-rays and CT scans) reveal the overall structure of the brain, and *functional* neuroimaging provides a visual representation of the brain as it processes sensory information coming in and of commands going from the brain to the body. This processing is visualized directly as areas of the brain are "lit up" by increased metabolism, blood flow, oxygen use, or glucose uptake. Functional brain imaging can reveal neural activity in particular brain regions and networks of connecting brain cells as the brain performs discrete cognitive tasks.

Functional magnetic resonance imaging (fMRI): This type of functional brain imaging uses the paramagnetic properties of oxygen-carrying hemoglobin in the blood to demonstrate which brain structures are activated and to what degree they are activated during various performance and cognitive activities. During most fMRI learning research, subjects are scanned while they are exposed to, think about, and respond to visual, auditory, or tactile stimuli; the scans then reveal the brain structures that are activated by these experiences.

Graphic organizers: Diagrams that are designed to coincide with the brain's style of patterning. In order for sensory information to be encoded (the initial processing of the information entering from the senses), consolidated, and stored, the information must be patterned into a brain-compatible form. Graphic organizers can promote this patterning in the brain because children participate in creating relevant connections to their existing memory circuitry.

Gray matter: The *gray matter* refers to the brownish-gray color of the nerve cell bodies (neurons) of the outer cortex of the brain as compared with *white matter*, which is primarily composed of supportive cells and connecting tracks. Neurons are darker than other brain matter, so the cortex or outer layer of the brain appears darker gray and is called "gray matter" because neurons are most dense in that layer.

Hippocampus: A ridge in the floor of each lateral ventricle of the brain consisting mainly of gray matter that has a major role in memory processes. The hippocampus takes sensory inputs and integrates them with relational or associational patterns from preexisting memories, thereby binding the information from the new sensory input into storable patterns of relational memories.

Learning styles: *Learning styles* refer to the way children prefer to approach learning and how their brains most successfully process information. While *intelligences* are seen in *what* children relate to in the things, information, and people around them, *learning styles* are reflective of *how* children relate to what's around them. Learning styles also indicate the way of presenting information that is most likely to stick with a child's neural-network patterning.

Learning strengths: A categorization used in this book that incorporates both multiple intelligences and learning styles. There are several different ways to look at learning, including multiple intelligence designations and learning-style preferences. These two approaches overlap—the learning proficiencies that are the hallmark of specific intelligence strengths often match the learning-style preferences found in children with those intelligences. In order to designate which brain-friendly strategies in this book will help your child best, I have classified them according to learning strengths.

Limbic system: A group of interconnected deep brain structures on each side of the brain involved in olfaction (smell), emotion, motivation, behavior, and various autonomic functions. Included in the limbic system are the thalamus, amygdala, hippocampus, and portions of the frontal and temporal lobes. If the limbic system becomes over-stimulated by stress-provoking emotion (seen as very high metabolic activity lighting up those brain areas), the information taught at that time will be poorly transmitted to the thinking brain and will be less likely to be stored in the long-term memory networks.

Long-term memory: Created when short-term memory is strengthened through review and meaningful association with existing patterns and prior knowledge. This strengthening results in a physical change in the structure of neuronal circuits (plasticity).

Metacognition: Knowledge about one's own information processing and strategies that influences one's learning and optimizes future learning. After a lesson or assessment, when children are prompted to recognize the successful learning strategies they used, that reflection can reinforce the effective strategies.

Myelin: The fatty substance that covers and protects nerves. Myelin is a layered tissue that sheathes the axons (nerve fibers). This sheath around the axon acts like a conductor in an electrical system, ensuring that messages sent by axons are not lost as they travel to the next neuron. Myelin increases the efficiency of nerve impulse travel and grows in layers in response to more stimulation of a neural pathway.

Myelinization: The formation of the myelin sheath around a nerve fiber.

Mnemonics: A strategy that uses the pattern-seeking brain to look for associations between the information it is receiving and what is already stored. Mnemonic devices are associations we use to help us remember facts. Because the brain looks for relationships, when your child can attach facts to personal, meaningful, or even humorous sequences, facts will be more easily remembered.

Multiple intelligences: *Multiple intelligence* theory suggests that rather than being an all-or-nothing entity, intelligence is made up of distinct learning proficiencies that can work individually or together. There are generally eight agreed-upon classifications of multiple intelligence strengths. All of us are presumed by this theory to have all eight intelligences in varying amounts. Your child's learning may be most efficient and successful when he applies his strongest intelligence to the task. Here's a quick overview of those eight intelligences:

Linguistic intelligence includes sensitivity to sounds, rhythms, and words. Proficiencies in this intelligence include organizational abilities;

logical deduction; memory sensitivity to spoken and written language; mnemonics, and structured, sequential notes or instructions.

Logical-mathematical intelligence includes proficiencies in logic, patterning, conceptualization, and abstraction.

Musical-rhythmic intelligence includes sensitivity to auditory tone, pitch, and rhythm. Proficiencies include auditory patterning and auditory memory.

Visual-spatial intelligence includes sensitivity to the relationships of objects, concepts, or images in different fields or dimensions. Proficiencies in this intelligence include mentally creating and visualizing spatial relationships, as in mapping or diagramming, starting with a big-picture conceptual overview before filling in details.

Bodily-kinesthetic intelligence includes sensitivity to physical, spatial, or sequential movement through time and space. Proficiencies include sense of time, proportion, prediction of sequence, and visualization of movement.

Interpersonal intelligence includes perceptiveness and sensitivity to others' moods and feelings. Proficiencies include the ability to interact with and lead people by interpreting their intensions, needs, emotions, and desires.

Intrapersonal intelligence includes understanding of and confidence in one's own beliefs and goals. Proficiencies include an ability to reflect upon one's own thoughts and feelings, introspection, analysis, and reflection.

Naturalist intelligence includes perceptiveness of things existing in the natural world, such as plants and animals. Proficiencies include organizing things into categories, detailed observation, and pattern recognition.

Neuronal circuits: Neurons communicate with each other by sending coded messages along electrochemical connections. When there is repeated stimulation of specific patterns of stimulation between the same groups of neurons, their connecting circuits (dendrites) become more developed and more accessible to efficient stimulation and response. This is why practice (repeated stimulation of grouped neuronal connections in neuronal circuits) results in more successful recall.

Neurons: Specialized cells in the brain and throughout the nervous system that control storage and processing of information to, from, and within the brain, spinal cord, and nerves. Neurons are composed of a main cell body, a single major axon for outgoing electrical signals, and a varying number of dendrites to conduct coded information throughout the nervous system.

Neurotransmitters: Brain proteins that are released by the electrical impulses on one side of the synapse (axonal terminal) and then float across the synaptic gap carrying the information with them to stimulate the nerve ending (dendrite) of the next cell in the pathway. Once the neurotransmitter is taken up by the dendrite nerve ending, the electric impulse is reactivated in that dendrite to travel along to the next nerve. Neurotransmitters in the brain include serotonin, epinephrine, acetylcholine, dopamine, and others that transport information across synapses and also circulate through the brain, much like hormones, to influence larger regions of the brain. When neurotransmitters are depleted by too much information traveling through a nerve circuit without a break, the speed of transmission along the nerve slows down to a less efficient level.

Numeracy: The ability to reason with numbers and other mathematical concepts. Children's concepts of number and quantity develop with brain maturation and experience.

Occipital lobes (visual memory areas): These posterior lobes of the brain process optical input, among other functions.

Parietal lobes: Parietal lobes on each side of the brain process sensory data, among other functions.

Patterning: Patterning is the process whereby the brain perceives sensory data and generates patterns by relating new information with previously learned material or chunking material into pattern systems it has used before. Education is about increasing the patterns children can use, recognize, and communicate. As the ability to see and work with patterns expands, the executive functions are enhanced. Whenever new material is presented in such a way that children see relationships, they can generate greater brain cell activity (formation of new neural connections) and achieve more successful patterns for long-term memory storage and retrieval.

Plasticity (neuroplasticity): Dendrite and synapse formation and dendrite and neuron destruction (pruning) allows the brain to reshape and reorganize the networks of connections in response to increased or decreased use of these pathways.

Positron emission tomography (PET scans): Radioactive isotopes attached to molecules of glucose are injected into the blood. As a part of the brain is more active, its glucose and oxygen demands increase. The isotopes attached to the glucose give off measurable emissions used to produce maps of areas of brain activity. The higher the radioactivity count, the greater the activity taking place in that portion of the brain. PET scanning can show metabolism in the tissues of the working brain that reflect the amount of brain activity in these regions while the brain is processing sensory input (information). The biggest drawback of PET scanning is that because the radioactivity decays rapidly, it is limited to monitoring short tasks. FMRI technology does not have this same time limitation and has become the preferred functional imaging technique in learning research.

Prediction: Prediction is what the brain does with the information it stores in patterns. Prediction occurs when the brain has sufficient information in a patterned memory category to find similar patterns in new information and predict what the patterns mean. For example, if you see the number sequence 3, 6, 9, 12..., you predict the next number will be 15 because you recognize the pattern of counting by threes. Through careful observation, the brain learns more and more about our world and is able to make more and more accurate predictions about what will come next. Prediction is often what is measured in intelligence tests. This predicting ability is the basis for successful reading, calculating, test taking, goal-setting, and appropriate social behavior. Successful prediction is one of the best problem-solving strategies the brain has.

Prefrontal cortex (front part of the frontal lobe): The prefrontal cortex interprets, directs, and coordinates information flow, executive function, decision making, memory processing, and many other "higher" thinking activities.

Pruning: Neurons and their connections are pruned (destroyed) when they are not used. In prenatal development, the brain overproduces brain cells (neurons) and connections between brain cells (synapses) and then starts pruning them back around the age of three. The second wave of synapse formation occurs just before puberty and is followed by another phase of pruning. Pruning allows the brain to consolidate learning by pruning away unused neurons and synapses and wrapping more white matter (myelin) around the neuronal networks more frequently used to stabilize and strengthen their ability to conduct the electrical impulses of nerve- to-nerve communication.

RAD learning: An acronym used in this book that represents three brain systems that are keys to building better brains. The three systems referred to as *RAD* are:

R: *Reticular Activating System* (RAS)
A: *Amygdala*
D: *Dopamine*

Relational memory: Learning consists of reinforcing the connections between neurons when we learn something that adds to what we have already stored in memory. Relational memories expand on neuronal networks and categories of related memory storage already present in the brain.

Reticular activating system (RAS): This lower part of the posterior brain filters all incoming stimuli and makes the "decision" as to what sensory input is attended to or ignored and if the input will be directed to reflective (thinking) or reactive (automatic-fight/flight/freeze) brain centers. Categories that focus the attention of the RAS include novelty (changes in the environment), surprise, danger, and movement.

Rote memory: This type of memorization is the most commonly required memory task for children in school. This type of learning involves "memorizing," and soon forgetting, facts that are often of little primary interest or emotional significance to the child, such as lists of words.

Facts that are memorized by rehearsing them over and over, that don't have obvious or engaging patterns or connections, are rote memories. Without giving the information context or relationship to children's lives, these facts are stored in more remote areas of the brain. These isolated bits are more difficult to locate and retrieve because there are fewer nerve pathways leading to these remote storage systems.

Serotonin: A neurotransmitter used to carry messages between neurons. Too little serotonin may be a cause of depression and inattention. Serotonin secreted by the brain during certain hours of sleep helps enhance new dendrite growth.

Somatosensory cortex areas: Areas in each parietal brain lobe where input from each individual sense (hearing, touch, taste, vision, and smell) is processed and stored.

Synapse: These gaps between nerve endings are where neurotransmitters like dopamine carry information across the space separating the axon extensions of one neuron from the dendrite that leads to the next neuron in the pathway. Before and after crossing the synapse as a chemical message, information is carried in an electrical state when it travels down the nerve.

VSK learner: Visual-spatial-kinesthetic learners are children who show learning strengths of sensitivity to the physical, spatial, and temporal relationships of objects, concepts, or images in and through space and time. Proficiencies in this intelligence include mentally re-creating and visualizing spatial relationships, seeing the big picture, prediction of sequence, visualization of movement, good time-coordination sense, physical coordination in fine- and gross-motor skills, and putting together puzzles or broken objects.

Venn diagram: A type of graphic organizer used to compare and contrast information. The overlapping areas represent similarities, and the nonoverlapping areas represent differences.

Working memory (short-term memory): This memory can hold and manipulate information for use in the immediate future. Information is only held in working memory for about a minute. The memory working span of young adults (less in children and older adults) is approximately seven for digits, six for letters, and five for words.

RESOURCES

GENERAL RESOURCES

Graphic Organizers
Downloadable Templates for Graphic Organizers
http://www.edhelper.com/teachers/graphic_organizers.htm?gclid=CM
   yrxNeis4gCFSZmYwodvD8vhw
http://www.eduplace.com/graphicorganizer
http://freeology.com/graphicorgs
http://www.graphic.org/goindex.html
http://www.inspiration.com/productinfo/kidspiration/index.cfm
http://www.smartdraw.com
http://www.teachervision.fen.com/graphic-organizers/printable/6293.
   html

Computer Software for Graphic Organizers
http://www.inspiration.com/productinfo/kidspiration/index.cfm
http://www.smartdraw.com

Rubrics
http://janeconstant.tripod.com/Rubrics.htm
http://rubistar.4teachers.org/

Note Taking

Different types of note-taking formats are explained and offered as tutorials with samples:

http://backpack.blackboard.com/NoteTakingTutorial.aspx.

Interactive templates for traditional Cornell notes:

http://interactives.mped.org/view_interactive.aspx?id=722&title

Encouraging Questions

http://www.ask.com

VOCABULARY AND READING

Word roots, prefixes, and suffixes:

http://www.webenglishteacher.com/vocab.html

Word roots:

http://www.vocabulary.com

High-frequency words:

http://www.usoe.k12.ut.us/ATE/keyboarding/resources/presentations/
    1hfw50.ppt

Rhyming words for writing poems:

http://www.poetry4kids.com/modules.php?name=Rhymes

Oral pronunciations of word combinations in a variety of words:

http://www.fonetiks.org

Rhyming:

http://www.poetry4kids.com/modules.php?name=Rhymes

Vocabulary-building activities using a crossword format to create word challenges through a variety of learning style options:

http://games.msn.com/en/flexicon/default.htm?icid=flexicon_hmemail
    taglineapri107

Create a variety of crossword puzzles by inserting vocabulary words and one-word definitions:

http://www.puzzlemaker.discoveryeducation.com

Vocabulary work practice activities, including hangman, word search, hidden word, matching, word scramble, concentration, reproducible word cards, graphic organizers (word webs, concept circles, word squares), and crosswords:

http://www.sadlier-oxford.com/vocabulary/index.cfm
Website for vocabulary learning and reading comprehension strategies, with
  fiction and nonfiction texts at a variety of reading levels:
http://www.literacy.uconn.edu/compre.htm
Merriam-Webster's "Word of the Day" for English-language learners:
http://www.learnersdictionary.com
Newspapers of the world:
www.newspaperlinks.com/home.cfm

Books

Picture Books That Encourage Observation
Art Fraud Detective
Where's Waldo

Books to Entice Reluctant Readers
101 Ways to Bug Your Parents by Lee Wardlaw
101 Ways to Bug Your Teacher by Lee Wardlaw

Suggestions for Books
Some of My Best Friends Are Books by Judith Winn

MATH

Games
http://www.coolmath.com
http://www.shodor.org/interactivate/activities
Code-breaking games, such as S M T W T F S
(first letters of days of the week):
http://www.puzzlepixies.com/medium/medium/sherlocks-secret-code.
  html

Picture memory-sequencing match games:
http://www.prongo.com/match/index.html
Pattern matching:
http://www.primarygames.com/patterns/start.htm

Maze puzzles to build patterning skills:
http://www.prongo.com/maze/index.html
http://teacher.scholastic.com/fieldtrp/math/patterns_3_5.htm

Fact Practice

Individualized worksheets to print:
http://www.superkids.com/aweb/tools/math
The Math Fact Café for K–3 (samples are available on the website, but there is a charge for the software):
http://www.mathfactcafe.com

Metric

Metric-conversion ferris-wheel game:
http://www.walter-fendt.de/m11e/conversion.htm
Metric recipes:
http://www.learner.org/interactives/dailymath/meters_liters.html
Conversion tables and the British Nutrition Society website for recipes to convert and other math and cooking activities:
http://www.foodafactoflife.org.uk/Sheet.aspx?siteId=12&sectionId=49&contentId=131

Shapes and Patterning

Basic shapes:
http://www.bright-productions.com/kinderweb/tri.html
Tessellations (geometric shapes that fit together perfectly):
http://www.tessellations.org
Move shapes to build tessellations:
http://www.mathcats.com/explore/tessellationtown.html
Samples of tessellation art:
http://www.k4.dion.ne.jp/~mnaka/home.index.html

Math Humor

http://www.sonoma.edu/Math/faculty/falbo/jokes.html
Math riddles by children for children, plus a bit of math practice in each one:

http://www.jokesbykids.com/math

Progressive Individualized Instruction and Feedback

ALEKS (ALEKS.com) system for math practice and corrective feedback, with fee-based programs from elementary through high school:
http://www.aleks.com
A similar program, also fee-based, by McGraw-Hill:
http://www.acuityforschool.com

Graphing and Proportion

Download graph paper of different sizes:
http://nces.ed.gov/nceskids/createagraph/default.aspx
http://nlvm.usu.edu/en/nav/topic_t_5.html

Math and Sports

http://mathforum.org/library/topics/sports
http://oncampus.richmond.edu/academics/education/projects/
webunits/math/sport.html

Area and Perimeter

Basic area website:
http://www.shodor.org/interactivate/activities/AreaExplorer/?version=1
.5.0_07&browser=Mozilla&vendor=Apple_Computer,_Inc.
More advanced area and perimeter website:
http://www.freewebtown.com/weddell/mw/shape/area/area.swf

Stock Market Math

http://www.atozinvestments.com/more-wall-street-history.html
http://finance.yahoo.com (*past performances and current activity of stocks*)
http://pbskids.org/bigapplehistory/parentsteachers/business_lesson7.
html

Currency Exchange

http://www.x-rates.com

Other Math Websites

U.S. Department of Education's "Helping Your Child Learn Math":
http://www.ed.gov/parents/academic/help/math/index.html
Wolfram MathWorld:
http://mathworld.wolfram.com/PlatonicSolid.html
Math Forum Child Center website:
http://mathforum.com/children
Natural Math website:
http://www.naturalmath.com
Math games, grades 6–8:
http://illuminations.nctm.org/Activities.aspx?grade=3
http://nlvm.usu.edu/en/nav/grade_g_3.html
Math activities for projects:
http://mathforum.org/mathtools/sitemap2/m7
Math games and manipulatives:
http://nlvm.usu.edu/en/nav/category_g_3_t_2.html
National Library of Virtual Manipulatives:
http://nlvm.usu.edu/en/nav/topic_t_2.html
Jackson Pollock art design website:
http://www.jacksonpollock.org/
Downloadable polygon activities:
http://www.peda.com/poly/
Aplus Math Java Games (interactive bingo and concentration games that reinforce basic arithmetic facts:
http://aplusmath.com/Games/index.html
Mathematical Association of America Digital Classroom Resources: Free online learning activities, elementary through middle school levels.
http://Mathdl.maa.org/mathDL/3
Texas Instruments webpage with connections to math activities for children grades K-12. In additional to general investigations and practice programs, it also offers calculator activities for all ages.
http://education.ti.com/educationportal/sites/US/sectionHome/classroomactivities.html
PBS Kids:
http://pbskids.org/cyberchase/games.html

SCIENCE AND SOCIAL STUDIES

Visual images of the earth:

google.earth.com

Iditarod for kids:

http://www.iditarod.com

Pen-pals: Educational websites help you arrange email exchanges for your children so they can find out from someone their own age what the geography is like in the country or state they are studying.

http://www.iecc.org

http://www.planetpals.com

Bibliography writing instruction:

http://citationmachine.net

Simulations and virtual travel:

http://www.field-guides.com

http://www.tramline.com

The WorldWatcher website offers geographic visualization and data analysis programs best suited for students in upper elementary school or above and includes gridded, geographic data.

http://www.worldwatcher.northwestern.edu

Famous American trials:

http://www.law.umkc.edu/faculty/projects/ftrials/bostonmassacre/ bostonmassacre.html

Tactics and weapons of the Revolutionary War:

http://www.doublegv.com/ggv/battles/tactics.html

Practice country identification and facts about the country such as rivers, capitals, and mountains, etc.:

http://www.ilike2learn.com

The JASON Project, multimedia interdisciplinary science program for grades 4–9:

www.jasonproject.org

NASA Education Resources:

http://education.nasa.gov

Historical documents and recordings:

www.loc.gov

"This day in history" facts:

www.historychannel.com/thisday
Take and test water samples:
www.baylink.org/lessons/3fr_pollution.html
Country identification and facts:
http://www.ilike2learn.com

Science Books for Kids

The Cartoon Guide series, by Larry Gonick (*The Cartoon Guide to Physics, The Cartoon Guide to Genetics, The Cartoon Guide to the Universe, The Cartoon Guide to Communication,* etc.)

Einstein Anderson, Science Detective series, by Seymour Simon

Exploring Matter with Toys, by Mickey Sarquis

George's Secret Key to the Universe, by Stephen and Lucy Hawking

Great Minds of Science series

Science Around the Year, by Janice VanCleave (upper elementary)

The Science Chef: 100 Fun Food Experiments and Recipes for Kids, by Joan D'Amico and Karen Drummond

Scientists Ask Questions, by Ginger Garrett (lower elementary)

Social Studies Books for Kids (Elementary)

Books by Jean Fritz:
And Then What Happened, Paul Revere?
Around the World in a Hundred Years: From Henry the Navigator to Magellan
George Washington's Breakfast
Shh! We're Writing the Constitution
You Want Women to Vote, Lizzie Stanton?

GAMES

Preschool:
Dora the Explorer
Geoboards
LeapFrog
North Pole Camouflage Game

Early-elementary games:
Blokus Strategy board game
More advanced LeapFrog games
SET game
Tanograms
Upper-elementary games:
Brain Quest Around the World Game
Dino-Opoly
Learning Resources Planet Quest
The Making Inferences Game
MoneyWise Kids
Oceanopoly
Questionary
Risk
Scientific Explorer's Disgusting Science—A Kit of the Science of
    Revolting Things
Snap Circuits
Where in the World

BOOKS FOR PARENTS AND TEACHERS

*Most of these titles are all geared toward teachers, but parents can browse
    the ASCD.org website under "Publications" for detailed descriptions and
    sample chapters.*
Brain Friendly Strategies for the Inclusion Classroom, by Judy Willis
Brain Matters: Translating Research into Classroom Practice, by Patricia
    Wolfe
Developing Minds: A Resource Book for Teaching Thinking, 3rd Edition,
    by Arthur L. Costa
Educating Oppositional and Defiant Children, by Phillip S. Hall and
    Nancy D. Hall
Getting to Got It: Helping Struggling Students Learn How to Learn, by
    Betty K. Garner
Habits of Mind: A Developmental Series
How to Teach So Students Remember, by Marilee Sprenger
Learning and Memory: The Brain in Action, by Marilee Sprenger

Research Based Strategies to Ignite Student Learning, by Judy Willis

Schooling for Life: Reclaiming the Essence of Learning, by Jacqueline Grennon Brooks

Totally Positive Teaching: A Five-Stage Approach to Energizing Students and Teachers, by Joseph Ciaccio

Science and Math Books for Parents

Family Math, by Jean Kerr Stenmark, Virginia Thompson, Ruth Cossey

Science through Children's Literature: An Integrated Approach, by Carol Butzow, John Butzow, and Rhett Kennedy

Teach Your Child Math, by Arthur Benjamin and Michael Brant Shermer

General Parenting Books

The Irreducible Needs of Children, by T. Berry Brazelton and Stanley Greenspan

The Nurture Assumptions, by Judith Rich Harris.

Raising Cain, by Dan Kindlon and Michael Thompson

Raising Resilient Children, by Robert Brooks and Sam Goldstein.

Real Boys, by William Pollack

Mindful Learning Books

Educating People to be Emotionally Intelligent, by Reuven Bar-On, J.G. Maree, and Maurice Jesse Elias (Prager Publishers, 2007)

Emotionally Intelligent Parenting: How to Raise a Self-Disciplined, Responsible, Socially-Skilled Child, by Maurice J. Elias, Steven E. Tobias, and Brian S. Friedlander (Harmony Books, 1999)

Raising Emotionally Intelligent Teenagers: Parenting with Love, Laughter, and Limits, by Maurice J. Elias, Steven E. Tobias, and Brian S. Friedlander (Harmony Books, 2000)

Mindful Learning Website

http://www.thehawnfoundation.org

ACKNOWLEDGMENTS

To Paul, my college sweetheart, for inspiring me to write books about the neurology of learning because you want all parents to empower their children to discover the joys of learning combined with the love of supportive family.

To Norma Allerhand, my mom and mentor, who modeled for me her own love of learning and made discovery and enrichment part of my daily life. Your confidence in my ability to succeed gave me the encouragement to live my dreams.

To my beautiful daughter, Alani Willis, whose perseverance and humor melt my heart.

To my wise and dedicated daughter, and new second grade teacher, Malana Willis. You and your fellow teachers hold the future in your hands, and that makes me so hopeful.

To Goldie Hawn, who believes in the limitless potential of children when people care enough to guide them mindfully, with wisdom and love. You dedicate your inspiration, time, and unflagging effort so the Hawn Foundation will reach every child possible, and then some.

To Shana Drehs, my editor, and her co-editor, Sara Appino, at Sourcebooks who made my words so readable. You brought the wisdom needed to make this the reader-friendly book it now is. You both did a phenomenal job!

To my agent, Nancy Love, who nurtured my ideas into a presentation worthy of the talented professionals at Sourcebooks.

As always, to my students past, present, and future; their devoted parents and my colleagues at Santa Barbara Middle School, because you are all the diamonds in my wheels. I love you all.

INDEX

ABOUT THE AUTHOR

After graduating Phi Beta Kappa as the first woman to graduate from Williams College, Judy Willis, MD, MEd, attended UCLA School of Medicine, where she was awarded her medical degree. She remained at UCLA and completed a medical residency and neurology residency, including chief residency. She practiced neurology for fifteen years before returning to university to obtain her teaching credential and Masters of Education from the University of California, Santa Barbara. She has taught in elementary, middle, and graduate schools and currently teaches at Santa Barbara Middle School.

Association for Supervision and Curriculum Development (ASCD) published her first book for education professionals, ***Research-Based Strategies to Ignite Student Learning: Insights from a Neurologist/Classroom Teacher,*** in August of 2006, and her second book, ***Brain-Friendly Strategies for the Inclusion Classroom,*** in May 2007.

Dr. Willis presents at educational conferences nationally and internationally in the field of learning-centered brain research and classroom strategies derived from this research. She was a distinguished lecturer at the ASCD national conference in March 2008 and will co-present the Distinguished Lecture at the 2009 National Conference with Goldie Hawn. Dr. Willis writes extensively for professional educational journals and was honored as a 2007 finalist for a distinguished achievement award for her educational writing by the Association for Educational Publishers.

Dr. Willis is a research consultant and member of the board of directors for the Hawn Foundation, an international foundation developed and directed by Goldie Hawn to develop and implement evidence-based mindfulness education programs through collaboration with learning theorists, educators, scientists, and professionals. She is on the management team of the First Move Program, a foundation that provides teacher instruction in the use of chess as learning tool to teach higher-level thinking skills, advanced math, and reading ability, and to build self-esteem in elementary-school students. The program is sponsored by America's Foundation for Chess.

When not teaching, writing, consulting, or making presentations, Dr. Willis is a home winemaker (with her husband, college sweetheart, and fellow neurologist, Paul) and writes a weekly wine column. She is the mother of two daughters: Malana is a new second grade teacher, and Alani attends the University of California.